MODERN SELVES

MODERN SELVES

Essays on Modern British and American Autobiography

Edited by
PHILIP DODD

FRANK CASS

820.9
M689

First published 1986 in Great Britain by
FRANK CASS AND COMPANY LIMITED
Gainsborough House, 11 Gainsborough Road,
London, E11 1RS, England.

and in the United States of America by
FRANK CASS AND COMPANY LIMITED
c/o Biblio Distribution Centre
81 Adams Drive, P.O. Box 327, Totowa, N.J. 07511

British Library Cataloguing in Publication Data

Modern selves : essays on modern British and
    American autobiography.—(Prose studies, ISSN 0144-
    0357; v. 8, no. 2)
    1. Autobiography   2. English prose literature—
    20th century—History and criticism
    I. Dodd, Philip, *1949–*   II. Series
    828'.91208'09   PR808.A9

ISBN 0-7146-3255-4   87-5515

This group of studies first appeared in a Special Issue, 'Modern
Selves: Essays on Modern British and American
Autobiography', of *Prose Studies*, Vol. 8, No. 2, published by
Frank Cass & Co. Ltd.

Printed in Great Britain by
Adlard & Son Ltd, Dorking

Contents

Notes on Contributors

Glen Cavaliero   Fellow of St. Catharine's College, Cambridge. Dr Cavaliero's recent books include *A Reading of E.M. Forster* and *Charles Williams: Poet of Theology*.

Philip Dodd   Lecturer in English, University of Leicester. He is the editor of the journal, *Prose Studies* and author of numerous essays on modern literature. He is currently contributing co-editor of *Englishness 1880–1920*.

Timothy Dow Adams   Assistant Professor of English, West Virginia University. He is the author of articles on biography and autobiography, and is working on a book on lying in contemporary autobiography.

Simon Dentith   Lecturer in English, University of Liverpool. Dr Dentith is the author of a forthcoming book on George Eliot.

Brian Finney   Lecturer in English, Department of Extra-Mural Studies, University of London. His publications include *Christopher Isherwood: A Critical Biography* and *The Inner I: British Literary Autobiography in the Twentieth Century*.

Carolyn G. Heilbrun   Professor of English, Columbia University. Professor Heilbrun's numerous publications include *Reinventing Womanhood* and *Towards Androgyny: Aspects of Male and Female in Literature*.

Judith Lee   Dr Lee, who was recently Visiting Scholar at the Center for Research on Women, Stanford University, teaches at Brandeis University. She is completing a book-length study of Isak Dinesen.

Sheila Lodge   Dr Lodge, whose PhD. was on *Edwin Muir*, was until recently managing editor of the journal *Cencrastus*.

Michael Mundhenk   Mr Mundhenk is at Simon Fraser University, has written several articles on modern literature and is the translator of American and Canadian poets into German.

Shirley Neuman   Associate Professor of English, University of Alberta. Her publications include *Gertrude Stein: Autobiography and the Problem of Narration* and *Some One Myth: Yeats's Autobiographical Prose*.

Martin Stannard   Lecturer in English, University of Leicester. Dr Stannard is the author of a number of essays on modern literature and editor of *Evelyn Waugh: The Critical Heritage*. He is currently writing a biography of Evelyn Waugh.

Preface

This volume has been organised into three informal sections after my opening essay. The first two sections are devoted to Gender and Autobiography and to the Politics of Autobiography. Each of these sections contains two general studies and an account of an individual work. The third section offers examples of other important ways of making sense of individual works or groups of works.

In selecting and organising this volume, I have been aware that the critical debate on modern autobiography has been based on the few autobiographies which have had bestowed upon them the honorific title, Literary Autobiography. To challenge the terms of the dominant critical debate, and to give a more adequate account of the varieties, meanings and uses of modern autobiography, I have mixed essays on "literary" and "non-literary" autobiography, radically different accounts of the same work, and conflicting arguments about the political potential of modern autobiography. The volume is devoted to Modern British and American Autobiography, with glances at the Irish tradition and recent autobiographical writing in Europe; the period of study is 1930 onwards.

It is important to state that the organisation of the volume is the editor's responsibility and not that of the contributors.

Philip Dodd

Criticism and the Autobiographical Tradition

Within university literature departments ... there is a constant resistance to the inclusion of modern works to study, and even when this battle is won, it doesn't necessarily help us or other writers, in that university English is a training in reading, not writing, literature. Even socialist and marxist theories of literature are formed in the university mould and are predominantly theories of criticism, of texts mainly from the past. ... a concentration on literature as tradition, as a mode of cultural consumption, is damaging because it rarely focusses on the question of the *production* of contemporary literature – how the literature of today is getting produced and is going to get produced, by whom, in what conditions and with what support.

The Republic of Letters: Working Class Writing and Local Publishing[1]

It seems appropriate to try to take the weight of part of this quotation at the opening of a volume of critical *readings* of one field of contemporary *writing*, autobiography. What is and ought to be the relationship between criticism and contemporary writing? What are the consequences of criticism's organisation of writing into the "literary" and the "non literary," and into traditions? Such questions are particularly pressing in any discussion of autobiography which has recently enjoyed increased status among writers and readers, and has become, during the same period, an object of academic critical discourse. What I intend to do in this essay is sketch briefly the dominant mode of critical address to autobiography, identify the "Autobiography" such an address constructs, show the (non-) relationship of that address to the most interesting contemporary autobiography, and draw some conclusions about what an adequate criticism of autobiography might be. Assuming editorial privilege, I draw my examples from outside as well as within the scope of the book (1930 onwards) in order to map the interests of the dominant criticism.

First, the perceived contemporary standing of autobiography. "Feminist autobiographies are all the rage right now," was the headline to a 1984 review of a number of women's autobiographies in the monthly journal, *New Socialist*.[2] The present success of a collection of women's autobiographies, *Truth, Dare or Promise: Girls Growing Up in the Fifties*

(1985), sold out within weeks of an original print-run of 7,000 copies, offers further anecdotal evidence for the claim that autobiography is important to women readers and women writers. Carolyn Heilbrun's essay in this volume provides substantial support for the same claim.

Working-class writers who have generated such ventures as the Federation of Worker Writers and Community Publishers are also wedded to the form, as the authors of *The Republic of Letters* make clear when they acknowledge "that certain forms predominate [in contemporary working-class writing and] are even, as in the case of autobiography, taken to be characteristic."[3] It is hardly surprising that autobiography should be important to contemporary women writers and to working-class writers, given their (very different) stress on experience as a source of knowledge and political resistance, and on the articulation of experience as the goal of writings.[4] The essays in this volume by Simon Dentith and Michael Mundhenk reflect on the political implications of autobiographical writing by marginalised groups.

Autobiography matters also to those whose literary credentials need no inspection. For instance, Graham Greene, as Martin Stannard's essay shows, has devoted many of the most recent years of his literary life to autobiographical writing. And Graham Greene is not the only eminent writer to write a number of autobiographical works. Consider, for example, V. S. Naipaul whose series of autobiographical travel books have recently culminated in two explicitly autobiographical pieces, *Finding the Centre* (1984). Or Stephen Spender, who said, in a recent interview, that a major remaining literary ambition was to revise and double the length of his 1951 autobiography, *World Within World*, and write a new autobiography.[5]

It is, of course, very difficult to judge whether there has been *more* autobiographical writing in the last forty years than in any other forty-year period. For instance, Thomas Carlyle in *Sartor Resartus* (1831) wrote of "these Autobiographical Times of ours." But there is not only the question of how many autobiographies are being written, but also how much we value autobiography as *a kind of writing*. One measure of the status of a form of writing or of an individual work, as a great deal of the literary theoretical work of the last fifteen years has taught us, is its place within the literary canon. What then is interesting about autobiography is that it has recently moved from the periphery towards the centre of the canon (this volume is, of course, confirmation of what I describe). Academic interest is as recent as Wayne Shumaker's *English Autobiography: Its Emergence, Materials, and Forms* (1954) and Roy Pascal's *Design and Truth in Autobiography* (1960). Perhaps not surprisingly, those committed to research on autobiography are clear that it generates great interest. James Olney, editor of *Autobiography: Essays Theoretical and Critical* (1980) says in his introduction that "within a few years of one another (and I believe quite independently) a number of people turned their critical attention to autobiography, found the same, new kind of interest in it and read it in the same, new sort of way, and that this number of people who share something of a common interest and understanding is increasing – has in the past years increased – very rapidly."[6] One can even find autobiography being proposed as *the* cornerstone of a prospective teacher's own education in Peter Abbs's *Autobiography in Education: An Introduction to the Subjective Discipline of Autobiography and Its Central Place in the Education of Teachers* (1974). What is of equal interest, and perhaps more compelling as evidence, is that a critic such as Edward Said, opposed to the dominant assumptions of American literary criticism, should lament the current emphasis on biography and autobiography, both of which, according to Professor Said, isolate the subject beyond his or her time and society.[7]

What, then, is the nature of the dominant criticism of autobiography and what "Autobiography" has it constructed? To phrase it briefly, but not unfairly, the dominant criticism of autobiography has tried to secure autobiography for Literature; it has identified autobiography as a *literary* genre with its own history (Tradition), as a distinctive kind of writing, which produces, does not simply express, meaning through a repertoire of formal and thematic conventions. Before sketching the usefulness and limitations of the dominant criticism, it may be well to emphasise two matters. First, the dominant criticism does not exhaust the range of critical address to autobiography, even though it is the dominant *literary* critical address. Second, the critical books referred to below have not been chosen to highlight their authors' "errors," but to make concrete the general case about the dominant literary discourse on autobiography. From the particular works themselves, I have often learnt a great deal.

The advance made by the dominant criticism, by the rejection of the earlier positivist assumption that autobiography is a simple transcription of antecedent reality, should not be underestimated. For instance, such an advance should prevent critics in the future from making the error of Ronald A. Duerkson in *Shelleyan Ideas in Victorian Literature* (1966) who used information from Leigh Hunt's *Autobiography* (1850) as part of his narrative on Shelley's last days:

> Being deeply religious, Shelley recognised that in religion, as in politics, a revolution was necessary. Touring Pisa with Hunt on 7 July 1822, he paused with his friend to listen to the cathedral organ and enthusiastically agreed with him 'that a truly divine religion might yet be established, if charity were really made the principle of it, instead of faith'.[8]

This is the passage in Hunt's *Autobiography* on which Professor Duerkson drew:

> He [Shelley] assented warmly to an opinion which I expressed in the cathedral of Pisa, while the organ was playing, that a truly divine religion might yet be established, if charity were really made the principle of it, instead of faith.[9]

Unfortunately, if one checks Hunt's 1828 account of the same incident, it differs from that in the autobiography:

He [Shelley] said to me in the cathedral at Pisa, while the organ was playing, 'What a divine religion might be found out, if charity were really made the principle of it, instead of faith'.[10]

Between the two versions, the speaker changes. What is as interesting is that only from Hunt's autobiography could Professor Duerkson work out the date of the occasion, 7 July 1822, the day before Shelley's death. There is no independent evidence against which to check Hunt's claim that Shelley, the famous atheist, the day before his death, moved close to Christianity; that Shelley became of Hunt's own mind. In short, the status of the anecdote as historical evidence is, to put it mildly, suspect. Sheila Hearn's essay on Edwin Muir in this volume offers further evidence of the consequences which ensue from accepting an autobiography as an unproblematic document.

To show the fruitfulness of seeing a particular autobiography as working within and against the conventions of a form (the strategy of the dominant criticism), consider briefly Edmund Gosse's *Father and Son* (1907). The passage I want to examine describes what Gosse himself called the "highest moment of my religious life," when he sat on a sofa by an open window inviting Christ to " 'come now and take me to be forever with Thee in Thy Paradise' ":

> This was the highest moment of my religious life, and apex of my striving after holiness. . . . Still I gazed and still I hoped. Then a little breeze sprang up, and the branches danced. Sounds began to rise from the road beneath me. Presently the colour deepened, the evening came on. From far below there rose to me the chatter of the boys returning home. The tea-bell rang, last word of prose to shatter my mystical poetry. 'The Lord has not come, the Lord will never come', I muttered, and in my heart the artificial edifice of extravagant faith began to totter and crumble.[11]

The meaning of the passage is inseparable from (but not of course reducible to) its working on earlier autobiographical writing. For instance, the dedication of the self to God – the discovery of vocation – is itself one of the traditional subjects of autobiography which criticism sees as originating with the *Confessions* of St Augustine. But there is more than this general connection between *Father and Son* and the *Confessions*. The boys' voices which recall Edmund to the world of nature at his most evidently religious moment echo the voice of the child, which is the occasion of St Augustine's dedication of himself to God:

> when all at once I heard the singing voice of a child in a nearby house. Whether it was the voice of a boy or girl I cannot say, but again and again it repeated the refrain 'Take it and read, take it and read'. At this I looked up, thinking hard whether there was any kind of game in which children used to chant words like these, but I could not remember ever hearing them before. I stemmed my flood of

> tears and stood up, telling myself that this could only be a divine
> command to open my book of Scripture ... *arm yourselves with the*
> *Lord Jesus Christ; spend no more thought on nature and nature's*
> *appetites* ... it was as though the light of confidence flooded into my
> heart and all the darkness of doubt was dispelled.[12]

St Augustine rejects nature for Christ; Gosse rejects Christ for Pan, the
God of Nature; St Augustine's acceptance of Christ releases light into his
darkness; Edmund's embrace of Nature floods his life with light. (This is,
needless to say, not to identify the nature of St Augustine and of Gosse.)[13]
One might say, then, that certain central elements of *Father and Son* are
the comic inflection of earlier autobiographical material. But vocation,
the subject of the passage from *Father and Son*, is central not only to St
Augustine's *Confessions*, but to Victorian autobiography, the immediate
autobiographical context into which Gosse wrote. The point of closure of
the dominant mode of Victorian autobiography is vocation, the resolution of self-determination and socialisation. And this is so whether one
examines the autobiography of the atheist J. S. Mill or the Catholic J. H.
Newman. What then is noteworthy about the quoted passage from *Father*
and Son is that it articulates an escape from vocation – as does the last
passage from the book:

> No compromise, it is seen, was offered; no proposal of a truce
> would have been acceptable. It was a case of 'Everything or
> Nothing'; and thus desperately challenged, the young man's
> conscience threw off once for all the yoke of his 'dedication', and, as
> respectfully as he could, without parade or remonstrance, he took a
> human being's privilege to fashion his inner life for himself.[14]

Unlike Victorian autobiography, where the discovery of vocation finds its
formal inscription in the identification of the "I" who narrates with the
narrated "I," *Father and Son* ends with their formal separation (Gosse
turns his young self into the third person – "his inner life for himself").
There is no discovery of a new vocation to replace that imposed by his
father. It is a very short distance from the end of *Father and Son* to Robert
Graves' *Goodbye To All That* (1929) which enables Graves to part "with
myself for good," and in which the younger self is seen adopting (and
failing to sustain) a series of vocations; or to Christopher Isherwood's
Christopher and His Kind 1929–1939 (1977) in which the self who narrates
and the younger self are wholly distinct ("Christopher's first visit to
Berlin ...").[15] It is then, I hope, clear that autobiography does work (at
least in part) by means of working within and against the resources of
earlier autobiographical writing (i.e. within a tradition). It has been the
burden of the above admittedly brief argument and of what I have called
the dominant criticism to demonstrate this.

Unfortunately such demonstrations have often taken place in the context of (perhaps it would be more accurate to say are the *effect of*) the
establishment of The Tradition of autobiography, which is incorporated

into the literary canon. The titles of two good recent studies, *Autobiographical Acts: The Changing Situation of a Literary Genre* and *The Forms of Autobiography: Episodes in the History of a Literary Genre* are symptomatic.[16] With such titles, autobiography (or at least the examples discussed in the books) are rescued for Literature, and the forms of autobiography are constructed as variants of a single story. The construction of a tradition works by a process of inclusion, exclusion and transformation, and is inevitably a radical selection from the actual autobiographies that have been written. The origin of the form, it has been generally agreed, lies with St Augustine's *Confessions* and the growth of the form – often seen in terms of evolution rather than, as it is, the construction by the present of the past – has been traced. Certain kinds of autobiography have been excluded entirely, or conceded only a subordinate place. For instance, women's autobiographies hardly appear at all (see Carolyn Heilbrun's essay in this volume for confirmation). In Paul Fussell's excellent account of First World War autobiographies, there is no mention of any female autobiography, and in Shirley Williams' introduction to her mother's autobiography, there is the claim that *"Testament of Youth* is, I think, the only book about the First World War written by a woman."[17] In fact autobiographies by women containing substantial accounts of the First World War are numerous. A recent unpublished study puts the number at around thirty.[18] What the tradition does not acknowledge does not exist. It is only recent feminist work that has excavated women's autobiographies and mapped the traditions of women's autobiography – although one must add that there is the ever-present danger that an alternative (single) women's tradition will be stabilised, which will reduce through a process analogous to that of the dominant tradition the actual variety and *traditions* of women's autobiography. For instance, Beatrice Webb's *My Apprenticeship* and Virginia Woolf's "A Sketch of the Past" were written within thirteen years of each other (1926; 1939), and yet they can be assimilated to a single tradition only with great difficulty. *My Apprenticeship* works within and modifies only slightly the dominant (male) Victorian form which is organised around a "conversion" and the discovery of a vocation. On the contrary, "A Sketch of the Past" with its commitment to accommodate simultaneously present consciousness and past events, its fragmentary and non-continuous character and its refusal to move towards a settled close, resists formally (as well as at the level of subject matter) the dominant (male) Victorian form whose nature is incarnated in J. .S. Mill's description of his *Autobiography* as the record of "successive phases of [a] mind which was always pressing forward."[19]

Neglect of gender has not been the only consequence of The Tradition; neglect of race and class have been others. For instance, an essay "Modern Black Autobiography in the Tradition" offers the autobiographies of De Quincey, Newman and Yeats as the tradition in which Richard Wright, Malcolm X and Eldridge Cleaver wrote their autobiographies.[20] Timothy Dow Adams' essay in this volume on Wright's

Black Boy shows how the question of the truthfulness of the work is inseparable from the questions of whom he addresses and how far he can trust his (white) readership. On the whole, working-class auto-biographies have been bequeathed to social historians;[21] they are not Literature. The cost of such categorisation is evident in the recent history of the attempt by the Federation of Worker Writers and Community Publishers to gain an Arts Council grant from the Literature Panel. That panel rejected the application and the FWWCP was encouraged to apply to the Community Arts Department.[22] In this case, the designation of certain kinds of autobiography as "non-literary" had very material consequences.

What I have said about The Tradition's exclusion of the determinants of class, race and gender may seem to be irrelevant when one considers the attention given to such determinants in autobiographical discourse by, for example, Black Studies and Women's Studies. But rather than damaging my case, such evidence helps to confirm it. It is precisely the surrender of responsibility of, for instance, gender criticism to Women's Studies that enables the dominant criticism to pursue its colonisation of certain autobiographies as Literature.

But it is important to recognise that the Autobiographical Tradition does not only affect those works it excludes but shapes the works accommodated within The Tradition in determinate ways. Focussed as it is on the mapping of the characteristics and history of a particular form of writing, the dominant criticism effectively neglects that writing's relationship to other writing and to non-literary practices. Intent to rescue (some) autobiography for Literature from the charge of literalness, the dominant criticism has misinterpreted its ambitions and interests.

Consider, for instance, a group of autobiographies written between 1950 and 1960 by a number of male writers whose work was associated with the 1930s: *World Within World* (1951) by Stephen Spender; *Arrow in the Blue* (1951) and *The Invisible Writing* (1954), both by Arthur Koestler; *An Autobiography* (1954) by Edwin Muir; and *The Buried Life* (1960) by C. Day Lewis.[23] if one temporarily suspends attention to their form (in order to understand better why autobiography may matter to a particular group at a particular moment) and pays attention to when they were written (the early 1950s, with the exception of *The Buried Life*), and the period they discuss (the 1930s), the autobiographies then appear to be contributing to the early 1950s debate about the political and literary significance of the 1930s. That debate was prosecuted across a range of writing, from the criticism, fiction and poetry of the Movement writers who used the 1930s writers to define what they themselves were not, through *Scrutiny* which used Spender in essays such as "Keynes, Spender and Currency Values" (1951) to sustain its rejection of the 1930s, to openly political volumes such as *The God That Failed: Six Studies in Communism* (1950), which included essays in autobiographical form on communist politics in the 1930s.[24] To the last of these publications Koestler and Spender contributed, and their essays help to clarify why autobiography seemed such an appropriate form for those who wished to distance themselves from their earlier communist commitment. (It is worth noting that Hamish Hamilton was the publisher of four of the six volumes, a publisher whose commitment to Anglo-American relationships would inevitably have political implications during the Cold War.)[25] For Spender and Koestler, Communism entailed belief in the immutable laws of history, in the inevitability of the revolution. Given such laws, the agency of the self had no place. Koestler, writing of the Stalinist purges, noted his acceptance of the "necessary sacrifice of a whole generation in the interest of the next – it may all sound so monstrous and yet it was so easy to accept while *rolling along the single track of faith*"; and Spender noted the Communists' belief in the "automatism of history."[26] Day Lewis' and Muir's convictions were very similar. In *The Buried Day* Day Lewis confessed that Communism appealed to "that part of me which revolted against the intolerable burden of selfhood"; and Edwin Muir in *An Autobiography* rejected what he saw as the common error of Fascism and Communism, their belief in the "impersonal and the inevitable."[27] With such an understanding it becomes clear why autobiography, a form which might seem to guarantee the agency of the self, should be deployed by such writers to articulate their rejection of Stalinism, which denied the self any agency. What characterises each of these works is the representation of the self's discovery that it is not simply an effect of history, but "free." In Muir's case, such a self is discovered through an acceptance of Christianity, in Spender's case by the resuscitation of the notion of a sovereign liberal self surrounded but uncontaminated by the mess of history:

> Surrounded by a lacquered screen of fire [he was serving as a fireman], I felt enormously at peace, settled in the centre of the element ... It was as though a cycle of living was completed, and in the fire I stood in the centre of a wheel of my own life where childhood and middle age and death were the same.[28]

One can see, then, that to restore autobiographies, however briefly, to their original conditions of production may help to understand a particular work, the ideological import of autobiographical discourse at a particular moment, and the significance of the representation of the self inscribed in a particular work. Concentration on the evolution of a single Literary Tradition effaces or at least marginalises such matters.

This brief survey of the effect of the Autobiographical Tradition on women's autobiographies, on those of the working class, and on the perception of the ideological significance and uses of autobiography should make it clear that one cannot afford to find trivial what the opening quotation of this essay pointed to, the neglect by academic criticism of contemporary autobiographical production. Indeed so strong can be the authority of the Tradition that one can find critics who claim that the forms of modern autobiography are simply repetitions of past forms: "Although historical, philosophic, and poetic autobiographies are still being written today, the generic evolution that produced the divergent forms and so relates them to one another ... was complete a century ago."[29] What, then, is interesting is that the most important contemporary English autobiography, *In Search of a Past: The Manor House, Amnersfield, 1933–45*[30] cannot be accounted for by the Tradition. Its provenance is not the conventions of the Tradition, nor does it trace the evolution of an essential self which finds its realisation in the embrace or rejection of available social roles. The author of *In Search of a Past* is Ronald Fraser, an author who made his reputation as an oral historian, publishing among other books *Blood of Spain: the Emergence of Civil War 1936–1939* (1979). The publisher is Verso, the paperback imprint of New Left Books, distinguished for its translation of European (Marxist) theory.

What Fraser does not do in *In Search of a Past* is offer a narrative account of his childhood in the Manor House from the age of 3–15, nor does he, despite the allusion to Proust in the title, draw on established literary models. What he does is deploy two competing modes of constructing the past and the self, oral history and psychoanalysis. He weaves together and annotates a series of interviews with former servants of the House, and with his brother, with a series of encounters between himself and a psychoanalyst, and punctuates both by an account of his journey with his father to a nursing home:

> Unexpectedly, his [the psychoanalyst's] voice takes on a conversational tone. 'What purpose are you trying to achieve within the book?'
>
> Relieved to find myself in a zone of normality, I outline the newly discovered aim of combining two different modes of enquiry – oral history and psychoanalysis – to uncover the past in as many of its layers as possible. 'At first, I thought I wanted your help to overcome the difficulty of writing about the past; now I see that the difficulty is part and parcel of the past. This "voyage of inner discovery", as I think you once called it, has to be combined with the account of the other voyage into the social past ...'
>
> 'Uh-huh ...' After a time, he adds: 'Yes, through them you set out to discover the external objects; now, through analysis, you're seeing the internal object.'
> 'And the two don't always coincide,' I reply. 'That's my split vision. Formed by a past, a person is also deformed by it.'[31]

The book is divided into three parts and, within these parts, sections are identified by pronouns: "We," "They, She/He/She/You," "We, Us, I". There is no simple unified self, but one split between, for instance, competing mothers, between parents and servants. The lack of coincidence – indeed the contradictions – between the meanings of class and of gender generated by oral history and by psychoanalysis is not resolved. Unlike Arthur Koestler who in his 1954 autobiography, *The*

Invisible Writing, excluded passages from his 1937 *Dialogue With Death* on the grounds of their stylistic and ideological incompatibility with his present work,[32] Fraser in *In Search of a Past* acknowledges in the formal organisation of the book that "the difficulty of writing about the past . . . is part and parcel of the past."

If the dominant criticism might find it hard to account for *In Search of a Past* (note, not *the* Past), the book might seem to be more at home with what one might call the emergent (as opposed to dominant) criticism of autobiography, a poststructuralism which sees all meaning, including the meaning of self, as an irreducibly textual matter simultaneously caught and lost in language.[33] My reasons for not conceding this view of *In Search of a Past* would be not unlike those Terry Eagleton advances for resisting poststructuralism:

> Meaning may well be ultimately undecidable if we view language contemplatively, as a chain of signifiers on a page: it becomes 'decidable', and words like 'truth', 'reality', 'knowledge' and 'certainty' have something of their force restored to them, when we think of language rather as something we *do* . . . It is not of course that language then becomes fixed and luminous. On the contrary, it becomes even more fraught and conflictual than the most 'deconstructed' literary text. It is just that we are then able to see, in a practical rather than academical way, what would *count* as deciding, determining, persuading, certainty, being truthful, falsifying and the rest – and see, moreover, what beyond language itself is *involved* in such definitions.[34]

What the poststructuralist and the dominant criticism of autobiography share is an emphasis on the consumer (i.e., reader) and on the reduction of a literary practice to a series of literary texts. In contrast, to use Eagleton's terms, *In Search of a Past does* a number of things. Consider three. First, it restores subjectivity to oral history, making it clear that the interviewer does not simply afford untroubled access to the past but is an agent in the "making" of the past. Second, through its substantial incorporation of the memories and words of others, it minimises the "special pleading" of autobiography which it has been claimed tends to reduce all other persons to their place in the life of the central figure.[35] *In Search of a Past* tries to acknowledge that "the past is a collective experience" and to move in formal terms towards a "perspective in which each stood equally witness to a past you had in your different ways shared."[36] And third, implicit in the first two, it interrogates not only the past, but also two of the major discourses which offer to articulate the past. *In Search of a Past* shows that past, and what self, psychoanalysis and oral history produce, what each of the discourses can do, what each cannot, and the adequacy of the questions each asks of the self.

In Search of a Past's expansion of what an autobiography can do is not exhausted by my brief description – one might note, in addition, its rewriting of, and opposition to, the country-house between-the-wars idyll which has recently in books and in such television dramas as *Brideshead Revisited* and *Upstairs Downstairs* threatened to be instituted as the national past.[37] Only one recent critical book comes near to the ambition of Ronald Fraser's book. Bernard Sharratt's *The Literary Labyrinth: Contemporary Critical Discourses*[38] is as far as I know a unique act of criticism. Sharratt's book which takes the form of an issue of a journal, *New Crisis Quarterly* mixes experiments with literary forms themselves (for example a rewriting of *Four Quartets*) with reviews of imaginary works. The section on autobiography takes the form of a review by "Anne Arthur" of "W. Armstrong's" *Objectives: a Materialist Autobiography* which highlights, through passages of self-writing and critical reflections upon them, what autobiography can do.

Of course, to restrict criticism of autobiography to this function would be to confine its domain to the contemporary and to deny it a role in relationship to autobiographies of the past. There *is* need for a criticism which encourages what has been called reading competence – what we need to know in order to read, say, African or Afro-American autobiographies in ways which do not simply appropriate them in Eurocentric ways, or to ensure that we do not read seventeenth-century autobiography exclusively by the conventions of mid-twentieth-century autobiography. But to become an adequate criticism, we must reject the Autobiographical Tradition and its implicit division of autobiography into the literary and the non-literary. The variety of autobiographical traditions and their determinants – of, for example, class, race and gender – will have to be identified; autobiographies will have to be returned to a wider literary and cultural history; the uses of autobiography by certain groups will have to be mapped; and contemporary autobiographical practice will have to be given attention – not referred back to some regulatory Tradition, but rather seen as a source of knowledge of what an adequate contemporary criticism of autobiography might be. Only with such a criticism will it be possible to persuade sceptical critics such as Edward Said, quoted near the beginning of this essay, that he has confused autobiographies and the Autobiography constructed by the Tradition, and that the wealth of autobiographies cannot be summed up in the judgement that they elevate the individual above history. What an autobiography such as *In Search of a Past* shows, and what a good critical practice would show, is the nature of autobiography's entry into history.

PHILIP DODD

NOTES

1. *The Republic of Letters: Working Class Writing and Local Publishing*, ed. Dave Morley and Ken Worpole (London: Commedia, 1982).
2. Ros Coward, "Cautionary Tales," *New Socialist*, July/Aug. 1984, pp. 46–7.
3. *The Republic of Letters*, p. 87.

4. "Experience" is a central term throughout *The Republic of Letters*; Bernard Sharratt in *Reading Relations: Structures of Literary Production: A Dialectical Text-Book* (Brighton: Harvester P., 1981), pp. 237–309, discussed how the stress on experience by figures such as E.P. Thompson may have helped to revivify the concern with auto-biography. The emphasis by the women's movement on "experience" and on the "personal" extends from Sheila Rowbotham in *Women's Consciousness, Man's World* (Harmondsworth: Penguin, 1973), pp. 23–5 to Florence Howe in her demand for auto-biography in criticism, *Images of Women in Fiction*, ed. Susan Koppelman Cornillon (Bowling Green, Ohio: Bowling Green U.P., 1972), p. 255.
5. See the interview in *Writers at Work: "The Paris Review Interviews"* 6th Series, ed. G. Plimpton (London: Secker & Warburg, 1981), p. 60.
6. "Autobiography and the Cultural Moment: A Thematic, Historical and Bibliographi-cal Introduction," *Autobiography: Essays Theoretical and Critical*, ed. James Olney (Princeton: Princeton U.P., 1980), p. 11. Olney's very useful introduction confirms with substantial evidence the recent upsurge in academic writing on autobiography. My differences from Professor Olney are two. First, he seems content to map the range of critical approaches without wanting to identify which criticism is dominant. Second, he is unconcerned with what is important to my essay, the ideological implications of what Frank Kermode has called the Institutional control of interpretation: see *Essays on Fiction 1971–82* (London: Routledge & Kegan Paul), pp. 168–84.
7. Edward Said, "Opponents, Audiences, Constituencies and Community," *Critical Inquiry* 9 (1982), p. 17.
8. Ronald A. Duerkson, *Shelleyan Ideas in Victorian Literature* (London, Hague, Paris: Mouton, 1960), p. 19.
9. Leigh Hunt, *The Autobiography of Leigh Hunt with Reminiscences of Friends and Contemporaries* (1850), II, 133.
10. Leigh Hunt, *Lord Byron and Some of his Contemporaries with Recollection of the Author's Life and of his Visit to Italy* (1828), p. 176.
11. Edmund Gosse, *Father and Son: A Study of Two Temperaments*, ed. James Hepburn (London: O.U.P., 1974), p. 165.
12. *St. Augustine, Confessions*, trans. R.S. Pine-Coffin (Harmondsworth: Penguin, 1961), pp. 177–8.
13. For an account of "nature" in *Father and Son*, see Philip Dodd, "The Nature of Edmund Gosse's *Father and Son*" *ELT* 22 (1979), 270–80.
14. *Father and Son*, p. 178.
15. Robert Graves, *Goodbye to All That: An Autobiography* (London: Jonathan Cape, 1929), p. 439; Christopher Isherwood, *Christopher and His Kind 1929–1939* (London: Magnum, 1978), p. 10.
16. Elizabeth Bruss, *Autobiographical Acts: The Changing Situation of a Literary Centre* (Baltimore: Johns Hopkins U.P., 1976). William Spengemann, *The Forms of Auto-biography: Episodes in the History of a Literary Genre* (New Haven and London: Yale U.P., 1980).
17. Paul Fussell, *The Great War and Modern Memory* (London: O.U.P., 1975). Vera Brittain, *Testament of Youth: An Autobiographical Study of the Years 1900–1925* (1933, London: Virago, 1978). The quotation is from Shirley Williams' preface, unpaginated.
18. Lidwien Heerkens, "Becoming Lives: English Women's Autobiographies of the 1930's," unpub. M.A., University of Leicester, 1984.
19. J.S. Mill, *Autobiography*, ed. J. Stilinger (London: O.U.P., 1971), p. 2.
20. Michael G. Cooke, "Modern Black Autobiography in the Tradition," *Romanticism: Vistas, Instances, Continuities*, ed. David Thorburn and Geoffrey Hartman (Ithaca and London: Cornell U.P., 1973), pp. 255–80.
21. See for instance, David Vincent, *Bread, Knowledge and Freedom: A Study of Nineteenth-Century Working Class Autobiography* (London: Europa, 1981).
22. For a full account, see Jim McGuigan, "The State and Serious Writing: Arts Council Intervention in the English Literary Field," unpub. Ph.D., University of Leicester, 1984.

23. *World within World* (London: Hamish Hamilton, 1951); *Arrow in the Blue: The First Volume of an Autobiography, 1905–31* (London: Collins, with Hamish Hamilton, 1951); *The Invisible Writing: The Second Volume of an Autobiography, 1932–40* (Collins, with Hamish Hamilton, 1954); *An Autobiography* (London: Hogarth, 1954); Cecil Day Lewis, *The Buried Day* (London: Chatto & Windus, 1960).
24. Blake Morrison, *The Movement: English Poetry and Fiction of the 1950s* (Oxford: O.U.P., 1980). Morrison discusses the importance of the 1930s and of *Scrutiny* to the Movement writers; *The God that Failed: Six Studies in Communism*, with an intro. by Richard Crossman M.P. (London: Hamish Hamilton, 1950). The contributors were, in addition to Koestler and Spender, Ignazio Silone, André Gide, Richard Wright and Louis Fischer.
25. *Mumby's Publishing and Bookselling in the Twentieth Century*, 6th ed., Ian Norrie (London: Bell & Hyman, 1982), p. 131.
26. *The God that Failed*, p. 69, p. 238.
27. *The Buried Day*, p. 209; *An Autobiography*, p. 195.
28. *World within World*, p. 322.
29. Spengemann, *Forms of Autobiography*, p. xvii.
30. Ronald Fraser, *In Search of a Past: The Manor House, Amnersfield, 1933–45* (London: Verso, 1984).
31. *In Search of a Past*, p. 118.
32. *Invisible Writing*, p. 337.
33. The most famous poststructuralist essay on autobiography is Paul de Man, "Autobiography as De-facement," *MLN*, 94 (1979), 919–30.
34. Terry Eagleton, *Literary Theory: An Introduction* (Oxford: Basil Blackwell, 1983), pp. 146–7.
35. The phrase "special pleading" is Raymond Williams', from *The Long Revolution* (1961: Harmondsworth, Penguin, 1965), p. 311. Williams is discussing first-person novels, but the phrase has often been used to describe autobiographies.
36. *In Search of a Past*, p. 6, p. 10.
37. A point also made in Neil Belton's review in *New Left Review*, 149 (1985), 125–8.
38. Bernard Sharratt, *The Literary Labyrinth: Contemporary Critical Discourses* (Sussex: Harvester P., 1984), pp. 137–57.

Woman's Autobiographical Writings: New Forms

Georges Gusdorf has written of autobiography:

> The man who takes delight in thus drawing his own image believes himself worthy of a special interest. Each of us tends to think of himself as the center of a living space: I count, my existence is significant to the world, and my death will leave the world incomplete.... The author of an autobiography ... looks at himself being and delights in being looked at – he calls himself as witness for himself; others he calls as witness for what is irreplaceable in his presence.

In earlier times, Gusdorf points out, in those periods and places where "the singularity of each individual life" has not yet evolved, there was no autobiography. Men have been writing autobiographies shaped by the contemplation of their own singularity at least since the time of St. Augustine. It is my intention in this paper to argue that women's self-writings were, until very recently, radically different from men's, and if the contemplation of one's own singularity is critical, scarcely deserve the name of autobiography, but that in the last decade women's autobiography has unmistakeably found its true form.

Here's how Gusdorf describes what we might call the pre-autobiographical era in human history: "the individual does not oppose himself to all others; he does not feel himself to exist outside of others, and still less against others.... The important unit is never the isolated being." And again: "Each man thus appears as the possessor of a role," and not as an individual.[1] Until very recently women lived in such a pre-autobiographical era, and though they occasionally wrote about their own lives, singularity was hardly to be boasted of. Even in the twentieth century, before the current women's movement, women had only what Patricia Spacks has called "selves in hiding." Their narratives of self were strictly bound in by convention and scarcely to be compared with those of the male autobiographer expressing, as Gusdorf puts it, "the wonder that he feels before the mystery of his own destiny." Autobiography in that sense has been possible for women only in the last two decades, and then probably not in what theorists of the genre would call its true form.

Only since 1980 in America have critics even bothered to speak of women's autobiography, and then in less than confident tones. As in academic departments of literature before the age of "equal opportunity" there had been an "honorary man," or "token woman" already on the premises, so in autobiography there had been Gertrude Stein. Apart from the obvious qualification that her autobiography was an account within the male norms of destiny, its indirect mode of discourse (it was presented as *The Autobiography of Alice B. Toklas*) doubtless provided a comfortable and "literary" angle from which to approach it. James Olney's collection: *Autobiography: Essays Theoretical and Critical*, published in 1980, included only one essay on the autobiographies of women, in this case four women dating from before 1700, whom its author, Mary G. Mason, called "early prototypes." The dialogue of these women was with God; thus they manifested Christian virtue, "an excellent thing in woman."

For secular women there was only one plot, though we have lately diversely named it: the erotic plot, the marriage plot, the romance plot, all the plots ending, as Nancy Miller has pointed out, with marriage or death: the euphoric or dysphoric plot.[2] The labels change, the outcome is the same. Henry James's words from *The Portrait of a Lady* suffice for the story of women's lives: "She was intelligent and generous; it was a fine free nature; but what was she going to do with herself? This question was irregular, for with most women one had no occasion to ask it. Most women did with themselves nothing at all; they waited, in attitudes more or less gracefully passive, for a man to come that way and furnish them with a destiny."[3] And as we know, Isabel Archer, for all her intelligence and generosity, is provided with a destiny by a man. What other story could there be?

James Olney, in a book published in 1972, took the maleness of autobiography for granted. "Autobiography," he wrote, "seems to mean the most to us because it brings an increased awareness, through an understanding of another life in another time and place, of the nature of our own selves and our share in the human condition."[4] Olney is interested, he goes on to tell us, in "why men write autobiographies, and have written them for centuries." It did not occur to him that half the human race did not share, in the way he described, in "the human condition." For women, their "condition" was female rather than human.

Albert Stone writes that "black autobiography vividly re-creates links between the singular self, the immediate community, and a wider world of sympathetic readers and fellow human beings." For women there were no such links to be recreated: their only "immediate community" were their family or neighbours to whom no doubts about their condition could easily be expressed. There were no sympathetic readers, at least none readily identified, and women were inevitably "other" to those "fellow human beings" whom Olney and everyone else referred to simply as "men."

But if the lack of any community or audience for their scarcely defined condition of storylessness was a hamper to women's autobiography, their own internalization of patriarchal standards operated more forcefully still. So, in the words of Patricia Spacks, writing of eighteenth century women's autobiographies, a fantasy of feminine strength, even if that were achieved, "transformed itself mysteriously into one more confession of inadequacy."[5] Spacks continues: "The nature of public and private selves ... is for women, in some ways, the reverse of what it is for men. The face a man turns to the world ... typically embodies his strength," while the only acceptable models for women "involve self-deception and yielding."[6]

By the time Spacks came, four years later, to publish her essay entitled "Slaves in Hiding", she had extended her observation of women's autobiographical disabilities to our own century. The women whose autobiographies she discusses are Emmeline Pankhurst, Dorothy Day, Emma Goldman, Elinor Roosevelt, and Golda Meir, each a profoundly radical individual, responsible for revolutionary acts and concepts, and possessing a degree of personal power unusual in men as well as women. But, Spacks notes, "although each author has significant, sometimes dazzling accomplishments to her credit, the theme of accomplishment rarely dominates the narrative." "Indeed," Spacks continues, "to a striking degree they fail directly to emphasize their *own* importance, though writing in a genre which implies self-assertion and self-display."[7] The women accept full blame for any failures in their lives, but shrink from claiming either that they sought the responsibilities they ultimately bore, or were in any way ambitious. Day, for example, has what Spacks calls "a clear sense of self – but struggles constantly to lose it." All of these autobiographies "exploit a rhetoric of *uncertainty*." And in all of them the pain of the lives is, like the successes, muted, as though women were certain of nothing but the necessity of denying both accomplishment and suffering.

All of these modern autobiographies, Spacks observes, "represent a female variant of the high tradition of spiritual autobiography."[9] One must be called by God or Christ to service in spiritual causes higher than one's own poor self might envision, and authorized by that spiritual call to an achievement and accomplishment in no other way excusable in a female self. So Florence Nightingale, in her desperate desire for an occupation worthy of her talents and desires, four times heard God calling her to his service. But if, for men, spiritual autobiographies resulted in personal satisfaction deriving from their spiritual achievement, this was not the case for women. As Mary Mason writes, "Nowhere in women's autobiographies do we find the patterns established by the two prototypical male autobiographers, Augustine and Rousseau; and conversely male writers never take up the archetypal models of Julian, Margery Kemp, Margaret Cavendish, and Anne Bradstreet." On the contrary, Mason writes, "the self-discovery of female identity seems to acknowledge the real presence and recognition of another consciousness, and the disclosure of female self is linked to the identification of some 'other.'" Identity is grounded through relation to the chosen other.[10] Without such relation, women did not feel enabled to write openly about themselves: even with it, they did not feel entitled to credit for their own accomplishment, spiritual or other.

The claim of achievement, the admission of ambition, the recognition that accomplishment was neither luck nor the result of the efforts or generosity of others, all continued, well into the twentieth century, to be impossible for women to admit into their autobiographical narratives. Jill Conway, in a study of the accomplished women of the progressive era in the United States (women born 1850–65), has remarked upon the narrative flatness with which, in their autobiographies, they have described their exciting lives. Their letters and diaries are quite different, reflecting ambitions and struggles in the public sphere and strong personal feelings; in their published autobiographies they portray themselves as intuitive, nurturing, passive, never managerial which, to have accomplished what they did, they inevitably had to be.

The autobiography of Jane Addams (who founded Hull House in Chicago, and was a prominent social worker and pacifist), Conway points out, is sentimental and passive: her cause finds her, rather than the other way around. Not so in her letters, where she takes over the family business and fights for her due. The money for Hull House, in the autobiography, fell in off the street: her letters reveal the truth. This same pattern, Conway demonstrates, is true of the autobiographies of Charlotte Perkins Gilman and Ida Tarbell. There is a wholly different voice in the letters on one hand and the autobiographical narratives on the other. All of the autobiographies begin confessionally, and, except for Gilman, report the encounters with what would be the life's work as occurring by chance: this was, in every case, quite untrue. Each woman set out to find her life's work, but the only script for women's life insisted that work discover and pursue them, like the conventional romantic lover. As Conway points out, there is no model for the female who is recounting a political narrative. There are no recognizable career stages in such a life, as there would be for a man. Nor have women a tone of voice in which to speak with authority. As Natalie Davis has said, women up to the eighteenth century could speak with authority only of the family and religion. These women had no models on which to form their lives, nor could they themselves become mentors since they did not tell the truth about their lives.

Ida Tarbell, for example, one of the most famous of the muckrakers, author of the history of the Standard Oil company, reports that the subject just "happened to be there," and, as Conway shows, Tarbell credits the idea of her work to others. This is wholly belied by her letters. Where anger is expressed in these autobiographies it is not, Conway believes, used creatively, as by black authors. The expression of anger has always been a terrible hurdle in women's personal progress. Above all, the public and private life cannot be linked, as in male narratives. This prevents women from writing exemplary lives: they do not dare to offer themselves as models, but only as exceptions chosen by destiny or chance.

What these women could least express in their autobiographies, Conway shows, is their love of other women. Jane Addams loved her college classmate and hated her stepmother, but none of this can be expressed. The unspoken law that women who "make it" must not identify themselves as women, nor dare to annoy men by their self-identifications as women, serves to erase from the record these women's love of one another, and their support of each other. Conway demonstrates that the only lively sections of the autobiographies she discusses are the accounts of childhood.[11] For girls, childhood is often the happiest and freest time. As Spacks has written: "For women, adulthood – marriage or spinsterhood – implied relative loss of self. Unlike men, therefore, they looked back fondly to the relative freedom and power of childhood and youth."[12] It is not only that in childhood girls were allowed to play with boys with a freedom later restrictions on female activity would prevent ever recurring, but that accounts of childhood were somehow freed from the terrible anxieties induced by adult female ambition and encounters. One notes, therefore, that in *The Autobiography of Alice B. Toklas*, Stein does not recount her childhood, but achieves a narrative of frank, mature accomplishment.

Eudora Welty's recent *One Writer's Beginnings*, a charming and popular recreation of her childhood, on the other hand, beautifully exemplifies this pattern. As a highly skilful writer, long and justly renowned for her ability to evoke pain and conflict in accounts of apparently ordinary events, Welty is able to suggest her parents' anguish; her own suffering is never recalled, nor are any facts mentioned that might spark such a recollection. She writes that "Of all my strong emotions, anger is the one least responsible for any of my work. I don't write out of anger." She has earlier dismissed her youthful anger as "all vanity. As an adolescent I was a slammer of drawers and a packer of suitcases. I was responsible for scenes."[13] But these outbursts of anger are mentioned no more.

A clue to the female displacement of anguish may be found in a sentence of Margaret Mead's, which Welty's memoir exemplifies. "There is much to be said," Mead wrote, "for the suggestion that the true oedipal situation is not the primal scene but parents talking to each other in words the child does not understand."[14] This, which is likely to be true for girl children especially, accounts for the sense that there is a secret to the world that has, because of one's inferiority, been withheld from one. It is far likelier that the girl child, like Welty, has witnessed, not the sexual intercourse of the parents, but their whispered consultations which suggested adult discourse. This is a condition experienced by children of both sexes, but likelier to result, in women, in the profession of writer, interpreter of that whispered, hard-to-perceive adult world.

Another point: Welty was clearly, like Charlotte Bronte and George Eliot, a plain, unpretty child. So was Catherine Drinker Bowen who has written: "I sometimes wonder why women do not write more about the condition of being born homely. It is something that colors a woman's life, almost from the moment of consciousness.... Every girl who lacks beauty knows instinctively that she belongs to an underprivileged group, and that to climb up and out she will have to be cleverer and stronger and more ruthless perhaps than she would choose to be."[15] Bowen goes on to say that many successful (and married) women have told her of this, and that many of them grew beautiful in their later years. But, like Welty, most women do not write of this, nor do they observe that not having been a natural sex object in youth may have turned out to be a very good thing. Childhood may be a happy time but, even as a writer like Welty recalls it, anxiety and unhappiness are not analysed. The desire to remember only the good things is perhaps not unconnected with Freud's ultimate conclusion that memories of childhood sexual assault were merely the fantasies of the women who recounted them: the women patients themselves may have conspired in Freud's desire to absolve parents from the charge of cruelty and sexual aggression.

In 1962, Lillian Smith, a revolutionary white novelist of the South, analysed the reasons why no woman had "as yet written a great auto-biography." Women, she wrote, "dare not tell the truth about themselves for it might radically change male psychology. So – playing it safe – women have conspired to keep their secrets."[16] Smith was right, but she missed, perhaps, what was most important, the degree to which women had internalized the "facts" dictated to them by male psychology. And when Albert E. Stone asserts, in *Autobiographical Occasions and Original Acts*, that there has been a remarkable outpouring of auto-biographies by American women since 1962,[17] he fails, perhaps from gallantry, to notice that the outpouring is more remarkable than the quality or courage or originality of the autobiographies. The two women Stone chose as exemplars of female autobiography from this period are Margaret Mead and Anaïs Nin: regrettable examples in many ways. Nin's diaries are, of course, diaries, and not "autobiography" at all. But even apart from this, Nin, while she has rebelled against the value and limits placed on those qualities defined as "feminine," has made no attempt to free herself from them, nor to redefine the possible "non-feminine" strengths of women.

As Betty Freidan wrote in 1963 of Mead's autobiography *Blackberry Winter*, Mead confirmed all the then dominant Freudian prejudices in her "glorification of the female sexual function. Those who found in her work confirmation of their own unadmitted prejudices and fears ignored not only the complexity of her total work, but the example of her complex life."[18] In a similar way, Helene Deutsch, the prime orchestrator of Freud's theories of female masochism and the dangers of female in-tellectuality and achievement, wholly ignored her own experience as an achieving, professional woman when laying down the law for other members of her sex. Norman Holland has written that "the basic dif-ference between our experience of fiction and our experience of non-fiction stems from the difference in the amount of reality-testing each asks from us."[19] Yet here, as with so many other statements from the male establishment, the opposite is true for women. It is likely that the amount of "reality-testing" women applied to non-fiction, that is, women's autobiographies, was much less than that they applied to fiction by and about women, precisely because the autobiographies confirmed them in their internalized patriarchal attitudes, and were therefore "real," while some of the fiction challenged these attitudes and could, therefore, be "reality-tested." It is interesting to note that even so "unwomanly" an autobiographer as Simone de Beauvoir is not, Alice Schwarzer observes, a "particularly introspective person."[20] But even had Beauvoir been able to view herself as the ground of profound struggle, rather than as an especially endowed individual who opted out of the usual female destiny, her account would not have changed the general picture. For, as Estelle Jelinek has observed, "As long as women were willing to operate within the system of female subjugation, to see evidence of their own excellence as exceptional, individual marks of courage or intelligence did not threaten the social fabric and perhaps even reinforced it."[21] Without class consciousness, and with few friends among women, Jelinek goes on to observe, women who recorded their own achievements were quick to express their reservations about other women, and men "were quick to foster this separation." For a classic example of this, Jelenik points to Swift, who observed that he "never yet knew a tolerable woman to be fond of her own sex."[22]

Extraordinary women's autobiographies have indeed been written in recent years, though not going back to 1962, Stone's watershed. These remarkable autobiographical accounts have, moreover, been tucked away into other forms, other genres, most of them new. The woman's autobiography as such has probably not changed greatly in recent years, though biographies of women certainly have. The remarkable break-through in women's life stories has come in the form of the "confessional," as it is often called with scorn, referring to a work in which the woman critic or writer refuses to adopt an olympian stance on the male model, instead of offering her own experience as example and evidence of commitment to other women. Especially important is the fact that women found a frankly autobiographical, "confessional" mode for their poetry and, for the first time in an extended way, discovered a form for their uninhibited autobiographical impulses.

Two generalizations appear to be valid concerning recent women's autobiographical writings, whether these writings are in the form of poetry or are embedded in other genres, such as social or literary criticism, the interview, or the essay focused on a particular element of women's life history. The first is that the poet is likely to have reached middle age before beginning upon a clearly autobiographical work. The second is that the autobiographical efforts are clearly outspoken, offering details of personal rebellion and sudden, dazzling recognition of too-easily accepted female servitude with a forthrightness unthinkable two decades ago. In the past, as Gilbert and Gubar have observed, women writers have created concealed plots, the story of "the woman writer's quest for her own story."[23] Now, women have begun to seize upon their own stories, and to tell them with a directness that shocks as it enlightens. This transformation can be seen clearly in the American poet, novelist, and memoirist May Sarton. Her *Plant Dreaming Deep*, an extraordinary and beautiful account of her adventure in buying a house and living alone, eventually dismayed her as she came to realize that none of the anger, passionate struggle, or despair of her life was revealed in the book. She had not intentionally concealed her pain: she had written in the old genre of female autobiography and then lived into a period which allowed the realization that she had, unintentionally, been less than honest. In her text book, *Journal of a Solitude* she deliberately set out to recount the pain of the years covered by *Plant Dreaming Deep*. 1973, when *Journal of a Solitude* was published, may be accounted the watershed in women's autobiography.

If women's writing until the last decade has been secretive, either wholly disguising the personal struggle, or encoding it in another story or form, readers have been no less unable to read or understand women's hidden stories. We, those taught by the patriarchal world, have not learned to read women's writings because, as Annette Kolodny put it, "we read well, and with pleasure, what we *already know* how to read; and what we know how to read is to a large extent dependent upon what we have already read (works from which we've developed our expectations and learned our interpretative strategies)." Nancy Miller, after quoting Kolodny, has pointed out that, for example, Henry James could not read Georges Sand, as opposed to Balzac, because he was not able to *re*-read Sand; he had not learned to read her in the first place.[24]

If women's writing was, in essence, dismissed as a female, and therefore valueless art, if women had neither the skills nor the courage to represent their own brutalization and dehumanization, their own despair and secret hopes, then the break into autobiographical expression which occurred in the last decade is the more astonishing and, of course, the more threatening, the more easily dismissed as "confession." It is, also, inevitable that the writers who made this break into the autobiographical mode should have been middle-aged when they did so. (We remember that Virginia Woolf recorded in her diary that she had at last, at forty, found her own voice.) Erik Erikson has said that autobiographies "are written at certain late stages of life for the purpose of re-creating oneself in the image of one's own method; and they are written to make that image convincing."[25] As is usual with Erikson's observations about life histories, this applies more easily to men. Women do not look back to recreate themselves in keeping with some finally perceived ideal; rather, they look back towards the moment at which they found the courage to move forward into as yet unnarrated and unexplored ways of living; they have no "image of one's own method."

In a recent collection of essays, *The Voyage In: Fictions of Female Development*, the bildungsroman is newly examined as a female form. Obviously, it differs from the male form, heretofore accepted as universal: the male pattern, for example, is that of apprenticeship, essentially chronological; for females, the pattern is often that of awakening, "deferred maturation." What is clear is that the male "evolution of a coherent self" has now become possible also for women, but in different ways, and at a different time of life. Women move "from introspection to activity," not the other way.[26] Women must recognize that their spiritual conformity is often a "death warrant," signed in the name either of marriage or other personal sacrifice. As Marianne Hirsch succinctly puts it, the "story of a female spiritual *Bildung* is the story of the potential artist who fails to make it."[27] Spiritual conformity for women is slavery; for men, it can be release into activity and moral revolution. And, in their fictions of female development, women often observe, as did Doris Lessing's Martha Quest, that "there was no woman she had ever met she could model herself on."

Small wonder, then, that it is only past youth that women begin to write the first uncoded, clearly expressed autobiographies. Virginia Woolf, in fact, was in the last months of her life when she wrote, "A Sense of the Past," her first wholly open autobiographical sketch; Quentin Bell had not seen it when he published his biography of her. It is a remarkably honest, almost searing memory, and, as with many such recollections in the past, it was disbelieved: Ellen Moers, to take but one example, regarded the memories of childhood sexual assaults upon Woolf as probably fantasy.[28] What is important, however, is that, exhausted, living in a country fearful of invasion, Woolf wrote her first outspoken autobiography, and then only for intimate friends in the Memoir Club. She was in her late fifties.[29] An American poet like Maxine Kumin did not begin writing poetry "as a woman" until she was middle-aged: her autobiographical prose came even later. In 1975, when she was fifty, she said in an interview: "I didn't really begin to be able to write womanly poems until, let's say, my consciousness was raised by my daughters.... I was programmed into one kind of life, which was to say: get a college degree, get married, and have a family.... And I came to poetry as a way of saving myself because I was so wretchedly discontented, and I felt so guilty about being discontented."[30]

Within the last two years, two volumes of essays have appeared, one in England and one in America, that present women in their new auto- biographical mode with a sharpness and clarity suggesting that, for the first time, women's autobiographical writing has become an exploration of painful experience rather than a denial of pain and struggle. The volumes are: *Fathers: Reflections by Daughters*, edited by Ursula Owen, published by Virago in England in 1983, and *Between Women: Bio- graphers, Novelists, Critics, Teachers and Artists Write About Their Work on Women*, edited by Carol Ascher, Louise DeSalvo, and Sara Ruddick, published by Beacon Press, Boston, 1984. There have, during this time, been other women's autobiographies that recount personal histories with the new honesty women have required. Of these, Ann Oakley's *Taking it Like a Woman* is a fine example. But because I can speak with more assurance of American autobiography, and because it happens that in the English collection on Fathers and Daughters, the essay by Adrienne Rich is the most searing and the most explorative, I shall limit my discussion to American autobiographers.

It must first be noticed, however, that for women examining with new awareness the hitherto mutely accepted constraints of their lives, their parents and other male and female figures are seen with sharp distinctions. One can generalize from these essays with only minor if any exaggeration that fathers, as representatives of patriarchy, are the pivot on which, usually in memory, the new awareness turns. Mothers have no obvious role in this change, but some other female mentor or figure, often not even known personally, operates in the new female plot to enhance the reaction from the father and encourage or inspire the awakening. Mothers may come to be recognized with a new, loving perception, but it is not mothers who free women from their fathers. Not, at any rate, as recounted in autobiographies.

Fathers have so clearly represented patriarchy to newly awakened feminists that, in 1983, Sheila Rowbotham felt the need to defend the individuality of fathers: "Because we were not dealing with abstractions of a vaguely defined 'patriarchy' but talking about actual men, a complex picture began to emerge of 'manhood' and 'fatherhood' and our contradictory needs and images of both. Because these were men with whom we were connected passionately and intimately, however painfully, it was impossible to settle for an oversimplified stereotype in which they could be objectified as 'the enemy' or even 'the other.' "[31] Yet a statement such as this, amounting to forgiveness of the father, or at least an understanding of him, which almost all women autobiographers, except those who have been actually brutalized or sexually assaulted by their fathers, seem eventually to reach, must not be allowed to obscure the great difficulty women have in coming to terms with this figure. As Maxine Kumin has said, the poem about her father was "the hardest poem I ever wrote." She wrote it originally in syllabics and rhyme, using these as a defence between her and the material of the poem: "That's how terrified I was of writing it."[32]

This terror of analysing one's relation to the father, as Kumin describes it, in no way denies, however, that until recently such analysis was the only way to female self-realization. Ellen Moers in *Literary Women* describes the influence other women's writing had in the past upon lonely and exceptional female creators. But for the ordinary woman, or the gifted woman who was not able, like Emily Dickinson or Madame de Staël, to become in herself a one-woman revolution, the father held the only possible key to female achievement, and the only available encouragement. Bell Gale Chevigny's essay in *Between Women* on Margaret Fuller clearly sets forth the conflict within a gifted woman like Fuller of the male example provided by the father, the female example provided by the mother, and the unbearable conflict between them for the daughter. As Adrienne Rich has observed: "It is a painful fact that a nurturing father, who replaces rather than complements a mother, *must be loved at the mother's expense*, whatever the reasons for the mother's absence."[33] The essays in *Between Women* demonstrate further that when the woman sought a female model for self-realization and achievement, she had to find it in a woman already dead (this is true of almost all the essays in the book), and she was enabled to find it, as the ages of the contributors testify, only with the encouragement of the current feminist movement. Without these dead women, and above all the feminist current bearing the lonely female swimmer along, the discovery and use of a female model would have been impossible.

Only two living women, May Sarton and Simone de Beauvoir, provided courage and inspiration for female achievement and are the subjects of essays in *Between Women*.[34] The latter is, of course, French, and Carol Ascher's essay is entitled "On 'Clearing the Air': My Letter to Simone de Beauvoir." Her letter, which attempts to clarify her own problems and does not set out to change Beauvoir's views, suggests the same relation between essayist and model as do the other essays. May Sarton provides the only other living mentor or model, and it is significant that Sarton has served so many women this way: she has done so not only through her writings in three genres, but by her life about which she has written in great detail. Her life devoted steadily to writing, lived for many years in solitude but encompassing a love for women, makes her a model both unique and available. Among the other essays for this volume, from Alix Kates Shulman's on Emma Goldman to Alice Walker's on Zora Neale Hurston, the dead woman as recorded in her own and others' writings seemed to replace the mother in affirming the daughter's right to her own destiny and her own opinions. It is now without question that these essayists will, in their turn, provide their daughters, or other young women of the age of daughters, with that encouragement that was denied them. Future women's autobiographies cannot but change profoundly in the light of this.

Side by side with the new examination of the influence of fathers, a widely represented group, and of accomplished women, a frighteningly small or hidden collection of rare individuals, went the new need to identify oneself, claiming, in a new multiple identification, a new freedom for seeking selfhood. Sheila Rowbotham, for example, would write: "Changes outside our immediate family have worked upon our lives.... I am a townswoman, educated at Oxford, part of the educated middle class, a Marxist, a feminist."[35] She defines herself as having undertaken a journey formerly inconceivable in one generation. But the multiple identification was not, in itself, enough. It matters whether the identifications are asserted or merely assented to. So Maxine Kumin wrote: "I began as a poet in the Dark Ages of the fifties with very little sense of who I was – a wife, a daughter, a mother, a college instructor, a swimmer, a horse lover, a hermit – a stewpot of conflicting emotions."[36]

Adrienne Rich, who more than any other woman has revolutionized women's autobiographical writing, has recorded how she sought again and again to identify herself in new ways, ways guaranteed to be upsetting to the neat, orderly world from which she came. Her most fundamental struggle was to recognize herself as a poet, and to mean by this that the quality of what she felt impelled to say in poetry was not diminished because it was thought to be female, political, and offensive. Rich, like all of us, grew up with anthologies of poetry we were convinced represented a "universal vision." "I still believed that poets were inspired by some transcendent authority and spoke from some extraordinary height." Although she had been born a woman, she "was trying to think and act as if poetry – and the possibility of making poems – were a truly universal – that is, gender-neutral – realm. In the universe of masculine paradigm, I naturally absorbed ideas about women, sexuality, power, from the subjectivity of male poets." Of course she was told that her sort of poetry, "that is, writing from a perspective which may not be male, or white, or heterosexual, or middle-class," was grinding a political axe, that what she was writing was "bitter," and "personal."[37]

Rich has written, in both poems and essays, of many women who preceded her, from Emily Dickinson to the Russian women's climbing team which perished. But while in the creation of her autobiography, which, it must be emphasized, is except for the essay in *Fathers: Reflections of Daughters*, always either a poem or part of some other not chiefly autobiographical work, Rich writes with loving attention of her female predecessors, it is her father with whom she has had to come to terms: it is her father who is the pivot upon which her autobiography ultimately turns. And, like Woolf, she is over fifty when she finally comes to terms with him in print, and identifies herself: she knows that in the rest of her life, "every aspect of her identity will have to be engaged. The middle-class white girl taught to trade obedience for privilege. The Jewish lesbian raised to be a heterosexual gentile. The woman who first heard oppression named and analysed in the Black civil rights struggle. The woman with three sons, the feminist who hates male violence. The woman limping with a cane, the woman who has stopped bleeding, are also accountable. The poet who knows that beautiful language can lie, that the oppressor's language sometimes sounds beautiful."[38] One can scarcely imagine a woman so identifying herself in print two decades ago: it is Rich who best demonstrates, in her writings, the new autobiographical form which permitted, indeed demanded, such a statement to be openly made.

Rich began her prose writings in the autobiographical mode in her profoundly important and shocking book, *Of Woman Born*. Her honesty in this book, her admission that women might at times hate their children, might even have murderous thoughts about them, so shocked the women who were its first reviewers that the book was denied much publicity and exposure that had, before the reviews, been offered.[39] Rich wrote at the beginning of her book: "It seemed to me impossible from the first to write a book of this kind without being often autobiographical, without often saying 'I.' Yet for many months I buried my head in historical research and analysis in order to delay or prepare the way for the plunge into areas of my own life which were painful and problematical." Rich asserted here, as she had previously, her belief that it is only the willingness of women to share their "private and often painful experience" that will enable women to achieve a true description of the world, and to free and encourage one another.[40] Feminist theoreticians like Elaine Showalter have, since then, defended this female mode, despite efforts to dismiss it by calling it confessional. "In comparison to this flowing confessional criticism," she wrote, "the tight-lipped Olympian intelligence" of such writers as Elizabeth Hardwick and Susan Sontag "can seem arid and strained."[41] They can also seem self-protective, and too readily conforming to the male model of distance and apparent disinterest.

Therefore, in *Of Woman Born*, Rich spoke many hidden truths: that only when visibly pregnant did she feel, in her whole adult life, not-guilty. That like so many women with "male" dreams in childhood, she had set her heart on a son, and had felt triumphant over her mother, who had brought forth only daughters, at the birth of her "perfect, golden, male child." That her husband was unusual in the fifties in "helping," but there was no question that the major career was his, all the initiative for domestic responsibilities was hers. She reports what she wrote in her journal in those years, the despair, resolutions, self-hatred, anger, weariness, bouts of weeping characteristic of so many women's journals. Nor was she willing to dismiss her despair during her children's early years as "the human condition." As she noted, "those who speak largely of the human condition are usually those most exempt from its oppressions – whether of sex, race, or servitude."[42]

By the date of this book (1976), Rich's poetry had already broken through the barriers of impersonality, and the propriety of autobiography in women's poetry. Contemporary male poets, principally Robert Lowell and W.D. Snodgrass, had chosen the same path. But it is chiefly in Rich's generation of women poets – Plath, Sexton, Kumin, Kizer, Levertov – that the T.S. Eliot ban upon the personal fell. These same women – certainly Plath, Sexton, and Kumin – began, like Rich, to explore in other genres their previously hidden resentments and experiences, guilts and sufferings. Novels, interviews, letters all served this impulse. But it is Rich alone who, in writing the essay devoted to her father, practised the new female autobiography directly, in prose.

The writing of this essay, "Split at the Root," seemed to her "so dangerous an act, filled with fear and shame," but nonetheless necessary. It is well to take these words at their face value. If women's autobiography has taken a great leap, it has not done so without great pain and courage on the part of women like Rich. What became central to Rich's account of her father was not only what was denied her as a woman, but what was denied her as a Jew. Her father's devoted belief in "passing," in making it into the gentile world by being so like gentiles that they would forgive him his Jewishness is what she chiefly remembers and resents about him: "With enough excellence, you could presumably make it stop mattering that you were Jewish; you could become the *only* Jew in the gentile world." "I had never been taught about resistance," Rich wrote; "only about passing." And to pass meant to be the right sort of Jew, one who exemplified "achievement, aspiration, genius, idealism. Whatever was unacceptable got left back, under the rubric of Jewishness, or the 'wrong kind' of Jews: uneducated, aggressive, loud.'"[43]

To disconnect herself from her family, Rich married a "real Jew." Perhaps she was simultaneously rejecting her Protestant mother and attempting to transform, to humanize, her father. But it is not really evident that her departure from her marriage, which followed her identification with the women's liberation movement, had a great deal to do with her father's Jewishness, although the essay is so finely written that one does not notice this. Yet there may be an indirect connection. Because in trying to state, to reveal, the truth about everything, particularly the fear of "seeming," let alone "being" Jewish, Rich suggests how profound is the feminist revolution, how it matters that one rethink everything once one has begun to think anew as a woman. She suggests, further, that the efforts of fathers to be accepted in the male world they do not question or challenge are vitally connected with their efforts to imprison their female children, however talented and encouraged, in the conventions of femininity.

The sense one has, in this essay, and in many of the others in this volume, is that in finding both themselves and their fathers these women have come home, have, in the concluding words of Rich's essay, cleaned up their act. The problem of mothers, except to forgive and understand them, is harder, perhaps impossible to solve. The new women autobiographers will probably be the first real mothers of achieving, self-realized women in the history of the world. It is a sobering thought, and one which reveals how new and revolutionary a form we are considering.

CAROLYN G. HEILBRUN

NOTES

1. Georges Gusdorf, "Conditions and Limits of Autobiography," in *Autobiography: Essays Theoretical and Critical*, ed. James Olney (Princeton: Princeton U.P., 1980), pp. 28–48.
2. Nancy K. Miller, *The Heroine's Text* (New York: Columbia U.P., 1980).
3. Henry James, *Portrait of a Lady*, I, vii.
4. James Olney, *Metaphors of Self* (Princeton: Princeton U.P., 1972).
5. Patricia Spacks, *Imagining a Self* (Cambridge, Mass.: Harvard U.P., 1976), p. 59. The reference in the previous paragraph is to "Introduction," *The American Autobiography*, ed. Albert E. Stone (Englewood Cliffs: Prentice Hall, 1981), p. 4.
6. *Imagining a Self*, p. 88.
7. In *Women's Autobiography*, ed. Estelle C. Jelinek (Bloomington and London: Indiana U.P., 1980), pp. 113–14.
8. "Selves in Hiding," p. 131.
9. "Selves in Hiding," p. 131.
10. Mary G. Mason, "The Other Voice: Autobiographies of Women Writers," in

Autobiography: Essays Theoretical and Critical, pp. 207–8, 210.

11. Jill Conway, Paper on Autobiographies of Women of the Progressive Era. Delivered at Workshop on "New Approaches to Women's Biography and Autobiography," Smith College Project on Women and Social Change, 12–17 June, 1983.

12. Patricia Spacks, "Stages of Self: Notes on Autobiography and the Life Cycle," in *The American Autobiography*, ed. Albert E. Stone, p. 48.

13. Eudora Welty, *One Writer's Beginnings* (Cambridge, Mass.: Harvard U.P., 1984), p. 38.

14. Margaret Mead, *Blackberry Winter* (New York: Morrow, 1972), p. 211.

15. Catherine Drinker Bowen, *Family Portrait* (Boston: Little Brown, 1970), pp. 127–8.

16. Quoted in Albert E. Stone, *Autobiographical Occasions and Original Acts* (Phil: U. of Pennsylvania Press, 1982), p. 194.

17. *Autobiographical Occasions*, p. 195.

18. *Autobiographical Occasions*, p. 200.

19. *Autobiographical Occasions*, p. 320.

20. Alice Schwarzer, *After the Second Sex*, trans. Marianne Howarth (New York: Pantheon, 1984), p. 20.

21. Jelinek, p. 24.

22. Jelinek, p. 34.

23. Sandra Gilbert and Susan Gubar, *The Madwoman in the Attic* (New Haven: Yale U.P., 1979), p. 76.

24. Nancy K. Miller, "Arachnologies: Representing Writing," forthcoming.

25. Erik H. Erikson, *Life History and the Historical Moment* (New York: W.W. Norton, 1975), p. 125.

26. Elizabeth Abel, "Introduction," in *The Voyage In: Fictions of Female Development*, ed. Elizabeth Abel, Marianne Hirsch, and Elizabeth Langland (Hanover: U. Press of New England, 1983), pp. 11, 13.

27. Marianne Hirsch, "The Beautiful Soul as Paradigm," in *The Voyage In*, pp. 26, 28.

28. Ellen Moers, *Literary Women* (New York: Doubleday, 1976), p. 105.

29. See my "Virginia Woolf in her Fifties," in *Virginia Woolf: A Feminist Slant*, ed. Jane Marcus (Lincoln: U. of Nebraska Press, 1984), pp. 236–53.

30. Maxine Kumin, *To Make a Prairie* (Ann Arbor: U. of Michigan Press, 1979), pp. 31–2.

31. Sheila Rowbotham, "Our Lance," in *Fathers: Reflections by Daughters* (London: Virago, 1983), p. 213.

32. Kumin, p. 27.

33. Adrienne Rich, *Of Woman Born* (New York: Norton, 1976), p. 245.

34. Elizabeth Kamark Minnich's essay on Hannah Arendt, written after Arendt's death, recounts Minnich's meetings with her in life. The subject's death offers distance and freedom.

35. Rowbotham, p. 215.

36. Kumin, p. 106.

37. Adrienne Rich, "Blood, Bread & Poetry: The Location of the Poet," *The Massachusetts Review* 24 (1983), 521–40.

38. Rich, "Split at the Root," in *Fathers*, p. 186.

39. See Kathleen Barry, Reviewing Reviews: *Of Woman Born* in *Reading Adrienne Rich: Reviews & Re-visions 1951–81*, ed. Jane Roberta Cooper (Ann Arbor, U. of Michigan Press, 1984), pp. 300–3.

40. *Of Woman Born*, pp. 15–16.

41. Showalter, p. 189.

42. *Of Woman Born*, pp. 26, 193, 223, 27, 30, 34.

43. "Split at the Root," pp. 170, 178, 175, 179.

Sexual Identity in
Modern British Autobiography

I

Why focus this essay on the autobiographies of members of sexual minorities? What I wanted to write about was the modern autobiographer's tendency to portray the self in the light of his or her sexual history. How has the genre been affected by the admission into its spectrum of that most private of human activities, sex? For the most part, however, autobiographers have not seen in their sexual behaviour the key to their identity, the search for which is a central obsession with writers of this century. Although reticence about disclosing intimate details of both their own lives and those of their sexual partners has undoubtedly played its part, most autobiographers, because they belong to the heterosexual majority, tend to treat their sexual lives as something they hold in common with most of their readers rather than as clues to the uniqueness they seek to identify within themselves. Even the few heterosexual autobiographers who have given special prominence to their sexual identity, such as Frank Harris, feel compelled to dramatise and exaggerate their sexual encounters so as to demonstrate the uniqueness of their own experiences. Harris's sexual gymnastics reveal more about his neurotic need (a leftover from childhood) to excel in his father's eyes in whatever he turns his mind to than about the inner workings of his psyche. In fact his sexual feats occupy a relatively small portion of *My Life and Loves*, and this is true of most heterosexuals' autobiographies which, like H.G. Wells's for example, attempt to include their sexual history as a prominent element.

So it is not surprising to find that only in the autobiographies of members of sexual minority groups is sexuality seen as a key to their sense of identity. Members of a repressed minority group, they find that the social ostracism which accompanies their sexual tastes produces in them an acute crisis of identity. In fact this crisis places them in a situation which is very similar to that experienced by numerous earlier autobiographers, the situation of the outsiders, of the socially ostracised who are compelled to reject the culture and beliefs of the majority in order to justify their lives. One immediately thinks of all those religious confessions written by protestant sectarians during the seventeenth and eighteenth centuries with their appeal to an inner light by means of which they justify themselves in face of their rejection by the bulk of their fellow Christians. Many of the most celebrated autobiographies are written by individuals who see themselves as outsiders – in religion, in the advancement of scientific knowledge, in the world of politics, or in the literary spectrum.

The confessions of religious converts merge with those of famous criminals in their writers' desire to reconcile their own pattern of existence with the expected norm. Almost invariably the reader is treated both as confessor and as representative of the social norm. As Michel Leiris points out in his earliest volume of autobiography, "every confession contains a desire to be absolved."[1] But this desire is at odds with the outsider's need to assert his own sense of identity, one which places him in conflict with the reader whose absolution he seeks. Rousseau's *Confessions* is a brilliant attempt to reconcile these conflicting needs. But he is sufficiently attentive to the genre to appreciate the impossibility of such a reconciliation and adroitly changes the object of his confession from the society of his own day (which he despairs of winning over) to a revolutionary society of the future from which he would win absolution because he would no longer be an outcast from it.

So the tradition of the outsider's autobiography naturally places its writer in the position of either a social outcast or a social revolutionary, and frequently both. To assert one's socially unacceptable sense of individual identity normally involves adopting a radical stance towards the society of one's day even while one is seeking to win its approval. It is the paradoxical nature of this predicament which I want to explore in this essay. Most of the autobiographies discussed here display a structural ambiguity which reflects their ambivalent relationship to the hetero-sexual majority. The situation is further complicated by the mixed if not muddled attitudes adopted by the majority towards the "deviants" in its midst. For instance the majority, which has a tendency to scoff at the findings of psychoanalysis in most cases, tends to accept its diagnosis of sexual deviancy, whereas almost all those to be considered here reject the theories of the childhood origins of their pattern of behaviour offered by Havelock Ellis, Kraft-Ebbing, Freud and his successors. The genre itself imposes strains on its practitioners because of its tendency to reveal more than they intended and because it encourages self-criticism on the part of the writer. One modern British autobiographer who is a bisexual has, in my opinion, responded to these generic characteristics by exploiting them rather than by trying to evade them. This is Stephen Spender in his autobiography, *World Within World* (1951). For this reason I have de-voted the latter portion of this essay, after a survey of a number of other "sexual" autobiographies, to a more detailed, if still highly selective, consideration of this work. Like Rousseau he confronts the paradox of his situation head-on and makes of the conflicts inherent in that paradox the substance and form of his outstanding autobiography.

II

It is possible to discern among the autobiographies of outsiders a re-current pattern which reflects the outcast's need to win some form of social acceptance without abandoning his or her restless search for individual identity. Consider for a moment the autobiographies of black writers living in a predominantly white society. I am thinking of writers like Malcolm X, Richard Wright, Ezekiel Mphahlele or Maya Angelou. A very similar pattern of behaviour can be discerned in all of them. As members of an oppressed minority their early reactions are likely to include fantasies about finding themselves members of the dominant majority and bouts of self-accusation and guilt at their failure to earn acceptance from the white majority. Both traits betray a fundamental need to belong to the dominant social grouping so as to allay their latent feelings of childhood anxiety. Failure to achieve this and the threat this failure poses to their whole sense of identity leads them to seek a sense of belonging from within their minority group, usually by raising its (and therefore their) status in their eyes to one at least equal to that of the larger group which is responsible for their crisis in identity. A moment arrives when they do finally achieve a sense of their collective identity as blacks among blacks who are proud of their kind. Maya Angelou, for instance, has this experience on her high school graduation day when the senior black graduate turns his back on the platform with its hypocritical white politician and leads the year's class in an impromptu rendering of the black national anthem. This realisation of a collective identity appears to be an essential preliminary to the continuing search for individual identity. A sense of belonging to a wider social grouping releases the individual from a feeling of rootlessness and a consequent lack of normal self-esteem.

A similar pattern can be traced in the autobiographies of members of sexual minority groups. Jan Morris, a transsexual who felt him/herself from early childhood to be a woman born in a man's body, echoes, in her autobiography, *Conundrum* (1974), the feelings of her fellow exiles that her sense of disquiet came from her lack of any sense of identity which coincided with the identity conferred on her by society: "I was not to others what I was to myself."[2] This condition she sees as the exact opposite to the dictionary definition of identity which she quotes – "the condition or fact that a person or thing is itself and is not something else." In his autobiography, *The Naked Civil Servant* (1968), Quentin Crisp, a homosexual, describes how he found himself in a similar predicament as a child, torn between his sexual fantasy that he was a woman, and the fact that he was biologically a boy. The fantasy is similar to that of the black child imagining that he or she is really white. In Crisp's case he took the fantasy to unusual lengths in his late teens by declaring his feminine proclivities in the form of nail-varnish, lipstick and what he calls "effeminate" dress. "By this process," he argues, "I managed to shift homosexuality from being a burden to being a cause. The weight lifted and some of the guilt evaporated."[3] Crisp goes on to find his own kind in the Black Cat, a drab Soho café where flamboyant homosexuals would meet over tea to argue how homosexuality had been a source of national culture: "The great names of history from Shakespeare onward were

fingered over and over like beads on a rosary" (30). Here at last was a
group of men – like some minority religious sect – united by their desire to
be feminine and by the persecution they suffered as a consequence of this
innate desire. Yet even after meeting them his sense of group identity is
extremely tenuous. He describes the group in the Black Cat as "pseudo-
women in search of pseudo-men." And he points to a paradox underlying
their sense of identity. Homosexuals of this kind "set out to win the love
of a 'real' man. If they succeed they fail. A man who 'goes with' other men
is not what they call a real man" (62).

It is worth recalling here the difference between sex and gender. Sex
refers to the biological distinction between "male" and "female," while
gender is a psychological and cultural distinction between "masculine"
and "feminine." The last two terms may be applicable quite independently of biological sex. Gender identity can be the product of social
conditioning and can refer to the sense an individual has of him- or herself
as belonging to one sexual group or the other. It is ironical that
psychoanalysts like Robert Stoller, John Money, and John and Joan
Hampson, who did much of the pioneering work on problems of gender
identity, also subscribe to the view that transsexualism and homosexuality are gender "disorders."[4] They argue that male transsexuals and
homosexuals have identified with their mothers far more closely than so-
called "normal" men. It is claimed that transsexuals' sense of gender is
wholly unseparated from that of their mothers, which is consequently
directed to other men.

This explanation finds little corroboration in the autobiographies of
transsexuals or homosexuals. Christopher Isherwood, for example, in his
autobiography of the nineteen thirties, *Christopher and His Kind* (1976),
maintains that his homosexuality was an assertion of defiance against his
mother and society at large: "*My* will is to live according to my nature,
and to find a place where I can be what I am."[5] He sees his homosexuality
as a conscious choice adopted not out of any unconscious identification
with his mother but out of his need to remove himself from her
domination. Of course one can argue that this interpretation is mere self-
delusion, since few people care to believe that they are the unthinking
products of some abnormality in their childhood development. Nevertheless Isherwood's account of his childhood in *Kathleen and Frank*
(1971) contains little evidence to suggest that he was unduly identified
with his mother during the first eleven years of his life. He saw more of the
servants than of her.

Isherwood, the adult autobiographer, is patently concerned to construct his own myth around his sexual identity and shows impatience with
psychoanalytical diagnoses of his condition. In the opening chapter of
Christopher and His Kind Isherwood cheerfully quotes the Jungian
psychoanalyst, John Layard, whom he met in Berlin, and who claimed,
according to Isherwood, "that *anything* one invents about oneself is part
of one's personal myth and therefore true" (4). For Isherwood, as for
most autobiographers, the writing of this autobiography constituted an

additional stage in his life-long endeavour to make his life conform to the myth or myths which had helped him to make sense of it. He has described an early draft of *Christopher and His Kind* as "an attempt, influenced by Jung, to explore one's personal sexual mythology and identify one's sexual archetypes."[6] His own dream lover is a foreigner and, unlike him, from the working class. In uniting with embodiments of this sexual archetype Isherwood achieved some kind of solidarity against the English upper-class culture from which he came and from which he desperately wanted to detach himself. By becoming homosexual he could at a stroke outlaw himself from his family, class and country. Homosexuality gave him an identity he could accept – that of the rebel, the wandering exile, the social outcast whose sense of freedom came from his rejection by the majority culture. It is interesting that Quentin Crisp also talks of the way homosexuals (by which he means those with a feminine sense of gender) "clutch with both hands at the myth of the great dark man."[7] This masculine lover, however, in Crisp's case proves constantly elusive and is a source of life-long disappointment. Crisp and his compeers achieve a dubious kind of negative collective identity in their shared experience of perpetual frustration. Crisp's sexual archetype represents the shadow of Isherwood's conscious and positive projection. But both need an ideal male lover around whom they can construct a counter-culture within which they can achieve a sense of their identity.

One of the most subtle and readable autobiographies in which a homosexual identity plays a key role is Elizabeth Wilson's *Mirror Writing* (1982). Early on in the book she displays many of the fantasies and suffers much of the guilt to be found in black autobiographies. Her early years as a teenager and young adult are marked by a series of poses she adopts which contrive to hide her lesbian nature behind the fashionable androgyny of the sixties. "Both trendy dolly and pretty boy," her aim became that of a generation – "to fuse, narcissistically, the glamour of the sexual object with the glamour of the sexual predator."[8] In her striped trouser suit and huge-brimmed yellow Biba hat, she felt part of the majority culture, accepted as what she appeared to be. But behind this pose lay ambiguity and confusion, she realises in her retrospective review of the multiple mirror images she had adopted in the course of her life. Again and again she is confronted by reflections of past selves which simultaneously display and screen her inner self. Mirrors frequently form key images in women's autobiographies. While the traditional male artist uses the mirror for self-portraiture, women find themselves painting their faces in the looking-glass to conform to a male-formulated image of femininity which deprives them of their own sense of identity. Elizabeth Wilson recalls one reflected image after another which she adopted in her desperate search for a socially acceptable identity. But her homosexuality constantly undermined her acceptance by others, especially as she was not prepared to settle for either traditional gender role in her lesbian relationships:

My place was with the girlfriends and the wives – or was it? Yet I didn't belong with the men. So I often felt threatened by a kind of social extinction. I was a nothingness, neither masculine nor feminine. (90)

So acute was this feeling of negation that she tried reverting to heterosexuality. When the man cast in the role of her saviour rejected her she turned to psychoanalysis. But this concentration on individual identity failed to meet her needs at the time. This was partly because she could not subscribe to the Freudian concept of an unchanging identity and partly because she still lacked any sense of collective identity without which her various personal masks failed to find acceptance outside herself. Then in 1971 she participated in the formation of the Gay Liberation Front. This movement combined political revolt, sexual protest and a rejection of the psychoanalytical treatment of homosexuality as a perversity. "I was no longer a Fairy Carabosse," she recalls with relief (123). The first taste of sexual solidarity soon evaporated as the women found it necessary to detach themselves from the male gays and re-group under the Women's Movement. Nevertheless Gay Liberation at its height was the time, she claims, "when my lesbian identity achieved a kind of unitary coherence because it fused my socialism and my sexual politics" (129–30). Thereafter she felt free to abandon her three-year course of analysis and to pursue her quest for individual identity along lines of her own choosing.

The gender issue, she realises, had merely been an imposition from without. Her "most authentic self," she writes, "was not particularly a gendered self at all" (142). But what is that inner self? The "soul"? The author of her own autobiography? The observing self that can only be observed in the course of its observations? She calls it "the threshold between private interiors – worlds of fantasy – and the public domain where we became performers" (152). This begs as many questions as it answers. As if she recognised this, Elizabeth Wilson ends the book not with a definition but with an image of individual identity as a process, a continual becoming which can therefore only be discerned by retrospective reflection, by a leap into a room of mirrors which reflect back the leaper's image into infinity. Like so many autobiographers before her she feels compelled to resort to the indirection of symbolism when confronted with the enigma of her identity. That leap with which the book ends is as much an act of faith as any form of religious belief, just as the ungendered self could easily be taken as a description of the traditional concept of the soul.

At one point in her autobiography Elizabeth Wilson rather surprisingly claims that lesbianism was meant to give her "a transcendent identity that would melt masculinity and femininity together in some new and potent sense of self that improved upon both" (144). This search for wholeness in the face of an externally imposed gender is characteristic of most autobiographies written by members of sexual minority groups. Heterosexual couples have, to this way of thinking, simply succumbed to the sexual conditioning of their society and settled for half their full range of potentialities. This common rationalisation stems from that sense of nothingness which Elizabeth Wilson experienced when she was feeling imprisoned by the expectations of a gender role which she could not accept. Jan Morris had a similar experience in early adult life: "If I could not be myself, my subconscious seemed to be saying, then I would not be."[9] Out of this sensation grew her mystical belief in the integrity of a self that transcended the limitations of the two genders. She represents the conundrum of her life as a quest for unity by the soul. In wishing to be transplanted as a boy into a female body she claims that she "was aiming at a more divine condition, an inner reconciliation" (18), and cites the ancients' belief that there was "something holy in a being that transcended the sexes" (23–4). The book ends with a prayer that one day she might transcend both her earlier life as a man and her later life as a woman.

Yet behind her spiritual desire to go beyond the gender differences which have made of her life one long ambiguity one can trace her original boyish adoration of womankind in preference to the male sex. This preference (or prejudice) no doubt originated in the mother's wish that her son had been a daughter and in the boy's unconscious desire to fulfil her wish so as to win her unreserved love. Her sexual bias repeatedly surfaces, as in her comparison between the repugnance she felt for the male world of the successful career on which she turned her back when still living as a man and her cultivation of the "impotent" but "real" world of women. Seen in this light, her opposing myth of transcending differences of gender appears to be answering her longing to win approval from her society for her transsexuality. Her reticence about her relations with her parents and her refusal to probe into the original circumstances from which her obsession with changing sex arose point to her use of the genre for self-justification. André Maurois has observed that even "the severest autobiography remains a piece of special pleading."[10] In *Conundrum* Jan Morris is far from severe on herself. In "Introductory" she goes so far as to admit that she is "disinclined to self-analysis." This is necessarily a disability in the field of autobiography.

Is this what accounts for the feeling of dissatisfaction with which the book leaves one? On the other hand is it possible for any transsexual who has gone through the complete surgical change of sex to allow him- or herself to examine his or her psycho-sexual history without bias? There is a strong probability that the psychological investment is too great to allow radical questioning of such a powerful obsession. Yet by its nature autobiography is self-referential and cannot help providing evidence of the writer's evasions and blindnesses. To assert, as Jan Morris does, that her compulsion to think of herself from early childhood as a woman was "sui generis" suggests an underlying fear of what she might find if she were to delve into the murkier depths of her sexual identity. To do this would entail asking such awkward questions as, why was it that only after her sex change did she allow herself to see men as desirable? Instead she offers a kind of pseudo-mysticism in which she becomes in her own eyes "a figure of fable or allegory" (15).

In *A Man's Tale*, the autobiography of John Pepper, a transvestite, *Conundrum* is dismissed with the comment: "how sad, he'd merely switched one half-personality for another."[11] Not that Pepper himself didn't spend much of his life switching roles alternately from one gender to the other. But he was never prepared to settle for either in isolation. He resented from childhood the gender conditioning to which he was subjected, likening it to an amputation, but of the psyche. In reaction he found himself at the age of six or seven trying on his mother's underwear. As a young man, like most transvestites, he lived out what appears to have been a healthy heterosexual sex-life. But he found that his affairs with the opposite sex only led to what he calls "emotional imperialism" (34). In seeking in the other for the missing feminine half in himself he simultaneously found himself trying to chain her to him so as to maintain the sense of wholeness she gave him. "However," he points out, "imprisoned people couldn't ever be whole; they'd have to keep trying to escape to find their wholeness. Thus the proverbial war of the sexes" (33).

To reach this insight took him years of what he terms "pairings of cripples" (75). Meantime he compensated himself for the limitations of the masculine role he felt forced to play by continuing to spend periods of time dressed as a woman. On joining the Beaumont Society for transvestites he invented a feminine persona for himself whom he named Angela Summerfields. As in the case of Jan Morris, Pepper cites the ancients' view that – in this case – transvestism is a sign of divine endowment. To him it felt far more than a mere matter of dressing up in women's clothes. The act gave him a sense of god-like androgyny. When, for instance, he went out dancing as a man he simultaneously felt like "the whirling goddess"; it was as if, like a hermaphrodite, he had fused sexually into his own flesh (37). Psychoanalysts would probably identify this sensation as retarded sexuality of the narcissistic kind. Pepper's frequent use of imagery drawn from the pantheon of the classical gods reveals what it was about transvestism that appealed to him – the sensation it gave him of having transcended the limitations of his gender conditioning.

It is therefore not that surprising that he finally turned to Tibetan Buddhism for a spiritual answer to his needs. For, "seeking to fuse the dynamic opposites of all creation, the male and female ... was what the transcendental rites of the East were all about" (112). Buddhism incidentally offered him that sense of belonging to a like-minded group which has played so important a part in the autobiographies of other members of social minority groups. The effect of Buddhist teaching on Pepper was to give him a completely different understanding of what heterosexual love could become. With his latest female lover "the revived male" in him was able "to be more aware than ever of her Eve-ish charms, while the female alongside could know what it was like to *be* her" (137). This androgynous state of mind caused Angela, the transvestite, to start fading away. It appears that she was finally exorcised by the writing of the autobiography itself. Pepper concludes the book celebrating the "psychic unity" he realises he had been seeking all his life, a unity he considers indistinguishable from "a state of gracefulness" or "the completeness that precedes all creation" (137). It is for the reader to decide whether the autobiography represents a radical critique of the gender roles that the majority of us play out unthinkingly or whether it is another example of retrospective rationalisation. When, for instance, Pepper, dressed as a woman, says to himself, "If only my father could see me now," one cannot help speculating how far he was attempting to rival or alternatively to identify with his mother. Is *A Man's Tale* yet another example of an elaborate edifice constructed by an adult unwilling to face the source of his identity-crisis in an arrested stage of childhood sexuality? And if this is so, is it another instance of art born out of repression? If this is the case then it is also true that this particular genre exposes more than others the sublimation involved.

Classical psychoanalytical theory sees all the sexual stances considered here as arrested stages of normal child development, defence mechanisms which enable "deviants" to enact sexual impulses which the neurotic represses.[12] But they still represent arrested development at an infantile stage of sexuality. Members of sexual minorities, on the other hand, judging from the testimony in their autobiographies, are convinced that their unusual sexual proclivities are inborn or, as Isherwood would have it, self-chosen. The heterosexual majority mostly prefers to accept the explanations of Freud and his followers on this question and to see sexual minorities as unnatural, childish and therefore at best to be pitied and tolerated with condescension. Perhaps this ready acceptance of psychoanalytical theory by the prejudiced majority partly explains why most members of sexual minorities refuse to confront the application of that theory to the origins and circumstances surrounding their own sexual identity. Most of them mention the theory only to dismiss it with derision. Even Quentin Crisp, who admits in humorous fashion how he and his parents had constructed the classic Oedipal triangle "for all the world as if we had read the right books on psychology," immediately distances himself from the Freudian explanation by asserting that he soon came to require of his mother "not love so much as unconditional obedience."[13] These autobiographies are partly the twentieth century inheritors of the tradition of the apology, the justification of a life, of which the greatest English example is Newman's *Apologia Pro Vita Sua*. But they normally combine self-justification with the urgent modern search for a sense of identity. The tradition of the apology encourages them to seek the sympathy and approval of the heterosexual majority who read their autobiographies, while the urge towards discovering their identity drives them to assert the culture of the minority groups they join as a defence against that same majority. The two traditions pull them in opposite directions, while neither encourages them to examine with any rigour the psychological roots of their sexuality.

III

An exception to most of these generalisations is Stephen Spender's *World Within World* (1951). This remarkable autobiography is not confined to a search for sexual identity alone. Poetry and politics play equally prominent parts. But his exploration of bisexuality features prominently. As a practitioner of autobiography he takes himself extremely seriously, describing himself as "an autobiographer restlessly searching for forms in which to express stages of my development."[14] He also appears to be unusually honest about himself, and is quite prepared to expose himself to ridicule. His account of his childhood and parents is highly revealing, perhaps more so than he was aware of, and provides the reader with ample evidence on which to draw his or her own conclusions about the origins of his sexual conduct. The book, as he explains, begins, revolves around and ends with his childhood, so that its form reflects a belief that the key to his adult identity lies in his earlier years.

Spender's brief description of his parents comes within the opening pages and offers a pattern which, he proceeds to show, determined his subsequent development either positively or as a model against which to react. Often his reaction was a complicated mixture of positive and negative attitudes which, however self-contradictory, he courageously reveals in the hope that out of such mixed material a harmony might emerge. His autobiography, then, is genuinely exploratory in its search for a meaning that he will not allow himself to reach by over-simplification. A good example of this is his highly ambivalent relationship to his father. In the opening section he portrays his father as a man imbued with an abstract mind whose sense of unreality terrified the young Stephen. By turning everyday schoolboy tasks into such weighty issues as the Battle of Life, Honour or Duty, he implanted in his son a desire for the ideal at the expense of the real. Much of Spender's early adult sex life was the product of both of his parents' fear of discovering some shameful depravity in their son. In reaction to their fear that he might turn out to be some moral outcast he spent his early adult life taking various outcasts for lovers.

Spender warns his readers that his portrait of his father may be over-simplified by the fury of adolescence since his father died when he was seventeen. But in fact no such simplified response emerges from the book taken as a whole. When Spender was twelve his mother died and his father remarked to his headmaster how untouched his son was by this event because of his youth. Spender recalls longing for his father to die so that he could demonstrate his grief to him as his father watched him from the grave. This complex fantasy can be interpreted either as the son harbouring a death-wish for his judgemental father or alternatively as an indication of his need to win his father's approval even at the expense of losing the flesh-and-blood reality. There is plenty of evidence to show that the father continued to make his ghostly presence felt in the years that followed. Spender's thirst for publicity is a straight reproduction of his father's own thirst for fame either for himself or for his son. It was his father who first implanted in him the seed of poetry when he was nine years old. Clearly the son is closely identified with a figure he ostensibly turned against in his late teens and this creates a fascinating tension within him between the ideal and the real, admiration and contempt. Christopher Isherwood, in reviewing *World Within World*, acutely observed the way in which the young son's fascinated hatred for his father became indistinguishable with the passing of time from love.[15]

Spender's paradoxical relationship to his father re-surfaces in the paternal role he assumed in his homosexual affairs with Walter and Jimmy Younger. In Walter's case he saw his lover's faults as projections of his own guilt, a guilt which originally had been implanted in him by his father. Walter was the moral outcast his father had so dreaded discovering in his son. By taking Walter as his lover Spender was simultaneously rebelling against the memory of his father and yet internalising his father's disapproval to such an extent that he felt compelled to treat the outcast's failings as his own. His longer account of his more committed affair with Jimmy Younger reveals the way in which he cast Jimmy in the role of himself as a boy by playing out the role his father had performed in his earlier life. As he writes, "Jimmy had really become the son whom I attempted to console, but of whom I was the maddening father" (182). It is as if he casts his male lovers in the role of outcast sons in order to confront the father in himself with the moral depravity he so feared – not just confront him with it but have him understand and forgive it. This desire to turn his internalised father into the good and lovable parent would square with classical Freudian theory which would expect him in his homosexual phases to identify with his mother's erotic feelings for the father.[16] He also claims to have played out a paternal role in his first disastrous marriage with Inez. But the scenario between them is entirely different in that she became, according to him, a substitute daughter to him rather than an embodiment of his earlier self.

Clearly his mother, of whom he remembers less, also played a key role in his unusual childhood. A semi-invalid, with a tragic perception of life, she was given to violent fluctuations of mood. In the course of describing the way in which she habitually put him down, Spender implicitly indicates the extent to which he nevertheless identified with her: "She recognised in me someone as hypersensitive as herself and snubbed me accordingly, being, like many sensitive people, unable to resist wounding those as vulnerable as herself, in revenge for wounds she suffered from the seemingly invulnerable" (3). When he meets Elizabeth, who becomes his lover, the first thing he notices about her before they have even spoken to each other is her resemblance to photographs of his mother taken before he could remember her: "In her appearance there was a look of her having suffered at some time" (193). Subsequently he sees in her suffering "something which after all I could console" (195). This is a very different way of relating to a lover than the entangled web of guilt and blame he spun around his relationships with the male lovers in his life. It is as if he wants to replay his brief early years with his mother and this time win her whole-hearted love by consoling her for all the hurts she received from the harsh outside world.

His affair with Elizabeth ran side by side with his continuing relationship with Jimmy who was completely dependent on Spender at this time. Spender recalls his own deep-seated ambivalence during this period of his life, his constitutional inability to choose between his two lovers of opposite sexes. He appears to blame himself for this lack of decisiveness and the guilt that ensued. This is at odds with a declaration he makes earlier in the book in favour of bisexuality. There he asks whether people should feel forced to choose between homosexuality and heterosexuality. This was never felt necessary, he argues, in the past, for instance in Shakespeare's time. He is even-handed in his condemnation of the artificiality of such a choice, denouncing the homosexual chauvinism which he undoubtedly met among friends such as Auden with as much vigour as he scorns conventional heterosexuality. He also offers a definition of "normal" that is at variance with the psychoanalytic understanding of normality: "what is 'normal' for the individual is simply to conform with his own nature" (68). What he means by his own nature is something he sets out to uncover in the course of the autobiography. It is complex, not simple, bi- rather than uni-sexual, and often self-contradictory.

The presence of self-contradiction in the book suggests that Spender is attempting a more honest portrait of his own vacillations and changes in direction than is usual. He is prepared to abandon narrative consistency where his own past inconsistencies come into conflict with it. One of the most glaring inconsistencies in the book is that between his early championing of bisexuality and his later evaluation of the relative rewards that hetero- and homosexual relationships have to offer. Ostensibly he argues that each type of relationship has a mutually exclusive set of properties. Relationships between men express a need for self-identification, one in which their work, ideas, play and physical beauty correspond with each other. Relationships between opposite sexes, on the other hand, according to Spender express the need to relate to all that is opposite and different from the self. It seems more than likely that Spender was indebted to D.H. Lawrence for his concept of woman as "otherness," the unknown. This concept, however, leads him, as it did Lawrence, into a negative definition of homosexual relationships, since men reach "a static situation where everything that is possible to be known between two people is known" (185). On looking back at both types of relationship he decides that homosexual relationships are inherently destructive because they reach a point of stasis which prevents further development of the self. This seems a dubious conclusion. What he means by self-identification appears to be some form of total projection onto the male other. But surely the male other can be no more "knowable" than the opposite sex? Indeed at one point in the book he explicitly states that there is "some-

thing withdrawn, inaccessible and unexplained" about the motives of others of both sexes about whom he attempted to write "in the spirit of . . . exploring the unknown" (61).

His generalisations are evidently based on his own particular experience and are more interesting if taken as insights into his unique history than as observations about the nature of homo- and heterosexual love in the abstract. It becomes apparent in the course of the book that he unquestioningly accepts traditional gender roles and does not cast his male lovers into either stereotyped part. With women he bases his relationships on the difference in gender and uses the women in his life to play out the unexplored feminine side of his personality. That is why they come to represent for him "the wholeness of a life outside" him (186), the missing otherness which is "unknown" because unexplored in himself. He asserts that each kind of sexual relationship met needs in him which the other could not hope to do. Nevertheless he comes down in favour of his heterosexual relationships based on the difference between the two sexes because he found them "the most enduring" (318).

Even this definition of heterosexual relationships is at odds with the description he gives of his two marriages. The first marriage to Inez was a failure, he concludes, not because they failed to offer one another otherness, but because their love, he writes, "was not of a kind which made us feel as though we were always one person. We were never completely together" (257). His second successful marriage to Natasha was founded, he explains enigmatically, on "the research for a unity which was ourselves belonging to one another" (279–80). What is one to make of this chain of contradictions running all the way through the autobiography? Is it that Spender feels free to write what he believes while generalising but under the need to compromise when writing about individuals such as his second wife who were still alive when he was writing the book? After all, compromise for the sake of the living is an inherent characteristic of the genre. Or is it a conscious cultivation of subjectivity? Does he feel more comfortable with the contradictions experienced in the course of his life exposed for all to detect in the narrative of that life? Alternatively are these contradictions a reflection of that opposition between the real and the ideal which was implanted in him as a child? Ideally he would like to feel that both kinds of relationship contribute to a more integrated sense of identity than either does on its own. But in reality he appears to have found more fulfilment in his long-standing hererosexual marriage to Natasha which has survived to the present day.

Another motive also plays a part in the drama of his conflicting loyalties towards rival points of view. As a writer he shows latent fear of becoming alienated from the heterosexual majority by the exclusivity that the homosexual sub-culture tends to construct around itself. "For the artist to feel cut off from this warm flow of the normal general life, is to cut himself off from what absorbs other people, perhaps also to place himself too much in the company of those who feel cut off in the same way" (68).

In the same passage he argues that homosexuals really ought to do their best to adjust themselves "to the generally held concept of the normal" (68). This definition of the normal is in conflict with the definition previously cited, as he acknowledges. Does this need to contradict himself so blatantly indicate a further division of loyalties? Did his ambition as a writer induce him to adopt a partial stance towards genuine bisexuality? Just as Isherwood constructed a myth of romantic homosexual love to meet his need to break with family and country, so Spender appears to have constructed his theory about the superiority of heterosexuality to homosexuality to satisfy his desire to make his name as a poet in the heterosexual world.

My exclusive concentration on Spender's search for a sexual identity could be misleading. Equally important to him is the search for his identity as a writer. *World Within World* does not just describe this search; it enacts it. Towards the end of the book he defines what he understands by poetic form – "the struggle of certain living material to achieve itself within a pattern" (313). If life is a struggle to achieve a form of wholeness called "identity," then the narrative of his life mirrors this struggle. He argues that the "refusal of a poet to sacrifice what he means to a perfectly correct rhyme ... can more powerfully suggest the rhyme than correctness would" (313). In the same way his refusal to sacrifice the contradictory nature of his experience of life is able to suggest the wholeness or form he is seeking in his life and in his autobiography without bending the facts of his life to achieve it. In terms of sexual identity he is searching for an integration of the different senses of self that different kinds of sexual relationship can offer him. The search is what is important, even if the particular compromise he has reached is partial.

Whatever confusion he shows is the result of daring to experience more than most people do and then sharing his experience and his confusion with the reading public. His struggle to find his sexual identity interacts with his struggle to achieve literary form within the autobiography which itself constitutes a further stage in his search for identity. His confusions and contradictions contribute to a self-portrait which partly depends for its effect on the humour with which he depicts his own conflicting nature. The humour which he employs in the book is not simply a literary strategy but a reflection of an attitude towards life. In his review of the book Isherwood shrewdly claimed that Spender's comic exaggeration of the clownish, self-mocking elements in his own character was a way of protecting himself from becoming the fool his father made of himself in public appearances. At the same time it prevents him from taking himself and his sexual search too seriously. One recalls, for instance, the comic scene in which an overladen Moroccan donkey reminded him of the way he had lumbered Jimmy Younger with "loads of ideas, of music, of literature, of politics" (217). No one in the book is more the object of satire than himself. Yet the comic element never prevents Spender from offering penetrating analyses of characters or situations. V.S. Pritchett, himself a master of comic autobiography, called the book "sincere farce."[17] It is this combination of seemingly opposed elements that allows Spender to admit self-contradiction within his struggle to find form. Ultimately it is as much his skilful employment of the formal elements in the autobiography as its unusually honest exposure of his emotional and sexual experiences that is responsible for its high repute within the genre.

IV

It has already been shown how autobiographies concerned with sexual identity seem generally to be constructed around two contradictory needs – the need for self-justification in the eyes of the heterosexual majority, and the need to establish an identity of kind which inevitably involves championing the minority group in the face of the majority. Many of the contradictions that I have identified in *World Within World* stem from this clash of sub-genres. The desire of the apologist to confess and win absolution conflicts with the longing to belong to a social group of similarly inclined individuals. In Spender's case the desire to confess stems largely from his wish to win literary recognition from the "normal" world, while his need to explore hetero- and homosexual forms of relationship places him not in a sub- but a supra-culture. What distinguishes Spender's contribution to the genre is the greater frankness with which he traces these conflicting sets of needs back to their origins in his childhood scenario. His need for praise, like his need to embrace the sexual outcast, can both be traced back to his parents, the father in particular. By revolving his autobiography around his childhood Spender provides us with primary evidence (however much he has shaped it for his own purposes) from which we can judge for ourselves the extent to which classical psychoanalytical explanations of sexual "deviation" appear valid. Most of the other examples examined in this sub-genre withhold the evidence needed to make such a judgement. Because autobiography by its nature is self-referential, omissions as glaring as these only serve to expose the partiality and defensiveness of the majority of autobiographers in search of a sexual identity. They provide fascinating insights into the by-ways of human sexual behaviour and the myths that are constructed around them. But ultimately they tend to evade the issue of normality, abnormality and their origins, and leave in the reader a sense of disappointment that they have failed to rise to the full potential of the exacting genre they have been using.

BRIAN FINNEY

NOTES

1. Michel Leiris, *L'âge d'homme* (Paris: Librairie Gallimard, 1939); *Manhood*, trans. R. Howard (London: Jonathan Cape, 1968), p. 13.
2. Jan Morris, *Conundrum* (London: Hodder & Stoughton Coronet, 1975), p. 45.
3. Quentin Crisp, *The Naked Civil Servant* (London: Fontana & Collins, 1983), p. 33.
4. Ann Oakley, *Sex, Gender and Society* (London: Temple Smith, 1972), pp. 158–72.
5. Christopher Isherwood, *Christopher and His Kind* (New York: Farrar, Strauss & Giroux, 1977), p. 12.
6. Brian Finney, *Christopher Isherwood: A Critical Biography* (London: Faber & Faber, 1979), pp. 277–8.
7. *The Naked Civil Servant*, p. 63.
8. Elizabeth Wilson, *Mirror Writing* (London: Virago Press, 1982), p. 15.
9. *Conundrum*, p. 58.
10. André Maurois, *Aspects of Biography*, trans. S.C. Roberts (Cambridge: Cambridge U.P., 1929), p. 159.
11. John Pepper, *A Man's Tale* (London: Quartet Books, 1982), p. 78.
12. Cf. S. Freud, *Complete Psychological Works*, ed. J. Strachey (London: Hogarth Press and The Institute of Psycho-Analysis, 1916–17), XVI, 340. Freud himself was heavily influenced by Havelock Ellis, *Studies in the Psychology of Sex* (London: The University Press, 1897), Vol. I.
13. *The Naked Civil Servant*, p. 12.
14. Stephen Spender, *World Within World* (London: Hamish Hamilton, 1951), p. 138.
15. Christopher Isherwood, "Autobiography of an Individualist," *The Twentieth Century*, 149 (May 1951), 406.
16. Cf. *Complete Psychological Works*, Vol. VII, 141–4.
17. V.S. Pritchett, untitled review of "World Within World", *New Statesman* 41 (14 April 1951), p. 427.

The Mask of Form in Out of Africa

Critical discussion of Isak Dinesen's *Out of Africa* has centred on the question of whether it can be called an "autobiography." Noting the way Dinesen rearranged, blurred, and omitted details of her experience managing a coffee plantation in Kenya from 1914 to 1931, critics have found it to be more myth than history, calling it a pastoral, a tale of sojourn, a travel book, a memoir, and "not quite an autobiography."[1] This confusion is understandable because *Out of Africa* is neither a chronicle of the times nor an account of Dinesen's private experience; it is comprised of anecdotes, character studies, meditations, descriptions, and information about the farm. In addition, Dinesen portrays herself as a figure without the interiority we might expect from a speaker who says she will "write down as accurately as possible my experiences on the farm."[2] Nevertheless, the disagreement about what to call *Out of Africa* raises questions both about what meaning we give to the term "auto-biography" and about what we assume constitutes a "life."

Out of Africa can be called an autobiography if we remember that as a theoretical construct "autobiography" names texts in which we cannot make a simplistic distinction between the protagonist and the author, as we might be able to in speaking of, say, autobiographical fiction.[3] In fact, *Out of Africa* confronts us with the paradox central to the study of autobiography: the protagonist both is and is not the author. An autobiographer does not create a persona that can be defined simply as imaginary or historical, nor does s/he create a life that can be interpreted as either fiction or documentary.[4] Rather, s/he creates another life, one that is analogous to the life lived, not a transcription of it. The crucial problem in reading autobiography is not the accuracy of the account, but the basis upon which the author chose to include some details and exclude others.

If we read *Out of Africa* as an autobiography, we assign ourselves the critical task of deconstructing, if you will, the difference between the author and the protagonist. The form Dinesen has given to the infor-mation about her experience constitutes a "mask," and our understand-ing of the life she represents depends not upon "unmasking" the speaker but in closely examining the lines and contours of that mask. Two related questions must be addressed: what mythos, or underlying narrative pattern, determines the form of the life Dinesen has created? And what idea provides the basis for Dinesen's use of that mythos? Before turning to the text itself, we shall first establish that Dinesen used the myth of Lucifer's rebellion as a paradigm for her experience as a woman, and that she used this paradigm to develop an idea of her life that was in harmony with Kierkegaard's definition of tragedy.[5]

I

In the heroine of *Out of Africa* Dinesen accommodates both an identity
she imagines for herself and an identity shaped by the social and moral
norms of a particular time and place. And yet the myths imposed on
women in a patriarchal culture do not acknowledge any discrepancy
between the life a woman imagines and the life she lives.[6] In response
to this lack, some women have created a persona whose imagined identity
has not been compromised by social norms, as Edith Wharton did in *A
Backward Glance* and Edna Ferber in *A Kind of Magic*. Others have
posed as speakers for whom the discrepancy is not problematic. In *The
Woman Within*, for instance, Ellen Glasgow created a protagonist who in
her introspection seems to ignore any contingencies inherent in her
identity as a public figure; more recently, Kate Millet's appropriation of
the diary form in *Flying* represents a denial of any discrepancy between
her imagined and historical self. Maxine Hong Kingston has been most
successful, perhaps, in mythologizing her life as a woman; in *The Woman
Warrior* she incorporates the Chinese mythology available to her through
the stories she learned as a child to portray a heroine who is able to live
out an identity that accommodates both her private imaginings and the
social norms that must govern her behaviour.[7]

Quite differently, Isak Dinesen created a mythos for her autobiography by revising the central myth of our culture. Critics generally agree
that *Out of Africa* retells the Genesis myth, depicting the irrecoverable
loss of an idyllic time and place.[8] If we situate this work within the context
of Dinesen's fiction and letters, however, we will discover that she found
the Genesis myth inadequate as a paradigm for female experience
because it tells of a place where Eve was neither autonomous nor
sovereign: since there can be no story of Eve's unfallen existence, there
can be no story of Eve's "fall." This assumption is presented most
explicitly in the voice of the Baron von Brackel in "The Old Chevalier":

> Adam had a time, whether long or short, when he could wander
> about on a fresh and peaceful earth, among the beasts, in full
> possession of his soul, and most men are born with a memory of that
> period. But poor Eve found him there, with all his claims upon her,
> the moment she looked into the world. That is a grudge that woman
> has always had against the Creator: she feels that she is entitled to
> have that epoch of paradise back for herself.... [Hence women feel
> that] no woman should allow herself to be possessed by any male.[9]

Dinesen found in the Genesis myth a paradigm which describes what she
perceived to be the paradox of every woman's existence: since she has
always existed in a world in which there is someone else, she can only be
herself in relationship to an other, specifically to a man; at the same time,
she can fulfil her nature as an autonomous being only by acting out an
identity that is not available to her and which she must imagine.

In revising the Genesis myth in this way, Dinesen subordinated it to the myth of the rebellion of Lucifer; this myth provided Dinesen with a paradigm in which rebellion, not loss, is central to the human condition. For Dinesen, Lucifer represented the refusal to remain bound to his prescribed place and the recognition that one can fulfil one's own nature only by claiming one's own domain. As she explained in one of her letters from Africa:

> By the symbolic expression Lucifer ... I conceive ... truth, or the search for truth, striving toward the light, a critical attitude, – or indeed what one means by *spirit*. The opposite of settling into the studied calm, satisfaction, and uncritical atmosphere of Paradise. And in addition to this: work ... a *sense of humor* which is afraid of *nothing* but has the *courage of its conviction* to make fun of everything, and life, new light, variety.[10]

As a figure who represented the primacy and the validity of the desire to be free of the "Paradise" of convention, Lucifer provided Dinesen with an alternative to the figure of Eve as a model to use in giving form to her own experience.[11] *Out of Africa* is a story of loss, but it is an act of defiance in which the author reclaims sovereignty over both her experience and her identity.

The question remains, however, whether Dinesen's Luciferian portrayal is narcissistic in glossing over any consideration of the moral and political ambiguity of her participation in a colonial system of exploitation.[12] We expect some consideration of the historical circumstances which have made a life noteworthy; even writers like Lillian Hellman (*Pentimento*) and Gertrude Stein (*The Autobiography of Alice B. Toklas*) whose autobiographies, like Dinesen's, focus on relationships rather than events and do not follow the conventions of historical narrative, address the moral and political issues that shaped their experience and their story.

Dinesen, however, enlarges upon her particular experiences as a woman whose existence inevitably consists of a continual tension between the identity she designs for herself and the identity others prescribe for her by drawing upon Kierkegaard's conception of tragedy.[13] Kierkegaard proposed that a person is capable of living in two ways: "aesthetically" – that is, as if one's life were one's own work of art, or "ethically" – that is, according to one's social responsibilities. Only a hero can balance these two opposing modes of living and such heroism is tragic because it can lead only to despair, for the aesthetic and the ethical, the duty to others and the duty to oneself, are fundamentally incompatible. Indeed, Kierkegaard suggested that a woman would be the exemplary modern tragic hero because she would inevitably experience the incompatibility between her idea of herself and the mandates of her social position.[14]

According to Kierkegaard, the modern "Antigone" differs from the classical tragic heroine. The classical Antigone's "ambiguous innocence" derives from her bond with the social and political order, and her fall is tragic because it constitutes the collapse of a world and the fulfilment of an inherited destiny. In contrast, the modern Antigone internalizes the conflicting values which in classical tragedy are dramatized in the heroine's relationship to her gods, her state, and her family; her "ambiguous innocence" derives from her sense of dissociation from the bonds of family and state, and her fall is tragic not because it causes her destruction but because it actualizes her isolation and marks her chosen destiny. Thus, while the classical heroine reveals the ultimate incompatibility of the values governing her world, the modern tragic heroine, because she internalizes those conflicting values, reveals her own incompatibility with the world. She does not belong to the world in which she finds herself and she must, like her classical counterpart, inevitably experience the despair of recognizing that she cannot maintain the delicate balance to which she aspires: she must at some point choose between her ethical responsibilities and her loyalty to herself, between her moral ideals and her ideal of herself.

Dinesen portrayed herself as a tragic figure in these terms, and in so doing she redefined, and invested with singular significance, the paradox of her particular experience as a woman. Isolated from her family and her culture, the heroine of *Out of Africa* attempts to balance the values in conflict around her. Even though she feels "at home" in Africa, she does not "belong" there, and her final dislocation confirms her isolation within her world. Her innocence is ambiguous because the sovereignty she believes to be hers is illusory: to believe that she can, as a woman, be sovereign and autonomous in a world she has not created is a Luciferian act of hubris.

Uncovering the Kierkegaardian paradigm in *Out of Africa* will reveal the modifications made necessary by the fact that Dinesen was creating a world in which female, rather than male, experience is the norm. Kierkegaard, as an aristocratic man, presumed that the individual remained a free agent, and that any choice was between conflicting responsibilities; Dinesen, as a woman, recognized the illusory nature of such independence, and presumed that any choice was necessarily between dependence and isolation. What Kierkegaard posed as a free choice Dinesen posed as a necessary choice. As a result, what in Kierkegaard's paradigm constituted a "fall" – the loss of some degree of freedom – in Dinesen's paradigm functions as an awakening to her actual and inevitable lack of independence.

Dinesen's letters from Africa provide a touchstone against which to measure her use of Kierkegaard's conception of tragedy to give form to her life. True, the voice in the letters shifts to accommodate different audiences and thus is in a sense no more "true" than that of the storyteller; but the letters provide a chronicle and an interpretation of events not mediated by any conception of tragedy. They are useful because they offer different perspectives, differences which cannot be accounted for by simply saying that *Out of Africa* was written in a different time and for a different audience. In short they reveal Dinesen's sense of herself as a private person while in *Out of Africa* she presents herself as a representative individual.

The most telling differences between the two accounts, those which clarify the form of the mask Dinesen assumes in her autobiography, are the stories of the shooting accident and Dinesen's relationship with the Kikuyu chief Kinanjui, her experiences with the Somali women who lived and worked on the farm, and her relationship with Denys Finch-Hatton. In the light of these discrepancies between the letters and the "myth," the section of *Out of Africa* entitled "From An Immigrant's Notebook" can be read as guide to reading the autobiography, for here, as we shall see, the speaker becomes a model reader of the protagonist as author and defines the meaning of tragedy. Finally, Dinesen's account of her final days on the farm implicitly justifies her creation of a mask that obscures as much as it reveals.

II

In *Out of Africa* Dinesen defines her life in terms of a set of relationships through which she both realizes herself and discovers her own limits.[15] Her three most important relationships – with the Africans, with other women, and with a man – show that what she does has significance primarily insofar as it constitutes an interaction by which she reconciles opposing values in a way that both valorizes and modifies her imagined autonomy.

Dinesen gives her account of the shooting accident a tragic design by using it to dramatize her awakening to the realization that she cannot remain solitary in her sovereignty. The first section describes an idyllic time and place in which Dinesen is both solitary and sovereign, in perfect harmony with her place and with those who live there. "Everything that you saw made for greatness and freedom, and unequalled nobility," we are told; "you woke up in the morning and thought: Here I am, where I ought to be" (4).

The accident tests this sense of belonging. A group of children find a gun which Dinesen's farm manager had carelessly left lying about, and it goes off in the hands of one of them, killing one child and badly wounding another. The repercussions of the accident are complicated by the long debate about what will be judged just restitution to the families of the wounded and the dead. Dinesen discovers that in fact her domain is made up of relationships which require that she modify her expectations. The difference between the response Dinesen shares in her letters and the response of her protagonist registers the difference between a person who feels limited by circumstances and a woman who discovers that she will always have a divided nature.

According to her letters, Dinesen heard the shot while taking a bath before dinner, and while disturbed by it, did not find it particularly unusual: "I always hate to hear [a shot]," she wrote, "especially at night, but I thought it was one of the white people shooting at a hyena" (*Letters*, 177–8). In *Out of Africa*, Dinesen changes the circumstances in which she learns of the accident: she hears the shot when she goes outside to enjoy the evening, and it jolts her out of her feeling of absolute freedom and sovereignty, the feeling that she was "the privileged person to whom everything is taken" (88). The shot in the night and the accident it signals are thus made to represent a moment of awakening, a sudden intrusion by which the mystery of the night becomes ambiguous, even disturbing. It also signals the intrusive and inexplicable presence of an other: "There is something strangely determinate and fatal about a single shot in the night. It is as if someone had cried a message to you in one word, and would not repeat it" (89). This "message," reiterated in the trip to the hospital with the wounded child and in the drawn-out councils to resolve the dispute that arises from the accident, is that Dinesen must accommodate her idea of her own sovereignty in order to meet her responsibilities as a social being.

The striking difference in the tone of the two accounts, which is more than the difference between momentary frustration and later tolerance, underscores Dinesen's purpose in portraying a heroine whose central problem is to negotiate her need to be both autonomous and responsive. The letters focus on her failure to adjudicate the dispute:

> I think all the Kikuyu customs in this kind of case are quite atrocious ... their aim is naturally to squeeze as much restitution out of the others as they can, so that the wounded boy's father can buy himself a new wife, and the boy himself will get nothing. I must say that I hate their 'kiamas'; they consist of only the old Kikuyu who just want to sit chattering, drinking, and eating endlessly, their judgements are completely worthless, I think they are absolutely fortuitous and dependent upon bribery. (*Letters*, 221–2)

In *Out of Africa*, however, Dinesen betrays no ambivalence; instead, her discussions with the elders on the arbitrary nature of their decisions illustrates the reciprocal openness of their interactions: "The old men listened attentively," she recalls, "they were pleased to hear, for once, an excellent principle put into speech" (104). Her capacity for reciprocity elicits as much respect as her autonomy. The bond between Dinesen and the Kikuyu is one which demystifies the differences between them and which requires no dissimulation.

In order to resolve the dispute, Dinesen decides to call upon the help of Kinanjui, chief of a Kikuyu tribe who lives several miles away from the farm. According to the letters, Dinesen seeks his help out of frustration at her own failure (*Letters* 222); according to *Out of Africa* she seeks his help because she recognizes in the witchcraft being practised by the wounded boy's mother a power and knowledge so fundamentally different from her own that she can respond to it only indirectly. She also recognizes her own responsibility in the insidious evil that has resulted from the accident: "I thought: 'This accident and the things which have come from it, are getting into the blood of the farm, and it is my fault. I must call in fresh forces, or the farm will run into a bad dream, a nightmare'" (140). She must awaken from the dream of her own autonomy to her actual and necessary dependence on another, specifically on an African man.

Kinanjui is portrayed as a kind of double to Dinesen, and their interactions measure both the fullness of her power and the depth of her tragic despair.[16] Since he was not born a chief but was made one by the English, Kinanjui's authority, like Dinesen's, rests in his ability to accommodate opposing forces. We see him dealing with the Kikuyu dispute as one in full command of his people, and able to adjudicate effortlessly simply because of his position.

Much later, during her last year on the farm, Dinesen's refusal to reciprocate in her relationship with Kinanjui is a sign of her recognition that she has lost her domain. When Kinanjui asks her to allow him to die in her house so that he will not be forced to die in the Mission hospital, she refuses out of simple weariness at the prospect of facing the government authorities in Nairobi should any legal complications arise from the fact that he had died on her property. In losing the farm she has lost her autonomy; Kinanjui must likewise surrender his place among his people and go the hospital to die: both must confront the tragic failure of the ideal balance between modern and primitive values to which they had aspired.

While the shooting accident and Dinesen's relationship with Kinanjui dramatize her attempt to accommodate the opposing values of the modern and the primitive, her activities as a hostess and her relationship with the African women, described in the third section of *Out of Africa*, dramatize her attempt to reconcile the moral differences inherent in distinguishing between the experience of men and the experience of women. Dinesen shows herself able to do "women's work" without being circumscribed by it and to recognize in "woman's place" a paradox without tension because she redefines the implications of a gender-bound moral order.

The heroine of *Out of Africa* has a "hybrid" nature in that she has qualities conventionally ascribed to both men and women, what Dinesen calls "womanliness" and "manliness." In her letters Dinesen explored at some length the moral implications of thinking of women only in terms of their relationships with men. At one point she wrote:

> A woman's 'morals' are understood to do purely with sex. An 'honorable man' is in general thought to be a man who understands and follows such clear and simple, human concepts as honesty, reliability, loyalty, fearlessness; an 'honest woman' is a woman who maintains certain traditions in her relationship with men. [But women's] morals should not be judged in one sphere only. (*Letters*, 261, 263)

The heroine of *Out of Africa* is honourable in more than one sphere: she is shown to be honest in her interactions with the Africans, reliable in her responsibilities as proprietor of the farm, loyal to those who work for her, and fearless in her love for the hunt, as well as "honest" in her relationship with men. For Dinesen's purpose in *Out of Africa* is not to express her private feelings or to use her account of events or relationships to reveal her personal values; rather it is to present a woman whose identity is not compromised by the norms of a particular time and place. The difference between the way Dinesen responds to the Somali women who live on her farm in her letters and the way she characterizes them in *Out of Africa* defines the moral norms by which the protagonist of *Out of Africa* must accommodate her own double nature.

According to her letters Dinesen found the limited lives of the Somali women utterly alien to her nature, almost incomprehensible:

> Of course I can see that there is something quite poetic in the Muhammadan view of woman and her position in life as its crown and the greatest treasure for man ... but it gives me the same feeling that I get with people who assure me that bull fighting is the finest sport and display of courage and dexterity and so on, — in a way I would gladly believe them, but I am instinctively against it all to such an extent that I have to give up any idea of getting much out of it from the outset; it is not merely that I would not go to a bull fight for anything in the world, I also think I could not live in a society that was so much concerned with it, and I cannot resist trying to get my Muhammadan women a little way out of their cage ... not even if in the eyes of the world I could become as lovely as the Virgin Mary herself would I give up the freedom of my relationship with nature and people and be confined to four walls and get the whole of life at second hand through one man. (*Letters*, 398–9)

In *Out of Africa*, however, Dinesen transforms the Somali women into mythic figures who are able to live out their paradoxical natures. They are owned without being possessed:

> These women cannot acquire a pair of slippers in any possible way except through a man, they cannot own themselves but must needs belong to some male, to a father, a brother, or a husband, but they are still the one supreme prize of life. (81)

The Somali women are thus doubly priceless: from one point of view they have no value, from another they have value without measure. They recognize the prescribed forms of social behaviour as rituals, and they achieve autonomy through the artistry with which they perform them:

> These daughters of a fighting race went through their ceremonial of primness as through a great graceful war-dance; butter would not melt in their mouths, neither would they rest till they had drunk the heart's blood of their adversary, they figured like ... ferocious young she-wolves in seemly sheep's clothing. (179)

Paradoxically, these women remain honourable by making of their lives a masquerade, for they live in a world in which they achieve authenticity only by appropriating the roles imposed upon them and by recognizing their fundamental and inevitable separateness from, and therefore in-comprehensibility to, their mates. Dinesen does not use this imagery to signify women who are hard or harsh, moreover, but to indicate that they are untamed by unavoidable constrictions that govern their lives.

The scarcity of detail in Dinesen's account of her relationship with Denys Finch-Hatton has prompted some critics to question the validity of calling *Out of Africa* an "autobiography."[17] But again, if we shift our focus from the amount of detail to the kind of detail that is included, and if we suspend our expectation that a woman's life is "complete" only when it is part of a man's life, we shall see that in describing this relationship Dinesen's purpose is to portray a woman who accommodates herself to the feminine role as defined by our cultural myths without compromising her own autonomy.

Dinesen's letters, of course, reveal many of the emotional ups and downs of the private relationship. They also reveal a curious ambivalence, not about Denys himself, but about how the relationship affects her own sense of identity. In her letters to her brother, Dinesen described a bond with Denys different from the one that she portrayed in *Out of Africa*: "I believe that for all time and eternity I am bound to Denys ... to be happy beyond words when he is here, and to suffer worse than death many times when he leaves," she wrote at one point (*Letters*, 224). In darker times her conflict became explicitly between being dependent and being iso-lated; if she could learn more about music, or if she had the funds to travel more, she wrote at one point, "then I would not feel so dependent only on him, and my feeling for him, and this makes me unhappy over the very thing that could make me completely happy" (*Letters*, 284). One such confession sheds particular light on her portrait in *Out of Africa*:

> I will not and cannot continue to go on living in this way, with this single element in my life; it is an intolerable situation and I find it impossible to allow my immediate future to take the form of six months of utter desolation, emptiness, and darkness, with the hope of seeing him again in the autumn, and being lifted up to the same unqualified happiness, only to be cast back into desolation and darkness—and so on and so on for infinity.... I have betrayed my angel Lucifer (*Letters*, 248–9).

In contrast, in *Out of Africa* Dinesen portrays a relationship which does not require that a woman "betray Lucifer," a relationship in which she and her mate are interdependent and enjoy an ideal reciprocity. To this end, she portrays only Finch-Hatton's arrivals, never his departures.

Indeed, the relationship Dinesen describes in *Out of Africa* is not the one she actually experienced but one she described as the ideal in a letter to her Aunt Bess:

> Where the relationship between men and women is concerned, a French author I have read says: 'To love a modern woman is homosexuality.'—and I think he is right ... sincere friendship,

understanding, delight shared by two equals, 'parallel moving' beings,—has been a human ideal that conditions have prevented being realized until now. In ancient Greece, when some of the most beautiful and noble relationships occurred between men and youths, may it not have been because their women were so handicapped by their sex that all their interests, the whole of their existence lay in spheres that were completely alien to the men? (*Letters*, 264)

The relationship described in *Out of Africa* is nonsexual in this sense. And Dinesen adapts her description of the three experiences she chooses as emblematic of this relationship in order to show a woman whose sphere is separate from but not "alien" to her mate.

The first anecdote, of a trip to Narok on which they together shoot a pair of lions, shows Dinesen participating easily in what is Finch-Hatton's domain – the bush. As a safari hunter, Denys spent most of his time here, where both human and animal are governed only by the laws of nature. As Dinesen puts it: "Hunters cannot have their own way, they must fall in with the wind, and the colours and smells of the landscape, and they must make the tempo of the ensemble their own" (17). On this particular ride to Narok, we know from the letters, Denys shot both lions (*Letters*, 332–3); but as Dinesen tells the story, he shot the lion and she shot the lioness. She makes of the scene a tableau which she likens to "the fifth act of a classic tragedy," the dead lions lying by the carcass of the giraffe on which they had been feeding, the hunters sitting by the side of the road eating almonds and raisins and drinking claret, the vultures circling overhead (230). Dinesen transforms her experience to portray a heroine who does not subordinate herself to her mate, and whose behaviour cannot be judged according to the moral norms of the "civilized" order.

The second anecdote, which tells of their confrontation with two lions who had killed two of Dinesen's oxen, locates the farm as the centre of the cosmic order that is created in *Out of Africa*. Dinesen's manager had wanted to lay out strychnine and poison the lions when they returned to feed on the oxen, but Dinesen felt this an unworthy death for lions. It makes no difference that in this case Denys did the shooting and Dinesen held the light so that he could see: "Africa, in a second, grew endlessly big, and Denys and I, standing upon it, infinitely small.... We did not speak a word. In our hunt we had been a unity and we had nothing to say to one another" (236–7). Just as she acts with ease in "his domain" of the bush, he acts with equal ease in "her domain" of the farm. And it is this interdependence which makes perfect union possible.

The two domains are combined in the third anecdote, Dinesen's account of her flights with Denys. Her descriptions recapture the perfect freedom of their relationship, the ease with which they enjoyed Africa as a playground, a land not to conquer but to claim as their shared domain. These descriptions echo those we find in Dinesen's letters, but Dinesen gives a new design to her story by ending it with the response of a very old Kikuyu: if, the old man remarks, they cannot fly high enough to see God, then he did not know "at all why you two go on flying" (245). This remark points to the tragic incompatibility between the absolute freedom they imagine themselves to have and the actual limits which define their existence. This is God's world, not theirs.

Dinesen's relationships with the Kikuyu elders, with the Somali women, and with Denys Finch-Hatton confront her with the fact that she must inevitably modify her imagined autonomy in a world she has not created. Her relationships themselves give a necessary form to her life which depends upon the authenticity of her interactions. In the section entitled "From An Immigrant's Notebook," Dinesen universalizes this tragic incompatibility between the actual and the real. This set of fragments – some parables, some meditations, some anecdotes, some portraits – imitates the randomness of a real "notebook," and yet it has an order which derives from the hybrid nature of the figures – male, female, and animal – it describes. Each is "proud" in Dinesen's sense of the word: "As the good citizen finds his happiness in the fulfillment of his duty to the community, so does the proud man find his happiness in the fulfillment of his fate" (261). In this redefinition of Kierkegaard's conception of a tragic hero, Dinesen implies that a figure is tragic not in possessing a tragic flaw, but in having to confront the conflicting demands of necessity and desire.

Dinesen also uses this "notebook" as a device by which she defines tragedy as a form which constitutes a way of seeing a character rather than as the imitation of an action or event. Fictions and observations are mixed together in her "notebook" because the "truth" of each piece lies not in its facts but in the authenticity of the figure at its centre. Each piece is a "reading" of a figure which becomes a model for our reading of Dinesen's heroine.

The two anecdotes of Dinesen's houseboy, Esa, provide a good example of how Dinesen makes her heroine a representative reader. The first anecdote tells of Esa's great fear of being conscripted into the Courier Corps during the war, a fear so great that it drove him back to the service of an employer he had had before working for Dinesen, despite his unhappiness there. Dinesen recognizes that in his fear Esa could be seen either as a foolish man or as a wild creature whose desire for freedom – however limited – is greater than his loyalty to her or his desire for short-term happiness, and that neither reading precludes the other.[18] The second anecdote tells of Esa's return to Dinesen's farm after the war, when by chance he comes upon good fortune and, believing he is to be blessed with new life, goes out and finds himself a new young wife. This new wife continually runs off to the city, howver, until she finally wins her freedom by poisoning Esa. Dinesen tries to "read" Esa as she sits by his deathbed:

> Would Esa himself hold his life to have been a success or a failure? It would have been difficult to tell. He had gone along his own little, slow, twined paths and had been through many things, always a peaceful man. (291)

All the characters in Dinesen's "notebook" are similarly unreadable: any judgement would acknowledge only half their nature.

The fable, "The Menagerie," points most explicitly to the larger meaning Dinesen is giving to tragedy here. The showman of the Menagerie points out that the hyena is a hermaphrodite and speculates as to whether its double nature diminishes or intensifies its consciousness of being caged:

> Would he feel a double want, or is he, because he unites in himself the complementary qualities of creation, satisfied in himself, and in harmony? In other words, since we are all prisoners in life, are we happier, or more miserable, the more talents we possess? (301)

The point is, of course, that happiness is beside the point. The hyena remains both caged and untamed, both male and female, immutable and unreadable. The hyena becomes a figure of the tragic hero as the archetype of a human existence defined by both infinite possibilities and absolute limits.

In describing her own moment of tragic despair in the final section of the book, Dinesen enlarges upon the meaning of her experience. That is, the heroine of *Out of Africa* suffers not because she is a woman, but because the identity she had created for herself proves incommensurable with her actual identity. In transforming the story about a tragic event – the loss of the farm – into a story about the loss of an illusion, she shifts emphasis from the irony of the heroine's incapacity to act to the irony of her incapacity to imagine. The final struggle is, for Dinesen, not just a struggle against relinquishing her dream of sovereignty, but a struggle against acknowledging that a design supersedes even her imagination:

> During these months, I formed in my own mind a programme, or system of strategy, against destiny.... For [I thought] in the end I shall still come out triumphant and shall keep my farm and the people on it. Lose them, I thought, I cannot: it cannot be imagined, how then can it happen? (329–30)

Ultimately, of course, experience proves the limits of the imagination:

> When in the end, the day came on which I was going away, I learned the strange learning that things can happen which we ourselves cannot possibly imagine, either beforehand, or at the time when they are taking place, or afterwards when we look back on them. Circumstances can have a motive force by which they bring about events without aid of human imagination or apprehension.... Those who have been through such events can, in a way, say that they have been through death,—a passage outside the range of the imagination, but within the range of experience. (386)

Dinesen is describing here a tragic awakening to the absolute limits, not just of being a woman, but of being human. Not only must she acknowledge that she has no domain except as she imagines it, but in so doing she must admit the larger truth that what she imagines must always be measured by experience. Her imagination will enable her to respond to necessity, but it will never enable her to transcend it.

As autobiography, *Out of Africa* treads the boundary between history and fiction, between fact and fantasy, is inherently a "hybrid" text. It is the story of a woman who must come to terms with the fact that she can fulfil her own nature only through acting out an imagined identity. At the same time, by using Kierkegaard's philosophy of tragedy, Dinesen objectified her life in a way that is unexpected and singular. Believing the book would be published under her own name, by telling the story of her life in this way Dinesen reclaimed both her name and the right to be known by her chosen identity.[19] She acted as a "daughter of Lucifer" by claiming her self as her own terrain in an act of redemptive rebellion.

And yet it is this very defiance which makes the book problematic. Is the conflict Dinesen poses between autonomy and dependence as serious as the conflict Kierkegaard poses between the ethical and the aesthetic? To anwer this question, we must reexamine our own assumptions about the possibility of achieving authenticity. To recognize any tragedy, we must acknowledge the plausibility and the validity of the hero's illusion. If we do not recognize the tragic structure of *Out of Africa*, we do not recognize the "unnatural" conditions of a culture in which anyone's only options are accommodation or artifice; we do not read the story Dinesen has told. Our reading of Dinesen's tragic myth must, in Barthes' words,[20] acknowledge that the story is "at once true and unreal," that its purpose and indeed its value rests in the form of its distortion.

JUDITH LEE

NOTES

1. Robert Langbaum calls *Out of Africa* "perhaps the best prose pastoral of our time," in *Isak Dinesen's Act: The Gayety of Vision* (Chicago: U. of Chicago Press, 1964, 1975), p. 119. I am indebted to Langbaum's discussion of Dinesen's mythmaking (pp. 119–54). In his review of this work, Hudson Strode called *Out of Africa* "a tale not of travel but of sojourn," in *The New York Herald Tribune*. 6 March, 1938; and Hannah Arendt proposed that it is too reticent about the actual details of Dinesen's life to be called autobiography, in her "Introduction" to Dinesen's *Daguerrotypes and Other Essays* (Chicago: U. of Chicago Press, 1979), p. xiii.
2. Isak Dinesen, *Out of Africa* (New York: Random House, 1965), p. 20. All references to *Out of Africa* will be to this edition and will be noted in the text.
3. Philippe Lejeune's suggestion that we presume the identity of the author, speaker, and protagonist in autobiography oversimplifies the problem of interpretation. The author and protagonist of autobiography exist in *dialogical* relationship. Lejeune's argument is, however, astute and stimulating; see "The Autobiographical Contract," in *French Literary Theory Today*, ed. Tzvetan Todorov (New York: C.U.P., 1982), pp. 192–222.

4. The theoretical implications of the ambiguous boundary between fiction and auto-biography is at the centre of, in particular, Paul de Man's "Autobiography as De-facement," *MLN* 94 (1979), 919–30 and Marc Eli Blanchard's "The Critique of Autobiography," *Comparative Literature* 34 (1982), 97–115. On the significance of form in autobiography see especially William Spengemann, *The Forms of Auto-biography* (New Haven: Yale U.P., 1980). I am also indebted to James Olney, *Metaphors of the Self* (Princeton: Princeton U.P., 1972), and Elizabeth Bruss, *Auto-biographical Acts* (Baltimore: Johns Hopkins U.P., 1976). Candace Lang offers an excellent critique of contemporary theories of autobiography in "Autobiography in the Aftermath of Romanticism," *Diacritics*, 12 (1982), 2–16.

5. Dinesen was familiar with Kierkegaard's work. Allusions to him appear regularly in her correspondence and her early tales; in fact, in one letter she specifically recommends that her brother Thomas read Kierkegaard, especially for his concept of the individual (*Letters*, 225–6).

6. The problem of form has become a central critical concern in the interpretation of autobiographies by women. For the most cogent analyses of this question, see the essays by Suzanne Juhasz ("Towards a Theory of Form in Feminist Autobiography") and Annette Kolodny ("The Lady's Not For Spurning: Kate Millet and the Critics") in *Women's Autobiography*, ed. Estelle Jelinek (Bloomington: Indiana U.P., 1980); Jelinek's "Introduction" provides a useful overview of the questions raised by dif-ferentiating women's autobiographies from those by men. Barbara Johnson suggests that some distortion is necessary for a woman writing of her life in "My Monster, My Self," *Diacritics*, 12 (1982), pp. 2–20.

7. Suzanne Juhasz provides an enlightening reading of *The Woman Warrior*, in Jelinek, pp. 230–37. I am also indebted to Elizabeth Winston, "The Autobiographer and Her Readers: From Apology to Affirmation," in Jelinek, pp. 93–111.

8. See especially discussions by Langbaum and Aage Henricksen, *Karen Blixen og Marionetterne* (Copenhagen: Wivel, 1952).

9. Isak Dinesen, "The Old Chevalier," in *Seven Gothic Tales* (New York: Random House, 1961), pp. 87–8.

10. Isak Dinesen, *Letters From Africa: 1914–1931*, ed. Frans Lasson; trans. Anne Born (Chicago: U. of Chicago Press, 1981), p. 249. All subsequent quotations from Dinesen's letters will be drawn from this edition and will be noted in the text.

11. Dinesen's conception of Lucifer and of the redemptive rebellion, it might be noted, differs radically from the "dark" Romanticism it echoes. For Dinesen's Lucifer is a form-maker rather than a form-breaker, and he remains an outlaw not because he will not be confined by convention but because he creates his own alternative domain, albeit one ironically subsumed within a larger, divinely ordered, cosmos. It is also noteworthy that Dinesen's "feminization" of Romanticism differs radically from the kind of accommodation and ambivalence that Mary Poovey sees reflected in Mary Shelley's *Frankenstein*; see her essay, " 'My Hideous Progeny': Mary Shelley and the Femi-nization of Romanticism," *PMLA* 95 (1980), 332–47.

12. Even to recognize the narcissism in the self-dramatization to be found in Dinesen's story is to recognize a singular critical problem in reading texts by women. For penetrating analyses of this question see Mary Jacobus, "Is There A Woman in This Text?" *New Literary History*, 16 (1982), 117–41, and Sarah Kofman, "The Narcissistic Woman: Freud and Girard," *Diacritics*, 10 (1980), 36–45.

13. Kierkegaard's conception of tragedy is developed most fully in "The Ancient Tragical Motif As Reflected in the Modern," *Either/Or*, Vol. I, trans. David F. Swenson and Lillian Marvin Swenson (Princeton: Princeton U.P., 1959), pp. 135–62, and in *Fear and Trembling*, trans. Walter Lowrie (Princeton: Princeton U.P., 1954).

14. Kierkegaard, *Either/Or*, Vol. I, p. 151.

15. I am indebted to Carol Gilligan's study of women's moral development, which points to the importance of relationships and the tendency to identify action with interaction in the lives of women; see her *In A Different Voice* (Cambridge, MA: Harvard U.P., 1982).

16. Judith Thurman proposes that Dinesen used this incident as a symbol of a "death of her

own." *Isak Dinesen: The Life of a Storyteller* (New York: St. Martin's Press, 1982), p. 243. I am indebted to Thurman's comprehensive account of Dinesen's life and relationships in Africa (pp. 113–249).

17. This assumption is most apparent in the discussions of Langbaum, Arendt, and Patricia Meyer Spacks, *The Female Imagination* (New York: Knopf, 1972), pp. 299–304.

18. This "reading" also demonstrates the way in which Dinesen mythologized the master-servant relationships in *Out of Africa*: Esa remains autonomous because he remains unreadable, as do Kamante and Farah. This recognition of the mystery of another being both reduces the power of the master and allows the servant to remain free. One reason why Dinesen remained genuinely blind to the moral ambiguities implicit in her role as a colonial, it must be remembered, was that she did not seek, or see herself as having, self-serving control over the Africans who lived and worked on her farm. See Thurman's insightful description of Dinesen's "paradoxical" attitudes toward the Africans (pp. 169–80).

19. With the success of her first book, *Seven Gothic Tales*, Dinesen revealed that "Isak Dinesen" was her pseudonym; indeed, the publication of her real name enabled her to begin work on an account of her life in Africa. She wrote to her American publisher, "Now that this secret [her name] is out in any case, I have got a few short, quite truthful recounts of my life on the African farm.... I have to have these published under my real name, as they deal with real facts and people." Quoted in Langbaum, p. 120. Only in the United States were *Out of Africa* and subsequent works not published under the name Karen Blixen.

20. Roland Barthes, *Mythologies*, trans. Annette Lavers (New York: Hill & Wang, 1972), p. 120.

Contemporary Working-class Autobiography: Politics of Form, Politics of Content

I

"Yes, Jerry, the assumption underpinning virtually all of this work IS that for working people to speak for themselves, about their own history, IS somehow a political act in itself."[1] These are the words of Stephen Yeo, an academic defender of working-class writing, replying to another historian who had suggested that local history needed to go "beyond autobiography" to more explicit socialist and theoretical modes of writing.[2] One of the issues at stake between the two writers is the adequacy of the autobiographical mode to expose the real determining instances in a person's life, and thus to carry a progressive political meaning. For Jerry White, Yeo's adversary in this argument, autobiography is in effect intrinsically inadequate; rooted in locality and confined to the language of reminiscence and common sense, it is incapable of comprehending those larger forces, especially economic ones, which are the final determinations of collective life. For Yeo, the implications of such an argument are authoritarian at least; for him, as my opening quotation asserts so strongly, it is enough for working people to speak for themselves to constitute a political act. However, what assumption underpins Yeo's assumption? For working-class autobiography to be defined as political presupposes that writing is already class divided, and that the political act consists in the simple fact of making a space for otherwise excluded or "underside" views of the world amongst dominant and received ways of viewing the past. The definition is not so much a categorical one as a pointer to the situation in which the writing occurs: politics is here to be understood in the sense of the politics of discourse. For Jerry White, by contrast, politics has a more traditional, narrower, but perhaps stronger meaning: overt class-conflict in the economy and society.

In what follows I want to explore this disagreement more fully, for the differences between Jerry White and Stephen Yeo are symptomatic of wider differences, both with respect to the adequacy of the autobiographical mode as a carrier of political meanings, and in attitudes towards popular culture more generally. I will explore these differences in connection with the varied, substantial and expanding body of writing that has been produced by local community publishers, most of whom are members of the Federation of Worker Writers and Community Publishers.[3] My discussion of these issues falls into two parts, respectively "historical" and "literary." Under the first heading, political questions are apparent: history-writing *must* presume a relationship between the language of generality which is used to explain the past (whether explicitly political or not), and political strategies directed towards the present.[4] Under the "literary" heading, however, political questions tend to be routed through the apparently non-political term, literary value; in the second half of the article I try to re-activate some of the political questions occluded by this routing, though finally I resist the simple description of all values as political, however tempting this may be.

"Federation autobiographies" have several distinctive features which make the discussion of these issues especially acute. They are by and large written by people with no experience of further education. They are thus very different from a number of commercially published working-class autobiographies which can bring to bear a range of educated concepts and techniques on the experience of childhood and youth in the effort to explain it.[5] By the same token, the Federation autobiographies are written by people who have remained within working-class communities; while often prompted by community workers or academics, their writing is addressed to and circulates within its originating constituency. Finally, this writing is often produced collaboratively, being produced from the transcripts of tape recordings, in Reading Centres, or in Writers Workshops. Roger Mills has put the point this way: "In practice, the Federation has never differentiated between autobiography/local history, poetry/prose and adult literacy. We have broken down the barriers that elsewhere still exist between these written forms."[6]

The narrower political case against simple notions of the value of working-class self-expression has also been put within Federation writing itself. Les Moss, for example, a lifelong political and trade-union activist, gives the following balanced but finally negative assessment of some of the writing published by QueenSpark, a Brighton-based community publisher:

> Now, this organisation, QueenSpark, is putting ordinary working people's views forward. These are undoubtedly going to be the future ideas. Working people are going to come out on top before very long. So reading this sort of thing is seeing the future, as I see it. There's the difference. Those other people – the Lady Barnetts – are making money out of it, spreading their ideas. QueenSpark is not. No one here is making money out of it. It's all coming from working people, showing the conditions of forty years ago and so on, when working people were starving, many of them.
>
> Perhaps QueenSpark could go a bit further. Perhaps I've gone a bit further than others with what I've recorded in this book. Those like me who are a bit more politically minded than others, I suppose, would put what I would call a better case. There's a *cure* for capitalism's conditions, which most of us have never even

thought of because we have been born under the system. We're supposed to accept these conditions without comment – that's the state of our mind generally speaking, under capitalism. The point is that if these books are just very simple and only respond to the ideas that the capitalists want, we'll never get any progress. The same status quo will remain. Whatever you write will just be the old ideas that capitalism wants you to write, to protect the ruling class. We live in a class form of society, and if you want to be progressive you've got to write according to working class needs.[7]

Les Moss's point here concerns the presence or absence of an explicit political discourse. His argument is familiar but no less important for that. The question is, however, how to make QueenSpark and the other Federation publishers "go a bit further" without reintroducing the authoritarian direction (or simple suppression) of working-class writing that the various projects were explicitly designed to circumvent.

It is an extremely difficult question, and one that points in many directions. One of them is towards a central political dilemma that has dogged left political parties throughout the twentieth century: how to connect both hard intellectual analysis and socialist ideas with the more commonsensical or "spontaneous" ideas of working people? At a more local and intimate level, the question exposes the relations of power between intellectuals (whatever their class origin) and worker writers, power relations created by differentials in technical skills and access to general ideas, and which cannot simply be wished away by the best will in the world. To come to grips with the question fully, that is historically, would require some answers to these difficult dilemmas couched in general terms, and also a discussion of post-War British education, the recruitment of working-class intellectuals and their experience of class-translation, and an evaluation of the answers put to this (and cognate) questions by both the old and the New Left, the Labour Party, and the parties to the left of it. I am not going to attempt that here.

Of course, it is possible to reject the question altogether. Those who take a generally positive attitude towards popular culture would naturally do so. Let us imagine two different ways in which such a rejection would be made – two different ways in which the fact of working people "speaking for themselves" is assumed, *ipso facto*, to carry a progressive political meaning.

The first of these would be not so much an argument as a simple rejoinder – in fact, it is Yeo's rejoinder to Jerry White: working-class self-expression constitutes a political act. However, the politics of "speaking for yourself" are clearly not sufficiently described without some reference to the context in which you speak, and the audience to whom your speech is addressed. For this reason, we need to make a sharp distinction between two different modes of working-class self-expression: the mode of academic oral history, and the comparatively unmediated form of the Federation autobiographies.

A consideration of academic oral history takes us momentarily away from Federation writing, but it too relies upon popular autobiography (or at least, popular memory) as its raw material. Moreover, it draws upon this fact for the very source of its authority; in terms reminiscent of Yeo's, Paul Thompson, one of the principal practitioners of oral history in England, has offered oral history as a site where ordinary people might speak for themselves and thus rejuvenate the practice of history:

> witnesses can now also be called from the under-classes, the under-privileged, and the defeated. [Oral history] provides a more realistic and fair construction of the past, a challenge to the established account. In so doing, oral history has radical implications for the social message of history as a whole.[8]

The Popular Memory Group at the Centre for Contemporary Cultural Studies, University of Birmingham, have pointed out some of the difficulties in this position, and in the theory and practice of oral history more generally.[9] Their argument points in two different directions. First, in what they describe as a deeply unpopular position, they criticize the empiricism implicit in much oral history; in effect, oral history takes people's memories at face value, and does indeed remain open to the charges of unreliability brought against it by more conventional historians. Instead, they argue that the deformations and repressions of memory should themselves be an object of study; they open up an opportunity for historians to reconstruct both the memories and, indeed, the study of history, as a relationship between past and present. Second, they argue that the characteristic form of oral history – quotations bound together by commentary and interpretation – in effect involves an interpretative foreclosure by the academic historians, which belies the claim that oral history lets people speak for themselves. It is this second aspect of their argument which especially interests me here, because it suggests the importance of context and mode of utterance in any discussion of the politics of autobiography.

The intercalation of quotation and autobiography is not necessarily damaging. Often the quoted autobiography is powerful enough to withstand or overwhelm the commentary brought to bear upon it, producing an open or polylogic text. An especially revealing example of this is Jeremy Seabrook's *Working-Class Childhood*, in which a number of reminiscences are organized and commented upon to support a general thesis: that in the course of the twentieth century a defensive working-class culture of poverty and solidarity has been eroded and finally abandoned for the (entirely understandable) sake of comparative affluence, but the abandonment of this culture has left the modern working class, and especially its children, prey to the brutalizing vagaries of the market and its sub-cultures.[10] It is a powerful and distressing book, perhaps also a sentimental one. In this context, however, what is striking about the book is the extent to which many of its quoted autobiographical passages exceed the general thesis that Seabrook is arguing. He is even conscious of this, and he includes accounts of violence and brutality by fathers in the "old" family which far exceed his explanation of it – that family discipline was in effect a preparation by loving parents for the much harsher discipline of the world of wage labour. It is to Seabrook's credit that he includes such passages; they make the texture of the book more open and multivocal than his interpretative strategy might otherwise permit. Nevertheless, this way of respecting the integrity of working-class self-expression is liable to become, in practice, a method which depends upon the interpretative or translating power of the historian to give sense or meaning to the autobiographical material it arranges. Seabrook for one is explicit about this; he writes after a collection of quotations from children that "When children talk in this way, they are, for the most part, talking in metaphors. They are trying to say something to the adult world in the only way that they can. They don't articulate it directly" (31). Seabrook sees it as part of his task to articulate for them. Such a historical practice, moreover, whether or not conducted by professional academics, is likely to take the material it draws upon away from the originating constituency which provides it – a point made very forcibly in the article on "Popular Memory." This has profound consequences for any assessment of what autobiographies might mean. It is not just a question of an assumed readership affecting what can and cannot be said; we have also to remember the material conditions in which reading occurs. Even a commitment to a notion of the general reader effectively excludes a working-class readership when price and point of sale are determined by commercial or academic publishing.

Hence the attractiveness of the Federation autobiographies, as a mode of writing in which the very fact of working people "speaking for themselves" can be thought of as providing a progressive political meaning. For the manner in which these autobiographies are both produced and distributed necessarily constitutes part of what they mean; the various Federation groups are indeed a response to a situation in which the writing, production and distribution of books occur outside the working class, even if the writing draws on material which refers to the working class and sometimes springs from it. It is therefore possible to take more seriously the claim that in Federation autobiographies working people are speaking for themselves because they are, in large part, speaking to themselves also. This is reflected in a number of aspects of Federation work. Many of the autobiographies are produced collaboratively; by virtue of deliberate policy they are kept cheap in price, sold accessibly, and can achieve remarkably dense sales in small areas. Ken Worpole has noted how "In Brighton . . . the Queenspark group sells the majority of its working class autobiographies and poetry anthologies door to door, hand to hand, and in so doing has achieved sales figures of a density which make the sales of Harold Robbins world-wide look rather lack lustre."[11] But it is not just a question of the *quantity* of sales; the very meaning of local history alters when it remains within the locality and is subject to community alteration, correction and elaboration.

Perhaps it is possible to romanticize all this, especially when, as I do, you view it from the outside. Middle-class intellectuals do have a mediating role in some worker–writer groups; doubtless there are relations of power which come into play when such intellectuals participate in editing and production. A more corrosive scepticism would minimize the effects of Federation autobiographies in returning to local communities a sense of their own history when matched against the powerful constructions of the past emitted by the mass media. Against such scepticism it is only possible to point to the very real success of many Federation groups in producing work of a real variety and substance, work that has plainly not been processed to a damaging extent.

Both oral history and the Federation autobiographies, then, can be adduced as instances in a rejoinder to the demand that autobiographies need to be more political, though the politics of production and distribution tend to weigh heavily in favour of Federation practice in giving substance to a claim of working-class self-expression. I will describe such a rejoinder as springing from a pluralist impulse; indeed, in the article from which I drew my opening quotation, Stephen Yeo rightly asserts that the demand for writing to be explicitly socialist is yet another authoritarian imposition. For him and doubtless for most workers in Federation groups, it is enough that working people have managed to overcome formidable obstacles in getting their lives down in print; this itself is a matter for celebration.

One way of suggesting the strength of this pluralist position would simply be to quote some of this writing. I have chosen two short extracts, which I hope are fairly representative; but of course the very fact of finding "quotable" passages, which must be free-standing, comparatively memorable, and of an appropriate length, covertly validates certain kinds of writing against others. At all events, this is Bert Healey recalling the pub opposite the house where he lived as a child:

> Opposite our house was a big pub which in those days, just before the First World War, kept open nearly all day, except for a break in the afternoon; then opened again up till 11 or 12 at night, according to business. My father, who made it a rule never to go in pubs near where we lived, sometimes gave a copper or two to a girl who ran errands for my Mum, to go and fetch a quart of bitter in a big jug, and a bottle of stout for my Mum. I sometimes went with her for company. In the bar called "Bottle and Jug" where we went were invariably two elderly women with glasses of stout by their sides, dressed in a man's cloth cap with a hat pin in it, a sack tied around their waists as aprons, long skirts and button-up boots, jawing away at one another like billy-ho. At their feet was a big enamel bowl, or sometimes a bucket, and into this they would be peeling potatoes, shelling peas, beans, onions, cabbages or whatever else they were peeling. They said it was "getting the old man's dinner ready", and away they would go, jawing, sipping the stout, saying, "Hallo,

Dearie" to me and the girl. Everytime I went in there with the girl, the two old girls would be sitting there, glasses of stout by their sides, saying "Hallo, Dearie", still peeling spuds, still peeling beans, still jawing, coughing, sneezing, drinking sips of stout. Dressed in the sack aprons and cloth caps and the button-up boots. I don't know what time the "old man's dinner" was got ready, but I should think they are still there now, jawing, sipping stout, still saying "Hallo, Dearie" to me and the girl. Yes, they are still there now, or their ghosts are, a real bit of Cockney London, the likes of which neither I or anyone else will ever see again, more's the pity.[12]

And here is another London reminiscence, less marked by Bert Healey's ecstasy of evocation:

Although I think my family, now fatherless, were perhaps in a worse plight than most of our immediate neighbours, the fact was they too were also generally hard up. Consequently, like my Mother, they also resorted to the Pawnbroker on Monday mornings, in order to try and make ends meet until the next pay day. As these establishments are still in existence today, I assume people still use them; certainly not as our parents did in those bygone days of general poverty. Shrewdly business-like and penny pinching as they were, they were a necessary means of salvation to the poorer classes. Youngsters of today listen to these times in frank disbelief if you tell them you did not wear your best suit, or your sister her prettiest dress, between Monday and Friday because it was hanging somewhere in a pawnshop. I often remember my elders poshing themselves up on Saturday or Sunday and being reminded as they went out "be careful of the suit, it has to go back on Monday."

In case you are fortunate enough not to know the function of these Pawnbroker establishments, I will tell you something of the procedure. Usually after the week-end, any garment, suit or dress, bowler hat, shoes, linen, in fact any article, umbrella, vase or ornament, providing it was in reasonable condition, were heaped together. A tablecloth, sheet or towel, depending on the size of the parcel, was used to wrap your personal treasures and fastened with a large safety pin or two. The rear part of the shop was divided into a number of small cubicles and you would take your bundle into, hopefully, an empty one. On reflection, they remind me now of a confessional box. In a way, I suppose that's just exactly what it was. A confession it was Monday morning and you were near broke, and as you handed your bundle over the high counter, a confession that you were parting with your most valued goods. Nervously you would ask "Ambrose", the broker, "Mum said can she have five shillings on them please?" Opening this bundle, he would cast a sceptical and practised eye over the contents, look down his nose and say shortly "three and sixpence". That was that, no bartering, take it or leave it! "Ambrose", with the addition of a bowler hat and a thin moustache, would have made more than a passing double for Oliver Hardy, but lacking of course his sense of comedy. Once he had stated his verdict, his word was law. As expected, you were given less than you asked, and in turn you had asked for more than you expected; always the Pawnbroker came off best. Having accepted his judgement, the tickets were written out in triplicate. I was always fascinated by this part of the proceedings. The three tickets, each about three inches by two and a half, were in one strip. The pen was just a normal shaped wooden handle with a steel nib. When this was raised in this writing contraption, two further steel needle-like nibs wrote in tandem with the first, so all three tickets were written simultaneously. One ticket was pinned to the parcel, one given to the client, and the third filed, so each had a record of date and articles pawned. A small rate of interest was exacted by the Pawnbroker. If the pledge was not redeemed after a reasonable stated period the goods became the property of the broker.[13]

These passages, so different in tone and style, spring from quite different impulses. The first pushes memory towards myth, where the vigour of Bert Healey's memory endows the two elderly women with a power almost to defeat the passage of time. The second passage, by George Cook, is by contrast perpetually conscious of the difference between then and now; the carefulness and relative formality of the language indicate the care being taken to recreate a now disappearing past for a new generation ignorant of these past and perhaps harsher realities. More extensive quotation is impossible here, but can be found in *The Republic of Letters*[14] or even in the original texts. Given writing like this, it does indeed seem an impertinence or worse to ask for more explicit political or theoretical input to take the writing "beyond autobiography."

To say this, however, necessarily involves a withdrawal from a certain kind of politics. Given a wide enough definition of politics, of course, anything can be seen as political; some of the current post-Gramscian definitions, which make the establishment of a "socialist commonsense" a political priority, could certainly accommodate an account of Federation publishing like the following:

> People are interested in themselves. Not in a selfish way – they want to share their lives. Writing in all its forms gives us the opportunity to make sense of it all.
>
> Federation groups and publications give working people the space to speak for themselves, the means of self-representation.[15]

The question is, however, what concepts people use to "make sense of it all"; how do they fill the space they have won to "speak for themselves"? It is after all clear that some concepts are already being employed. The passages from Bert Healey and George Cook that I have just quoted, for example, are tacitly organized around a positive or negative valuation of the past compared to the present; indeed, the "good old days/bad old days" alternation is the most widely used way of articulating an explicit sense of connection between then and now. Any political rhetoric must draw upon a sense of the past, and in doing so must, covertly or otherwise, include some sense of the good old days or the bad old days; for this very reason, however, we have to recognize that such valuations are politically entirely ambiguous.

Moreover, it is perhaps too easy to suggest that this writing speaks more unambiguously on political matters than is in fact the case. The quotations in *The Republic of Letters*, which display uniformly positive political positions, are certainly cannily chosen in this respect. But it is also easy to find other, less politically positive elements in some texts:

> When people went out to the theatre or to dance in those days, it was always in evening clothes, looking lovely, smart and clean. Nowadays, some of them look as though a good bath, and a change of underwear, not forgetting the horrible tattered and lousy-looking jeans that they wear, would do them good. I can't understand it, well-connected, good-looking, educated young men and women, walking about in those horrible jeans with patches on their behinds. Stupid long matted hair, growing past their shoulder. Bloody great boots with sole and heels like thick lumps of concrete. Smoking pot or whatever they call it. Staging demonstrations. Breaking into houses and calling themselves squatters. If that is modernisation under what is supposed to be a welfare, socialist state, then let me go back to the bad old days as they were supposed to be, and a good meal in a restaurant for a few coppers, instead of the pounds which you have to pay now, and for horrible stuff at that.[16]

You would of course have to be especially strait-laced to take strong exception to this, or to other passages like it which can be found in Federation autobiographies. The point is, however, that sub-political attitudes of this kind are easily available for more explicitly political cooptation; as indeed working-class autobiographies generally, when patronized by commercial publishing or broadcasting, can be fitted into some destructive ideological slots. The niches are there; publishing series which tell you that the past is pretty or quaint (Fred Kitchen's *Brother to the Ox* is published in the "Penguin Country Library"; in a tell-tale confusion of ideological values, Futura have a "Heritage" series which includes Margaret Penn's *Manchester Fourteen Miles*); local history pages in local papers for which the past is likewise a quaint tissue of old codgers' memories; or worst of all, a more widespread if institutionally unlocated desire for a return to discipline and law and order which might readily assimilate writing such as Bert Healey's.

Of course, it is impossible to write in such a way as to guarantee that your writing will be recuperated in the manner you want. The point here is not this more general one, but that there are contradictory elements within Federation autobiographies that are open for cooptation in different political directions. Stuart Hall's general description of popular culture is in this context relevant:

> Popular culture is one of the sites where this struggle for and against a culture of the powerful is engaged: it is also the stake to be won or lost *in* that struggle. It is the arena of consent and resistance. It is partly where hegemony arises, and where it is secured. It is not a sphere where socialism, a socialist culture – already fully formed – might be simply "expressed".[17]

I agree with this view; it is surely one which anyone adopting the "pluralist" position I have just outlined needs to consider very seriously.

Let us turn, then, to the second position which one can envisage as a defence against the view that Federation autobiographies fail to provide a sufficiently political view of the past; or at least, that their politics are couched in the language of common sense which necessarily excludes the theoretical understanding required by successful political interventions. One powerful rejoinder is to assert that certain characteristic popular cultural forms already possess an explanatory capacity, and a political charge, which may differ from the extended discursive forms of political and economic theory but which are all the more powerful as mobilizing forces for that. For example, in the context of a general defence of "slang" as a working-class medium of expression, Jim Wolveridge, a Stepney autobiographer, rightly insists on the cognitive power of certain slangy expressions:

> [Slang] had its serious side too, expressions like "I've only a shilling to last me till Friday", "it's all I've got between me and starvation", "I haven't had bit nor bite to eat all day", and "not a crust of bread has passed my lips since yesterday afternoon", said more about poverty than whole volumes of Mayhew, and "Nobody's been nigh or by for weeks" and "I haven't a soul in the whole wide world" says enough about loneliness.[18]

Much might also be made of the mobilizing capacity of anecdote and irony. With respect to the latter, for instance, the following comments on Jack Common's autobiographical novels are instructive:

> Ironic humour is in fact a distinctive tone of proletarian class– and self-consciousness, expressing moods that range from laconic res-ignation to buoyant self-confidence and pride. It is precisely this humour and irony that allow Common (like the working-class raconteur) to explore his own life at a distance and for its generality; Common is just as much interested in the representative nature of his fate as in his own unique and particular circumstances.[19]

The point is well made about Common's writing; what interests me here is the extent to which irony leads to an exploration of one's life for its generality. Irony might rather be thought of as allowing a suggestion of other perspectives without specifying them; it precisely suggests distance without recourse to a *language* of generality. It certainly is a characteristic tone of Federation writing, though perhaps especially so in the more explicitly political material that gets published in *Voices*. Here it is often used to establish the detachment of the narrative I, who has seen through the pretensions of the bosses, and perhaps some of the illusions of his mates (I notice I have characterized my putative ironic narrator as male. Female irony in this writing is typically more self-deprecating). Irony draws upon a reader's or listener's response to "get the point"; to draw out or make explicit the unstated perspective is to be heavy-handed or slow. It is of a piece with the "needless to say" in the following passage from Frank Deegan's autobiography:

> I remember seeing a blackshirt meeting in progress at the corner of Edgar Street and Bevington Bush off Scotland Road. Barny and I with other people were asking questions. Their usual thugs of stewards, not liking our remarks, prepared to remove us from the public open-air meeting. Needless to say they didn't have it all their own way. The police intervened, arresting us and protecting the Fascists. Mosley held another rally at the Liverpool stadium about April nineteen thirty-seven. It was a Sunday evening. I made my way alone. I entered the foyer. Inside were scores of Fascists, many of them officers. It was a military movement with plenty of police officials. Seeing them all pals together was too much for my temperament. I shouted "Down with Fascism". They must have had a ball. All I remember was finding myself halfway back to Bootle on the top of a tramcar, blood all over my face, black eyes, lumps everywhere. Heaven knows how I got on that tram. When I got off at Marsh Lane, I met Owen Kelly who asked "What happened to you?" When I told him he informed me the antifascists had agreed to boycott the meeting – what a time to find out![20]

The fact that this is the autobiography of a political militant reinforces the point that irony is a distinctive tone of proletarian *class-consciousness*, though the rueful humour at his own unnecessary beating-up is clearly a more widely available tone. At the risk of being heavy-handed, it is worth briefly spelling out Deegan's "needless to say." It arises from an unstated expectation that any man will respond to violence by fighting back. This unstated assumption stands in for a political strategy – however understandable or even personally heroic to resist Fascist provocation, street-fighting might or might not be the best answer, and to decide that question you need political analysis as well as personal courage. Irony is such a powerful mobilizing force for a class politics precisely because it draws on unstated solidarities and assumptions, but it cannot on its own provide political analysis.

Much the same can be said about anecdote, which is another characteristic organizing form in these texts. Again it would be pointless to deny the capacity of anecdote to organize experience retrospectively, and to provide politically mobilizing "examples" or "instances." The passage I have quoted from Frank Deegan serves as an excellent example; if you were to ask him what Fascism meant (and who better to ask, since he fought it not just in Liverpool but in Spain as well?), he could justifiably tell you stories like this. Anecdote is a way of mediating between rawer, unformulated experience and more general or formulated truths; it does so by turning such truths into narrative and character. To write anecdotally is to write from within a general position without stating it; anecdote typically works intertextually, taking its point from other stories against which it is directed. Thus, when Ernie Ross writes of his forty years in the NUR that "During all my time in the union, the NUR had an official strike of one day, and on that day I was on holiday abroad,"[21] his emphasis is directed against widely narrated stories of strike-happy unions; anecdote draws its authority, as in this brief (scarcely anecdotal) example, from the authenticating power of personal experience mobilized against inauthentic stories told elsewhere.

Both irony and anecdote, inflected in the ways I have suggested, are of course local forms of this writing. Their rhetorical force, equally, is apparent. Yet we also need a sense of the implicit meanings carried by the larger formal organizations of these texts, if we are to get any real understanding of their potential political charge. One of the striking characteristics of these texts is their organization around notions of locality. In this respect some titles are suggestive: "*Ain't it Grand" or This was Stepney*; *A Hackney Memory Chest*; *Hard Times and Easy Terms, and other tales by a Queens Park Cockney*. In other words, in seeking to define a sense of their own lives, many of these writers characteristically reach out for a public definition which locates that life in the particularities of a town, a district, or even a street. Thus the act of recovery that the autobiography constitutes is as much an act of social and historical recovery as a personal one. Similarly, many others of the autobiographies, especially those by men, are constructed around the writer's work. Again the titles are suggestive: *A Licence to Live*, written by a taxi-driver; *Tales of the Rails*, by a railwayman; *Hard Work and No Consideration: 51 Years as a Carpenter-Joiner 1917–1968*. In such writing a crucial moment will be the first experience of paid labour; the whole work, if written after retirement, will often amount to an assessment of changing conditions of work over a lifetime. If a characteristic experience of capitalist modernity is that of continuous dissolution and change, then these autobiographies constitute a resistance to that modernity which is not centred on notions of selfhood or identity, but are constructed instead around locality or workplace.

This is an important caveat to place against one thrust of the Popular Memory group's argument, which would certainly classify a local form like anecdote as a "humanist" figure of expression: "What Marxism or an explanatory social history will wish to treat as social relations or as social classes, these accounts tend to treat as persons" (244); they go on to add, rather nervously, "but there is no warrant here for thinking of humanist figures of expression and understanding as ideological through and through in all their manifestations" (248). Rather than worry about this as a problem of category, it would be more productive to see that these theoretical questions – both how to understand the relationship between abstract explanatory concepts and people's understanding of their own lives and how to understand the link between theoretical and other kinds of writing – also have a pressing practical aspect: can we find ways of linking such "humanist" figures of expression to explanatory concepts which, if they are worth anything at all, would enable people to link the past to the present and suggest ways of intervening in the conscious production of the future? For it is precisely questions of political strategy and direction that are ultimately at issue in this discussion.

I cannot stress too highly that these are not abstract questions, created in a discourse brought to bear upon this writing but having no echoes within it. These are difficulties that people live, in their education, their political confusions and occasional triumphs of solidarity, in the multiple ways in which they (we) are included and excluded in their (our) localities, work places, relationships and entertainments. Rebecca O'Rourke's fine autobiographical poem, *Class*, provides a knowledge of these difficulties as she has lived them; she too concludes by emphasizing the necessary connection between a knowledge of the past and hope for the future:

> I recognise that we are here, together,
> separate in our histories,
> separate in our reasons
> And I do not deny that we look to the same future
> We could be dead in five or fifty years
> It's important to me
> that we don't waste the time.
> There is nothing we can do to change the past,
> Maybe even the present,
> but we must be together in the ways the future asks.
> I want to know
> Where it was and wasn't the same
> I want to know the difference.
> It has to be the first stage.[22]

I hope it is clear that to assert that people *live* these apparently abstract questions does not amount to a validation of experience as the sole criterion of authenticity. Rather than run over the now only too familiar arguments about theory and experience, I simply want to make explicit what has been implicit in my discussion of the two ways of validating popular self-expression that I have envisaged – that explanatory theoretical concepts, which are one precondition of successful political strategy, do not arise naturally or spontaneously in popular culture, but are the product of theoretical labour which must to some degree be abstracted from that popular culture. To cross and re-cross the line drawn between popular culture and "theory" is of course, in a class society, to cross and re-cross a class line; properly epistemological debates about the status of experience have thus become contaminated with abusive counter-images of class. "My" theory can explain "your" experience. "My" experience is more "real" than yours.

Again, these are not only abstract worries. They are the reflection of a real history, which can be traced in the autobiographies themselves. Consider these experiences of two of the more politically conscious and active of the autobiographers:

> The CP had so many people in it who were professors and that sort of thing. They weren't even known as communists. They were secret members. All the things we industrial workers did they weren't involved in. Yet they were running the CP. You want some intellectual people to put forward Marxist theories but you also need industrial workers to do the donkey work. What I didn't like was that these people were pulling the strings and we were just the victims of it. Yet they weren't the active people. It wouldn't have happened perhaps in another branch, but I'm talking about locally. (Les Moss, *Live and Learn*, 74)

Despite this experience, Les Moss continued to be politically active. By contrast, Jim Wolveridge's comparable experience led to a partial political disenchantment:

> The trouble was that although a lot of the CP members were working class a lot were middle class. And the comfortably brought up who talk about the class struggle, sometimes irritate me. A lot of them never had to struggle for anything. And I found that I had a fatal weakness too. I didn't seem to be able to read and digest Marx, and this may sound like heresy. Long talks on Marx often bore me, so I could hardly call myself a Marxist. All I knew was that I was against the system, that at least came from the gut. I reckoned I was no use to anyone politically, so I dropped out entirely. (Jim Wolveridge, *"Ain't it Grand,"* 88)

In the context of local history, the "Popular Memory" group write that "the aim should be to generalise the skills of secondary analysis and ancillary research, not to hold them at bay in deference to a more accessible wisdom" (228); the same point could clearly be made with respect to other forms of writing. In the light of these accounts by Les Moss and Jim Wolveridge, perhaps no advice could be more pressing. I hope it is not defeatist to add that it remains a counsel of perfection.

II

The debates that I have been discussing, and the issues raised in them, have been aired most fully within the discipline of history where the question has been, what sort of contribution to historical understanding

(and therefore political strategy) can be made by working-class autobiography. It is not surprising that this should be the case; many such
autobiographies arise out of a broadly historical interest, whether prompted by academic historians or not. However this writing also constitutes a
challenge to current definitions of the "literary" or of "serious writing."
The issue is not only an "academic" one; an application by the Federation
for funding by the Arts Council Literature Panel in 1978–1979 was
refused on the grounds that Federation writing "didn't really for the most
part justify itself on literary grounds."[23] (The Federation persevered, and
eventually won funding for a "Literature Development Officer." The
Arts Council persistently wanted to hive off the Federation's application
from the Literature Panel to the "Community Arts sort of people" – a
move rightly rejected by the Federation as marginalizing their work.)
Clearly, "literary merit" – deliberately left unexplicated – is here being
used as the central term in a cultural politics that reinforces elite power
and privilege.

One rejoinder to judgments of this kind would simply be to ignore
them. Working-class writing is going to continue anyway; why worry if it
has not received the seal of approval from the literary establishment?
That establishment has its own apparatus of educational and commercial
institutions, all policed by the literary/non-literary distinction – why not
simply ignore it, and the English Literature courses, hardback novels,
King Penguins and Booker Prizes that go with it? The work of Raymond
Williams and others could be adduced in support of such an attitude.
Their demonstration of the historical nature of the concept "literature,"
of the way it has been forged in the changing discursive practices of a class
history, is powerfully suggestive of the covert (and sometimes not so
covert!) class-judgments that are being smuggled in under the universalist
concept of "literary merit."

As with the debate within history, a discussion of the issues raised here
could take you in a variety of different directions; the question I wish to
pursue here is the crucial one of value. I am tempted to answer this in a
way that would at least be rhetorically satisfying: simply to quote some
powerful writing and ask what criterion of literariness would wish to
exclude it. This however would be to reproduce the rhetoric of the Arts
Council Literature Panel; to assume that "literary merit" is indefinable
but you know it when you see it. So I will intercut my quotations with
some commentary.

My first quotation is from Hawtin Mundy's book *No Heroes No
Cowards*. Hawtin Mundy had gone blind when he wrote the book; it was
produced from transcriptions of tape-recordings. The most memorable
sections of the book deal with his experience as a soldier then prisoner-of-
war in the First World War:

> We climbed up the bank on the other side and we went a little way
> then we stopped and turned round and I looked across No Man's
> Land. There weren't a shot being fired, but it was lit up like daylight

because they kept firing Very lights in the sky. When we looked across there you could see all blokes laying dead all over the place, it were lit up as clear as that. If only a artist, a well known artist could have stood there with us and painted that scene as it was then there and took it back and hung it in the Cabinet headquarters of other countries, they'd never dare declare another war if they sat and looked at that. Years later when we got old, my old darling, she always used to read from the Good Book before we went to sleep. What I can recall mainly was the little bit she used to read "As I pass through the valley of the shadow of death I will fear no evil." I always remembered that and I used to say then, "I did pass through the valley of death and I felt no evil." Those people that I killed, deliberately killed, I didn't hate those chaps, I didn't know them, I didn't. I'm sorry and ashamed for doing it because those young chaps might have been nice young chaps with families with a couple of little kids and all that. It's awful. There's nothing brave about it, heroes and cowards, there's no such thing. I don't believe it.

This is certainly not literary in the way that, say, Robert Graves's writing about the First World War is literary. It gains some of its power from the urgent cadences of speech, with their evolving emphasis ("if only a artist, a well known artist"), shifts in tone and register, and the rhetorical finality of the concluding sentences, created by the rhythm of short and long phrasing from "The people" onward. It is not then simply that the impact of the experience itself is so powerful as to transmit power to the writing; rather, Hawtin Mundy has found a language in which to articulate and give rhetorical shape to that experience. However, to rest there would be to rest in a kind of formalism; I know that some of my pleasure in reading this (apart from being moved by it, and, yes, being proud of myself for being moved by it) derives from the fact that Mundy arrives at a kind of old soldier's pacifism with which I can sympathize. If Mundy had lapsed into jingoism I clearly would not have enjoyed the passage, or the book, so much.

It would perhaps be possible to concede the case of Hawtin Mundy without too much difficulty; he was twenty in 1914 and might be thought to be the inheritor of a vanished popular tradition which was not cut off from the literary tradition in the later twentieth century manner – note, for example, the references to the Bible, which certainly helps Mundy find a perspective on his experience which does not sell it short. Quite apart from the unwarranted and backward-looking organicism of this view, the point would nevertheless remain: however you account for Mundy's capacity to produce writing of this dignity and power, you cannot divorce the assessing of its value from what it says, by attending only to how it says it. I want to extend this simple point in two ways. First, it is worth reminding ourselves of the primary distinction between literary criticism as a mode of analysis, interpretation or appreciation (I know this list is both controversial and incomplete), and its object of study. Clearly, some of those formal terms deployed by literary criticism, especially perhaps simple ones like "rhythm" or "complexity," are helpful in discussions of value; that need not make the texts to which they apply "literary." Secondly, judgments of content are not only relevant, they are inevitable, so it becomes important to ask *what kind* of sense people make of their lives, not simply to assert the making of sense as a value in itself. We can see the question of "literary value" snaking back towards the political questions raised in the debate within history.

However, I would want to resist the full implications of that connection: that all values are ultimately political ones. Consider the following passage from Louise Shore's autobiography, which grew out of her attendance at Hackney Reading Centre. The book was produced in part from transcriptions from tape, and in part from Louise Shore's own writing; it is designed and printed to make it useful to people who do not find reading easy:

> Sue asked Louise, did she want people to read her story?
>
> "Yes, I want to tell it. If a person look at you, they don't know what really happen to you. They see you looking happy and going on sober, but they don't know what really happen. I've seen people that less things happen to than this, and they have breakdown.
>
> Sometimes I stand waiting for the bus, and I think over these things, what I would like to do and how I would like to help my family, and I full of grievement; and by the time the bus come, my eyes full of water. I no better and no worse. I still the same. My way of life it still the same.
>
> It's so painful, you don't want to remember all these things. If you often remember, is bring it into hate. Sometimes I feel I could hate anybody. I could see anybody go down the road, I just hate them, specially men. But I don't hate no-one. If I feel like hate, I call on God."[25]

According to the Introduction, this is the language of "a Jamaican speaking to white friends" (2). There is certainly no attempt to use all the resources of Caribbean English, as in much black writing; nevertheless, we can hear the rhythms of a distinctive culture in this brief extract, and this may in part help to explain its strength. As with the extract from Hawtin Mundy's book, however, it is insufficient to rest here; it is not just that this person is the bearer of a culture, but also that this culture is the bearer of a person. Especially given Louise Shore's openness about her feelings, one of the valuable things about this passage, and the book it is drawn from, is the sense it gives of this woman's courage and endurance. The courage to endure a hard life is not in itself a political value, though it can be endlessly drawn upon and exploited in a way that makes it one. Yet to write unselfconsciously *with* such courage, and to read *of* it, are valuable activities. To say as much is not to exclude a more directly political reading of the text; Louise Shore's collaborators clearly want to make manifest a latent feminism in the text ("her experience speaks directly to all women") – you may have noticed the reference to the special hatefulness of men in the quoted passage. Yet there is no need to confine an assessment of this text's value to that element in it.

The difficulty with this position – humanist, but not, I think ideological – is that it can seem to set up an opposition between "human" values and political ones. It need only do so if one thinks of a text embodying a single meaning and with it a single value; rather, one's experience of reading is one of negotiation with a variety of meanings, often pulling in different directions, so that one's final verdict is rarely one of continuous assent or dissent. In this situation it is impossible to make absolute judgments about the relations between relatively unpolitical values like courage and more directly political ones, since not only do different texts set up these relations in different ways (consider *Mother Courage*), but different readers assimilate texts in different ways also. This need not lead you into theoretical or analytic chaos, for both writing and reading have theories and are susceptible to theoretically informed historical analysis; but it does enforce a recognition of the social and historical specificity of value. To state the obvious, there is no trans-historical or asocial quality "literary merit" which is present in some texts on all the occasions of their reading. But equally, some texts serve their secular purposes better than others; some parts of some texts are more successful than others. Hawtin Mundy's book becomes more memorable and impressive when he begins to recount his experience of war; Louise Shore does not sustain that courageous clarity about herself and her situation throughout her writing. These are not judgments of literary merit but judgments based upon a comparatively instrumental notion of value.

My final quotation is from Ernie Ross's *Tales of the Rails*, which differs from both Hawtin Mundy's and Louise Shore's books by being much more self-consciously *written*. On the other hand it might not be thought to constitute a "proper autobiography," so much as a collection of anecdotes and reminiscences; but to make such a judgment is to assume that it is possible to discover some universal or generic definition of autobiography – perhaps that it "really" consists in the discovery of a self. Like many of these autobiographers, Ernie Ross has made another assumption; he has chosen to present a broadly chronological account of his life in which the significant events are the changing technical conditions of his work, the quality of the comradeship of his workmates, and the impact of large public events, like the war. Here is part of his account of one of his workmates:

> Fred was a strong sturdy man of somewhat ruddy complexion, piercing grey eyes, with a twinkle always lurking somewhere around, and an aura of solid dependability.
>
> Though he only worked on the small Wells branch line, he could handle a steam locomotive with almost unbelievable ease and

accuracy. He should of course have been on the main line expresses where he would have been a king, but he preferred the little Somerset branch line. His knowledge of nature was vast and did not come from books, but from his own observations. From me he got first respect and then admiration. In those days I gave respect to extremely few men, and admiration to practically none.

I knew Fred to make only one mistake in his observations of nature, he used to tell me there were eagles in the valley. He told me even where they nested. I told him that the only eagles in Britain were in Scotland but he said, "You will see." I kept a careful watch on any large bird and Fred several times asked if I had seen them and I had to say no. Then one Sunday morning I was in charge of the engineers track laying train between Warnstow and Witham. The engine had been detached and with the workmen had gone ahead and I was alone with the van and a couple of wagons. The bird flew down, folded its great wing span and sat upon a fence-post not 25 yards from me. It was a beautiful peregrine falcon; a splendid specimen. I told Fred what I had seen but I found no pleasure in correcting him. I repeat that it was the only time.[26]

All the book is written in this careful, even slightly deadpan way; Ernie Ross always locates his stories precisely with respect to time, place and frequency. The value of the text, however, is not only to do with qualities such as these, or even the economical way that Ross suggests his own embarrassment at correcting a man he admires. It is suggested in the book's blurb: "The book ... gives a fine unusual insider's account of working life on the railways." There is no dividing line where literary value ends and social-historical value begins; actual valuations are always affected by such "non-literary" attachments as one's interest in railways. There is no standing ground which is purely literary and which is purged of all such partial attachments. We are all made up of complex and contradictory combinations of partial considerations, and to attempt to abstract yourself from the web and to base literary judgments on this abstraction is to condemn yourself to idealism and others to ... the outer circle of Community Arts!

Much of this essay has consisted of commentary upon working-class autobiographies. I hope it has not reproduced the hierarchical ordering of discourse for which I earlier criticized some oral history, though I fear it has. For this essay too is of course caught in the divisive separations of discourse that I described earlier. As I have suggested, these divisions arise from real educational, social, cultural and political histories. But they are also partly self-created divisions, problems of category that can be argued through to some resolution. The politics of working-class autobiography are not reducible to their contents, but neither can you equate their politics with the simple fact of publication – in the end, as I have suggested, the two problems converge. Similarly, there is no abstract ground of "literary merit"; but that does not mean that you can do without some more secular notions of value. These are difficult distinctions to hold in practice, and indeed to make them practical presupposes the work of groups such as those brought together in the Federation of Worker Writers and Community Publishers. But they are distinctions that need to be held. Holding on to them in the academy might make the advice of the popular Memory group less of a counsel of perfection.

S. Dentith

NOTES

1. Stephen Yeo, "The Politics of Community Publications," in *People's History and Socialist Theory*, ed. Raphael Samuel (London: Routledge and Kegan Paul, 1981), p. 46.
2. Jerry White, "Beyond Autobiography," also in *People's History and Socialist Theory*, pp. 33–42.
3. A full and impressive account of the Federation can be found in Dave Morley and Ken Worpole, eds., *The Republic of Letters* (London: Comedia Publishing Group, 1982).
4. See Hayden White, "The Politics of Historical Interpretation; Discipline and De-Sublimation," *Critical Inquiry*, 9 (1982–83), 113–37.
5. There are many examples of working-class autobiographies of this kind. Some especially fine examples include Robert Roberts' two Salford autobiographies, *The Classic Slum* (Manchester: Manchester U.P., 1971), and *A Ragged Schooling* (London: Fontana, 1984); and John Holloway, *A London Childhood* (London: Routledge and Kegan Paul, 1966).
6. Roger Mills, "Through the Mangle," *Voices*, No. 31 (Autumn 1984), p. 1. *Voices* is the magazine of the Federation of Worker Writers and Community Publishers. Unfortunately the Autumn 1984 issue was the last.
7. Les Moss, *Live and Learn: A Life and Struggle for Progress* (Brighton: QueenSpark, 1979), pp. 119–20.
8. Paul Thompson, *The Voice of the Past: Oral History* (Oxford: O.U.P., 1978), p. 5.
9. See the Popular Memory Group, "Popular Memory: Theory, Politics, Method," in *Making Histories: Studies in History-writing and Politics*, ed. Richard Johnson and others (London: Hutchinson in association with the Centre for Contemporary Cultural Studies, University of Birmingham, 1982), pp. 205–52.
10. Jeremy Seabrook, *Working-class Childhood: An Oral History* (London: Victor Gollancz, 1982).
11. Ken Worpole, *Reading by Numbers: Contemporary Publishing and Popular Fiction* (London: Comedia, 1984), p. 93.
12. Bert Healey, *Hard Times and Easy Terms, and Other Tales by a Queens Park Cockney* (Brighton: QueenSpark, 1980), p. 16.
13. George A. Cook, *A Hackney Memory Chest* (London: Centerprise, 1983), pp. 11–12.
14. See note 3.
15. Roger Mills, "Through the Mangle," *Voices*, No. 31 (Autumn 1984), p. 1.
16. Bert Healey, *Hard Times and Easy Terms*, pp. 84–5.
17. Stuart Hall, "Notes on Deconstructing 'The Popular'," in *People's History and Socialist Theory*, p. 239.
18. Jim Wolveridge, *"Ain't it Grand" or "This was Stepney"* (London: The Journeyman Press, 1981), p. 42. The Journeyman Press is not a member of the Federation of Worker Writers and Community Publishers.

19. Michael Pickering and Kevin Robins," 'A Revolutionary Materialist with a Leg Free':
    The Autobiographical Novels of Jack Common," in *The British Working-class Novel in
    the Twentieth Century*, ed. Jeremy Hawthorn (London: Edward Arnold, 1984), p. 79.
20. Frank Deegan, *There's No Other Way* (Liverpool: Toulouse Press, 1980), p. 28. The
    Toulouse Press is not a member of the Federation of Worker Writers and Community
    Publishers.
21. Ernie Ross, *Tales of the Rails* (Bristol: Bristol Broadsides, 1984), p. 4.
22. Rebecca O'Rourke, *Class*, in *Voices*, No. 31 (Autumn 1984), pp. 9–13.
23. Charles Osborne, quoted in Jim McGuigan, "The State and Serious Writing: Arts
    Council Intervention in the English Literary Field," Diss. Leicester 1984, 234.
    McGuigan gives a full account of the Federation's application to the Arts Council.
24. Hawtin Mundy, *No Heroes No Cowards* (Milton Keynes: The People's Press, 1981),
    p. 54. The People's Press is not a member of the Federation of Worker Writers and
    Community Publishers.
25. Louise Shore, *Pure Running: A Life Story* (London: Centerprise, 1982), p. 63.
26. Ernie Ross, *Tales of the Rails*, p. 55.

Appropriating (Life-) History through Autobiographical Writing: André Gorz's The Traitor, a Dialectical Inquiry into the Self

I

> There is an entire mode of culture which is distinctly auto-
> biographical; autobiography is a manner of presenting, under-
> standing, and experiencing oneself. It enters into and shapes
> discourse, behavior, self perception, and political activity.
> (Rockwell Gray)

> The 'flight into inwardness' and the insistence on a private
> sphere may well serve as bulwarks against a society which
> administers all dimensions of human existence. Inwardness
> and subjectivity may well become the inner and outer space
> for the subversion of experience.... (Herbert Marcuse)

Herbert Marcuse's programmatic proposition as to the role of the individual in contemporary mass society[1] not only trenchantly outlines the
potential for subjectivity to develop a multi-dimensional critique of a
one-dimensional world, but it also addresses, on a more general level, the
prevailing autobiographical impulse in Western culture, a culture in
which, as Rockwell Gray contends, "autobiography appears all around
us."[2] By allusively calling his study "Autobiography Now," Gray estab-
lishes a link between the current surge of first-person testimonies and the
fascination with and propagation of an apocalyptic vision in "an age of
diminishing expectations,"[3] to quote the subtitle of a recent best-seller.

The preoccupation with the self can be looked at as a reaction to a
widely diffused feeling that the days of the individual person are num-
bered: people increasingly experience themselves to be powerless before
anonymous and virtually omnipotent corporations and institutions, and,
at the same time, are rendered superfluous by the rapidly advancing
automation of the sphere of work. This dehumanization of the modern
world is aptly epitomized by the fact that "TIME's Man of the Year for
1982, the greatest influence for good or evil, is not a man at all. It is a
machine: the computer."[4] A computer, however, does not have a mind of
its own and will therefore not be able to write its autobiography. Thus, in

order to secure their residual individuality, the otherness of their life experiences, from being standardized and hence effaced, the "outcasts of the rationality of our daily business"[5] can resort to expressing themselves autobiographically. In this sense, producing public autobiographical narratives[6] can always be an act of resistance against mass culture, a strategy of survival, a reaching out to others, and, by implication, a suggestion of a world different from that which is. If autobiography – the paradigm of bourgeois literature since it constitutes the "subjective center of the esthetic organization of life-historical knowledge"[7] – has indeed become the *modus vivandi* and *operandi* in Western bourgeois culture, then this phenomenon both attests to the threat to the individual provoked by the terms post-industrial society imposes on the self, and can also constitute a powerful challenge to this repression of selfhood.

Working through real human conflicts and experiences, autobiographical writing, which has become *the* major form of what Peter Sloterdijk calls a "literature debating our forms of living,"[8] provides a forum for a concrete social critique in and of an "emotionally crippled culture where there exist no forms of public lament, where people must banish their pain into cancer, madness, addiction."[9] In this sense, the sharp increase in the production and consumption of socially critical autobiographical writings in the last ten to fifteen years[10] attests to the pressing need to re-think and re-define one's position in relation to the world and to understand the objective obstacles that have so far prevented one from establishing oneself as a subject. The literary organization of one's life experiences constitutes both a rejection of the names the world has given one and an affirmation of the right to find one's own name and to speak it; it is thus especially suited to the needs of people who suffer from public discrimination. Rescuing the "forgotten peoples of the world from historical oblivion"[11] and making them more visible, this literature serves as a vehicle for its authors to come to an understanding of their historical and political situation in a predominantly oppressive, hostile, and hence intolerable world. Just as the Black slaves in the United States had, first of all, to "seize the word"[12] in order to be able to define their selfhood and ultimately to create a distinctly Black public self, today oppressed people in general must "seize the word," find a language that adequately expresses their experiences, and establish their own channels of communication in order to negate their depersonalization. The authors of autobiographical negative *Bildungsromane*[13] thus dramatize, oppose, and reject the loss or, rather, thwarting of their sense of identity as well as the corresponding state of non-identity. Ralph-Rainer Wuthenow writes: "Where the growing or even only 'inherited' self-confidence of the individual comes into conflict with a more and more intensifying experience of powerlessness, dependence, and self-estrangement ... autobiography can become a document of denied autonomy, of never-experienced freedom, of prevented socialization."[14]

The autobiographical work thus involves, of course, a struggle against the loss of memory. To embark on a *recherche du temps perdu* makes it necessary to take history out of the brackets in which it is put by contemporary mass culture. "'History is bunk'," said Henry Ford,[15] and this dictum bespeaks the utter uselessness that an industrial society assigns to memory.[16] In a significant essay on this shrinking of the consciousness of historical continuity, Ernest Schachtel distinguishes between "autobiographical" and "useful" memory. The former consists of the ability voluntarily to recover one's past experiences, whereas the latter is composed of the aptitude to recollect far more utilitarian, practical, survival-oriented skills like counting and recognizing objects, people, and words. Schachtel comes to the conclusion that in our culture the unfolding of autobiographical memory, which alone can provide the individual with a sense of the continuity of the self, is inhibited rather than nurtured: "In a culture oriented toward efficient performance of profitable activities, a society in which everybody has to fit like a cog in a machine and where powerful pressure is exerted to make people equal, in the sense of uniform, autobiographical memory is discouraged in its development and predestined to atrophy.... It would stand in the way of the process of equalization and uniformity since its very function is to preserve individual experience rather than repeat cultural and conventional schemata of experience."[17]

The non-formation and elimination of autobiographical memory, that is, the inducement of historical oblivion, thus profit the culture and powers that be. In a letter to Walter Benjamin, Adorno writes that "every reification is a forgetting"[18]; the reverse holds equally true: to forget means to decontextualize and to turn into a thing the living historical actuality in which that which is forgotten existed or occurred.[19] To not develop the autobiographical memory, therefore, means to aggravate our defencelessness and vulnerability in the face of the dominant fragmentation of reality, as Rockwell Gray unequivocally recognizes: "The person who is not conversant with his own history, or who has no memory-language with which to evoke it, is the victim of every manner of therapeutic fad or authoritarian political movement. Against the pressure to give himself away, as it were, to transfer to a person, a movement, or an ideology the actually ineluctable onus of his radical solitude, he may seek an anchor in the project of autobiography, which forces him to define for himself who he truly is."[20]

Consequently, the formation and recall of autobiographical memory can have a destabilizing impact on affirmative mass culture by strengthening individual consciousness. Firmly grounding the human being in the living continuum of history, remembrance contravenes reification, alienation, and fragmentation and thus proves to be a potentially subversive, emancipatory power. To engage oneself in an autobiographical act opens up the possibility of "Remembering, Repeating and Working-Through" one's past, to quote the title of an essay by Freud on the liberating use to which memory can be put in psychoanalysis.[21] Freud's maxim is echoed by Hans-Jürgen Syberberg in an autobiographical essay on the history of *Hitler—A Film from Germany*. He writes that the motivation for him to work on this film was to "grasp, understand, retell, and overcome us and our history".[22] This overcoming of (as opposed to the mere coping with) the unmastered past entails that the autobiographical author openly and critically works through and confronts subjective and objective history. Making the subject more immune to internal and external repression, this work of remembering[23] is an act of self-help. The autobiographical project[24] can serve, in the words of Herbert Marcuse, as a bulwark against the one-dimensional world which is: it gives us the opportunity to draw up a subjective balance sheet of objective history and to revolt against a society in which human beings are reified as objects in the exchange principle and in which subjectivity is buried under the objectivity of factual constraints. What is needed in this time of a comprehensive disenfranchisement of the human being is a reversal of the tendency to tie subjectivity to objective structures. Adorno writes: "It is on this emancipation, not on the subject's insatiable repression, that objectivity depends today. The superiority of objectification in the subjects not only keeps them from becoming subjects; it equally prevents a cognition of objectivity. This is what became of what used to be called 'the subjective factor'. It is now subjectivity rather than objectivity that is indirect, and this sort of mediation is more in need of analysis than the traditional one."[25]

Autobiographical writing can thus be the epistemological dock in which objectivity is stood by a subject laying charges against a world that hardly allows subjectivity to surface. In order that the indictment amounts to more than a diatribe of subjectivist trivialities, however, the autobiographical prosecutors must be careful not to isolate and fetishize the subjective moment and therefore to fall into the solipsistic trap of narcissism, but rather to bring their subjectivity to objectivity by anchoring it in the movement of objective history and by expressing this interaction in the testimony. Such an effort to work within the subject–object dialectic is, in the words of Russell Jacoby, "an objective theory of subjectivity," that is, given the alienation and depersonalization characteristic of the world that this kind of writing comes out of, "a theory of a subject-less subject—or a not yet liberated subjectivity."[26] This autobiographical, essentially concrete rather than abstract, writing bears witness against a society which "functions at the expense of suppressed life," exposes "the blocked and mutilated capacities of the human being," and thus shows "the price of the ruling praxis and, at the same time, the potential for possible change."[27] This potential lies, first of all, in the act of both becoming conscious of and negating our negation: "What is the human being? That which, although it does not yet know what it is, can know what it, as estranged from itself, certainly is not and which, therefore, does not want to remain that false or, at least, should not."[28] The potentially subversive knowledge of this estrangement, falsification, and negation of the self can be produced in the self-reflective, dialectical autobiographical act.

II

Already in his early *Notizen während der Abschaffung des Denkens*, a collection of culture criticism consisting of aphorisms, notes, and short essays, Ernst Herhaus, author of the subsequent autobiographical trilogy *Kapitulation, Der zerbrochene Schlaf*, and *Gebete in die Gottesferne* maintains that all theory "that does not also hand down, in its thoughts, the contemporary and personal conditions of its authors, is rhetorical over-subtlety and brainteasing in the form of deceitful finality."[29] In other words, a product of human beings for human beings, critical theory must admit and provide insights into its own human roots because at this present age of the abolition of the individual, one must begin to "talk truly and publicly" about oneself: "In any other form, theory does not make any sense any more."[30] Equating social theory with autobiography, two modes of investigation that traditional epistemology considers to be entirely antithetical (social theory being the objective, verifiable, and conceptual analysis of a given reality as opposed to autobiography, the subjective and arbitrary vision of the world), Herhaus recognizes the need for theoreticians to defetishize impersonal, systematic, and idealized thought, and to talk about the questionable conditions under which theory itself is being produced if, in the prevailing world of abstraction and indifference towards suffering, this theory is intended to be noticed or even actualized.[31]

The contemporary work in which the dilemma of being suffocated by a surplus of abstract theory is dramatized most unequivocally on both a theoretical and a life-historical level is André Gorz's intellectual monograph of himself *The Traitor*, an autobiographical narrative which Jean-Paul Sartre in a foreword characterizes as "*a work* in the process of creating *its* author."[32] Previous to this literary, self-reflective quest for identity, the history of André Gorz was the history of his obstinate escape from and negation of himself; his autobiographical work is informed by the predicament of an intellectual discovering that his abstract life-work, the monumental *Fondements pour une morale*, has denied him a concrete existence: "Writing had become a passion; he had purged himself of all problems; he had resolved them in the abstract. And when, after nine years, he had felt he was near the end, the beginning of the end, he had realized that the essential thing was eluding him. The essential thing: himself. He felt empty and bone-dry" (38). Instead of continuing theoretically to look at and solve the problems of humanity in general, Gorz now invests himself in "the autobiographical essay" which he considers "the best way of disinvesting himself from *the thing*."[33] Striving to overcome the dispossession and thingification of his thought and being, he embarks on an attempt to step out of the one-dimensionality of his alienated, universal, and conceptual life – that is, his non-life – and to establish himself as a particular, historical human being.

Hence *The Traitor* marks a turning point in Gorz's biography: searching for his own voice, he discontinues his almost lifelong practice of committing treason against himself. Growing up in the Vienna of the 1920s and the 1930s, a Vienna that was increasingly coming under the sway of German fascism, and raised by a Catholic mother and a Jewish father with entirely divergent and irreconcilable character traits and value systems – a situation which he experienced as "false from every point of view" (109) – Gorz was unable to develop any sense of belonging and identity; compared to his peers and classmates, "*he* was only half, half Jew, half Aryan, a half man—he felt like two halves that would never make a whole" (99). His world was one of rifts, splits, and contradictions: both the family and the city and country he grew up in were divided against themselves. In order to become complete and human, then, Gorz had, first of all, to disown his subjective being as well as the objective status quo and, at this juncture in time, his opposition to his life history and to world history converged. Developing a taste for "contradictory singularization" (134), young Gorz was an identity-less outsider living in an inner exile.

When this inner exile was, due to political developments, complemented by an outer exile – in 1939 Gorz was sent to a Swiss boarding school – his sense of being a useless nullity even intensified and his alienation became total: he began feeling that "man is a wound in which the world turns like a knife; and that between man and the world there was one term too many" (160). Not wanting to be knifed by a hostile reality, he shielded himself ever since from any direct involvement in the concrete corporeal world by cocooning himself in a layer of abstract theory, thus turning into a passive, analytical spectator of the life around him. As a result of this derealization, Gorz now feels "the earth giving way under his feet" (39): the gap between the residues of his self and the world has become too wide, too deep, and thus too obvious to camouflage.

This shock of experiencing his life as false and unlived and himself as an "abstract individual" (214) constitutes what Peter Sloterdijk, in his study of Weimar autobiographies, calls a "Stör-Erfahrung," a disturbing experience. According to Sloterdijk, such experiences challenge and unsettle the social and individual order, that is, the equilibrium between certain historical constellations, and therefore constitute a turning-point in one's life history if, rather than stealing away from them and repressing them, one " 'stumbles' over them, lets oneself be affected by them, and develops an interest in solving the contradictions brought to light" by these disturbances of the daily order.[34] For Gorz, the break with the hitherto self-evident continuity of his abstract existence marks the point at which a leap from his almost entirely alienated self to a self more identical with itself becomes a question of survival, and *The Traitor* constitutes this leap: *Hic Rhodus, hic salta* (37).

The crucial and vital questions for Gorz thus become: How can he introduce the world back into his self out of which it had fallen, and how can this self enter the world again? Should he try to arrive at a sense of reality for himself via the scientific, "affectively neutral" (50) path of objectivity, or should he acknowledge his "felt experience" (43) and pursue a course of subjectivity? Given his life-historical penchant for systematic thought and a theoretical intelligence, given "his way of *making himself* abstract, absent" (65), Gorz of course is drawn, first of all, to try to recover reality by distancing himself from everything that smells of the subjective. However, he quite soon comes to the painful realization that to be a "World Citizen" means to be "a man from nowhere (and not from everywhere)" (267). Hence he attempts to fill his "identity vacuum," as Erik Erikson calls this kind of non-existence,[35] with the help of previously repressed and shunned subjective knowledge. Instead of relying exclusively on universal arguments to create and communicate meaning, he now provides himself as well as the reader with a wealth of life-historical images which, rather than destroying reality by conceptualizing it, bring it to life through their particularity. Instead of theorizing himself out of existence from the safe and objectifying distance of social and psychological analyses, he now recontextualizes the issues in his life, concretizes his non-identity, and thus gives it a subjective, identifiable and experienceable colouring.[36]

In his attempt to constitute himself, Gorz does not, however, replace his depersonalized and alienating idolatry of objectivity with an equally estranging narcissistic cult of the self: inserting his abstractions into their concrete contexts, he restores the subject–object dialectic.[37] This inquiry into the self evinces two dialectical movements, one being vertical, as it were, and the other being horizontal. The former consists of Gorz sinking "into subjectivity until it hits bottom: society"[38] – to use an image of Russell Jacoby's – while at the same time probing into the social objectivity until it lays bare its integral part: the subject. This social objectivity is, in modern Western societies, governed by the principle of exchange according to which the universal (money) rules over the particulars (commodities) and Gorz, author of learned dissertations on the fetishism of money, knows this: "money [is] the annihilating transformation of the concrete into the abstract, of real products into currency ... the triumph of the imaginary ... over the real, the denial of diversity" (267). Living almost exclusively in his mind and knowing only "what he must want on principle" (250), Gorz is thus caught up, without realizing it, in the universalizing and levelling principle of the domination of the abstract. His principle of life *is* the life-destroying principle of the exchange process: "Men have come to be—triumph of integration— identified in their innermost behavior patterns with fate in modern society."[39] Just as people in general who are under the exchange principle are homogenized by the rule of money, Gorz's subjectivity in particular is levelled by the dominating currency of his reifying conceptualizations, and the latter process can be seen to be reflecting the former: the objective, desubjectivizing abstraction implicit in the exchange principle underlies and structures his subjective orientation toward objectifying and dehumanizing systems of thought. Gorz's autobiographical work thus unfolds how the principle of exchange underlies the central issues in his life-historical becoming, that is, his glorification of the mind and of will power at the expense of the body and of emotions, his desire to be Other, and his complex of non-identification.[40] His lifelong attempts to will himself Other, to become a somebody, while reflecting the objective rule of the exchange principle which does not allow any self-identity and makes people divest themselves of anything not commensurable with the social whole, end up turning him into a nobody split against himself. Negating who he is, he does not negate the world which imposes this self-denial; instead he follows its law, becomes identical with it, and is subsumed under its common denominator of universal alienation.

Expressing his existential non-identity in the form of an "autobiographical essay,"[41] Gorz brackets together his life-historical self-estrangement with its literary presentation, and it is this form of his search for self-identity that constitutes the second – horizontal – dialectical movement in *The Traitor*. Gorz's inquiry into the self consists of a mixture of, on the one hand, subjective, life-historical recollections, written in a concrete, graphic, and vivid language (autobiography) and, on the other hand, objective, abstract speculations, couched in scientific, conceptual terminology (essay), the two antithetical moments emphasizing and qualifying each other. Just as Gorz, "a half man" (99) always wanting to be Other, defies any unambiguous identity, the story of his life – a dialectical mediation between image and concept, theory and experience, literature and social science – does not allow any clear-cut classification: part essay, part autobiographical narrative, *The Traitor* is a half-breed. "Fallen apart is the identity of experience, the continuous and articulated life, which only allows for the posture of the narrator,"[42] Adorno writes, and Gorz's self-reflective, existentially uncertain, and episodic discovery of his complex of non-identification eloquently and painfully exemplifies this contention. It is exactly here, in the identity of the autobiographical narrator's experience, which has split asunder, that the vertical and horizontal dialectical movements in Gorz's work intersect, that the form of his writing and its content converge, so that the discontinuous narrative constitutes the discontinuous narrator who produces it.

The narrator's discontinuity does not only materialize in the fluctuation of *The Traitor*'s overall form, though, but also finds expression in his discontinuous use of the pronominal indicators of identity. It is, interestingly enough, only when he dramatizes his own non-identity that he does not fall victim to "the lie of representation"[43] and turns his own alienation itself into an aesthetic means of production: he attempts to constitute himself in a highly complex alternation of third-person and first-person singular narratives. Wanting to negate his crippling loss of selfhood yet not knowing who he is, he oscillates between assigning himself the status of an object and that of a subject. He predominantly uses the third-person singular in the past tense, thus distancing his writing self from his previous historical being; conversely, the first-person singular refers primarily to the present narrator who analyses his past existence and writes what could be called his own case study (e.g. 70).

However, the narrator also alternates at times between "he" and "I"
while simultaneously switching tenses, thereby attesting to a lack of both
a historical and psychological continuum; on the other hand, he occasionally employs both the third-person and the first-person singular either in
the past or in the present tense, thus indicating at least traces of continuity
and non-alienation.[44] Significantly enough, this complex use of pronominal and temporal indices becomes the *modus operandi* of Gorz's narrative chiefly when his primary *modus vivendi* – his loss of a sense of reality
as a result of his abstract, mental existence, which is, of course, the very
reason he embarks on this autobiographical project – and also the writing
of *The Traitor* itself, that is, his attempt to revert his complex of non-
identification, become the subject matter of his literary self-production.[45]
In other words, the "schizoid personality" (77) of the narrator presents
itself in the most disconnected and confused form exactly when its own
disconnectedness and confusion as well as their potential transcendence
are at issue.[46] It is exactly when he becomes aware of his primary complex
of non-identification, thus neutralizing the unconscious power this "terror of identification" has had over him, that Gorz is able to overcome his
personality split, to say "I," and also confidently to sustain his use of the
first-person singular.[47]

Gorz's autobiographical work, then, his process of appropriating (life-)
history, turns into reality Christa Wolf's demand that prose held "the
human being to become a subject."[48] At the end of his self-exploration
Gorz possesses a stronger sense of self, of who he is. This strengthening of
subjectivity is precisely also the goal of the therapeutic treatment of
psychoanalysis: "Where It was, there I shall become."[49] Although the
writer—particularly the autobiographical writer—and the analysand are
in a very similar situation (both try to make "the deliberate step out of
prehistory into history," as Christa Wolf puts it[50]), there is, however, a
fundamental difference between the autobiographical and the psychoanalytical pursuit; taking on the roles of analyst and analysand at the
same time, autobiographical writers are denied the possibility to engage
themselves in what psychoanalysts call "transference": their practice of
"remembering, repeating, and working through" their repressed past is
"only" an inner dialogue. Not therapeutic in strictly psychoanalytical
terms, writing autobiographically can, nevertheless, be a way of working
through the individual as well as the collective past and therefore of
surviving the as yet unmastered present in order that the future might be
more liveable. A self-rescue operation, Gorz's work on *The Traitor* thus
is what Kate Millett, referring to her own autobiographical writing, calls
"a safety valve of self."[51]

Hence the autobiographical act of self-help, releasing excess pressure
on the (non-)self from both inner and outer sources, is particularly
befitting a strategy of survival for exiles (be they "only" inner or also
outer ones[52]), that is, for those whose only liveable alternative to "the rule
and power of the whole, the superimposed, administered unification,"[53]
is to be "marginal in regard to society and history" (42), as Gorz puts it

with respect to himself. Gorz's repossession of his "internal foreign territory"[56] thus negates the officially sanctioned and induced historical oblivion and social amnesia. *The Traitor* is a time bomb in the locker of history: it explodes "the nightmare [*Schreckbild*] of a humanity without remembrance."[55] In an age in which individual experience becomes increasingly buried and distorted "under the cliché of the conventionally accepted,"[56] the dialectical search for life-historical experiences and knowledge is destabilizing and subversive of a repressive mass culture. The dissenting voice of the autobiographer Gorz thus has a utopian reverberation. Negating its negation, its refusal of the alienation and depersonalization of the world which is and has been constitutes a faint, germinal *Prinzip Hoffnung*. Attempting to speak rather than be spoken, to live rather than be lived, to be rather than not to be, Gorz makes the first step towards a responsible contemporaneity.

What he still owes us, of course, is some evidence as to whether he *can* actually be himself. That is to say, *The Traitor* is "only" a halfway house on the road to self-realization. Helping Gorz to become aware of the *raison d'être* of his non-identity and inspiring the confidence in him to take steps toward overcoming it, his concrete autobiographical work tears down the smoke screen of abstractions and objectifications behind which he had self-denyingly been eking out his false existence. It can thus be seen to be a *prise de conscience*, but not yet what Paolo Freire calls a process of "conscientisation":[57] not critically inserting himself into history, its author does not actively work on transforming the world that oppresses and instrumentalizes him. The foundation for a more self-identical life, Gorz's autobiographical coming-to-himself hence points beyond the literary realm towards a "practical transcendence of his global situation, which, instead of avoiding, he must act upon and thereby transform" (79). In this sense, the subjective investigation into the objective obstacles of his becoming a subject does not have an unburdened happy ending. The autobiographical negation of his negation declines "to be an end in itself" and instead tries "to transcend itself at the very moment it comes into being" (302). If Gorz's abstract treatise *Fondements pour une morale* contains the instruments for him to think himself,[58] then his concrete, dialectical autobiographical work *The Traitor* contains the tools for him to attempt, to the extent that this is possible in the life-denying exchange society we live in, to be himself: *Hic Rhodus, hic salta*.

MICHAEL MUNDHENK

NOTES

1. Herbert Marcuse, *The Aesthetic Dimension: Toward a Critique of Marxist Aesthetics* (Boston: Beacon P., 1978), p. 38. The motto by Rockwell Gray is from his essay "Autobiography Now," *Kenyon Review*, 4 (1982), 33. The present study is a considerably condensed version of a detailed analysis of both contemporary autobio-

graphical writing in general and André Gorz's *The Traitor* in particular.

2. Gray, 31. The current omnipresence of autobiographical expressions in Western middle-class culture – the examples in this essay are drawn from the literary productions in the Federal Republic of Germany, France, and the USA (for a comment on a similar trend in the UK see, e.g., Ros Coward, "Cautionary Tales," *New Socialist*, No. 18 [July/August 1984], 46–7) – is accompanied by a rapidly growing academic interest in forms of self-literature. Apart from Gray's essay, the studies most pertinent to an understanding of the scope and *raison d'être* of the contemporary autobiographical boom are: Michael Rutschky, *Erfahrungshunger: Ein Essay über die siebziger Jahre* (Köln: Kiepenheuer & Witsch, 1980); Hans Rudolf Picard, *Autobiographie im zeitgenössischen Frankreich: Existentielle Reflexion und literarische Gestaltung* (München: Wilhelm Fink, 1978); Sylvia Schwab, *Autobiographik und Lebenserfahrung: Versuch einer Typologie deutschsprachiger autobiographischer Schriften zwischen 1965 und 1975* (Würzburg: Königshausen & Neumann, 1981); Philippe Lejeune, *Je est un autre: L'autobiographie, de la littérature aux médias* (Paris: Editions du Seuil, 1980); Edmond Marc, "Le récit de vie ou la culture vivante," *Le français dans le monde*, No. 181 (Nov–Dec 1983), 72–83; "Récits de vie," two special issues of *Revue des Sciences Humaines*, Nos. 191 and 192 (July–Sept/Oct–Dec 1983); Juliette Raabe, "Le marché du vécu," in *Individualisme et autobiographie en occident*, eds. Claudette Delhez-Sarlet and Maurizio Catani (Brussels: Editions de l'Université de Bruxelles, 1983), pp. 235–48; Francis Russell Hart, "History Talking to Itself: Public Personality in Recent Memoir," *New Literary History*, 11 (Autumn 1979), 193–210. For further references, see also notes 3, 7, 10, 12, 13 and 17.

3. Christopher Lasch, *The Culture of Narcissism: American Life in an Age of Diminishing Expectations* (New York: Warner Books, 1979). Contemporary apocalyptic literature is also examined in Michael Rutschky, "Katastrophen-Literatur—die neueste Tendenz?," *Neue Rundschau*, 88, 4 (1977), 619–28.

4. Otto Friedrich, "The Computer Moves In," *Time*, 3 Jan. 1983, 10.

5. Hans-Jürgen Syberberg, *Die freudlose Gesellschaft: Notizen aus dem letzten Jahr* (München: Hanser, 1981), author's text on backcover (my translation).

6. The definitional dilemma of current research into autobiographical writing is succinctly summarized by Avrom Fleishman who, having surveyed the existing body of criticism, comes to the conclusion that "there are no agreed upon norms for a genre of autobiography" (*Figures of Autobiography: The Language of Self-Writing in Victorian and Modern England* [Berkeley: U. of California P., 1983], p. 35). Rather than adding to this literature yet another prescriptive and thus confining description of what a "real" or "true" autobiography is, I will keep the frame of reference broad and flexible by using the terms "autobiographical writing" and "autobiographical literature," the constitutive element of which is the—at least intended—identity of author and narrator or protagonist. The objective of this essay, therefore, is not to delineate the difference between various specific forms of autobiographical literature (e.g. diary, letter, essay, memoir, or novel), but instead to elucidate the dangers and the possibilities of the general surge of interest in self-writing prevailing in our culture.

7. Peter Sloterdijk, *Literatur und Organisation von Lebenserfahrung: Autobiographien der Zwanziger Jahre* (München: Hanser, 1978), pp. 5–6 (my translation).

8. Sloterdijk, p. 7 (my translation of "Literatur der Lebensformdebatte").

9. Karin Struck, *Kindheits Ende: Journal einer Krise* (Frankfurt: Suhrkamp, 1982), p. 548 (my translation).

10. The Frankfurt/M Suhrkamp Publishers have, e.g., started a whole series of what has been coined "Verständigungstexte" (a term that stresses the dialogical intent of this kind of literature) by men, women, parents, teachers and students, psychiatric patients, prisoners, and drug addicts. So far, eleven volumes of these "communicative texts" have been published; the pioneering ones were: *Frauen, die pfeifen*, eds. Ruth Geiger et al (1979); *Männersachen*, ed. Hans-Ulrich Müller-Schwefe (1979). For a concise statement on the communicative purpose of these texts, see Peter Sloterdijk, quoted in *Männersachen* (p. 212). However, the term "Verständigungstext" can be applied not only to these volumes but also to a host of other works, such as Peter Schneider's *Lenz*,

Verena Stefan's *Häutungen*, Bernward Vesper's *Die Reise*, Fritz Zorn's *Mars*, etc. For
an extremely helpful discussion of this literature, see Evelyne Keitel's essay "Verständigungstexte—Form, Funktion, Wirkung," *German Quarterly*, 56, 3 (May 1983),
431–55. Similarly in the United States a multitude of first person accounts has come out
of the Black and the women's movements. See, e.g.: Alex Haley, *The Autobiography of
Malcolm X* (New York: Random House, 1965); Eldridge Cleaver, *Soul on Ice* (New
York: McGraw-Hill, 1968); Julius Lester, *Search for the New Land: History as Sub-
jective Experience* (New York: Dial P., 1969); George Jackson, *Soledad Brother: The
Prison Letters of George Jackson* (New York: Coward-McCann, 1970); Maya Angelou,
I Know Why the Caged Bird Sings (New York: Random House, 1970); Ingrid Bengis,
Combat in the Erogenous Zone (New York: Knopf, 1972); Jill Johnston, *Lesbian
Nation* (New York: Simon and Schuster, 1974); Kate Millett, *Flying* (New York:
Knopf, 1974) and *Sita* (New York: Farrar, Straus and Giroux, 1977); Maryse Holder,
Give Sorrow Words (New York: Grove P., 1979); Michelle Cliff, *Claiming an Identity
They Taught Me to Despise* (Watertown: Persephone P., 1980).

11. Rockwell Gray, "Autobiography in Theory," rev. of James Olney, ed., *Autobiography: Essays Theoretical and Critical, Salmagundi*, Nos. 52–3 (Spring-Summer 1981),
177.

12. Houston A. Baker, "The Problem of Being: Some Reflections on Black Autobiography," *Obsidian*, 1, 1 (1975), 21. Black autobiographies have traditionally been
documents of and about self-help (see, e.g., John W. Blassingame, "Black Autobiographies as History and Literature," *The Black Scholar*, 5, 4 [Dec. 1973–Jan. 1974],
2–9).

13. Bernd Neumann, "Die Wiedergeburt des Erzählens aus dem Geist der Autobiographie?," *Basis: Jahrbuch für deutsche Gegenwartsliteratur*, 9 (1979), 101.

14. Ralph-Rainer Wuthenow, *Das erinnerte Ich: Europäische Autobiographie und Selbst-
darstellung im 18. Jahrhundert* (München: C.H. Beck, 1974), p. 214 (my translation).

15. Quoted by Theodor W. Adorno, "Was bedeutet: Aufarbeitung der Vergangenheit," in
Erziehung zur Mündigkeit: Vorträge und Gespräche mit Hellmut Becker 1959–1969
(Frankfurt: Suhrkamp, 1970), p. 13.

16. This reifying abolition of history and of the continuity of time, rather than considered an
oppressive condition to be transcended, is expressly embraced as a goal to be striven for
by structuralist and post-structuralist critics for whom culture in all its aspects is but a
language, a text. Correspondingly, the individual human being is a "textual, non-
subjective 'I'" (Jean Thibaudeau, "Le roman comme autobiographie," *Tel Quel*,
No. 34 [Summer 1968], 69 [my translation]). Thus Michael Sprinker, e.g., in fashionable apocalyptic style, boldly announces "the end of autobiography" and approvingly
discusses the modern fragmentation of time and the self in connection with "Kierkegaard's championing of the instantaneous, the momentary, the disruptive against the
Hegelian concept of mediation" ("Fictions of the Self: The End of Autobiography," in
Autobiography: Essays Theoretical and Critical, ed. James Olney [Princeton: Princeton
U.P., 1980], p. 329). Writing in general and autobiography in particular is not a
dialectical mediation of the historical world in which this intellectual/artistic (self-)
production occurs and of the historical possibilities and exigencies of the linguistic
means of this production, but instead pure discourse. In this unmediated universe, "the
impossible project, *vivre pour soi dans l'écriture*, determines the primary autobiographical activity" (Alain Finkielkraut, "Desire in Autobiography," trans. Christie Vance,
Genre, 6, 2 [June 1973], 223). Within the closed structuralist and post-structuralist
system of texts, in which the (autobiographical) author's identity is appropriated by
language – Barthes structures the fragments of his autobiography roughly according to
the law of letters, the alphabet (Roland Barthes, *Roland Barthes* [New York: Hill &
Wang, 1977]) – being is atrophied at the expense of becoming, that is, the sense of time
as a continuous movement where the present is the result of the past and the germ of the
future, is substituted by temporal atomism. In the words of Edward Said, "textuality
has ... become the exact antithesis and displacement of what might be called history.
Textuality is considered to take place, yes, but by the same token it does not take place
anywhere or anytime in particular. It is produced, but by no one and at no time." (*The*

World, the Text, and the Critic [Cambridge: Harvard U.P., 1983], pp. 3–4). See also notes 25 and 46 in the present essay.

17. Ernest G. Schachtel, *Metamorphosis: On the Development of Affect, Perception, Attention, and Memory* (New York: Basic Books, 1959), p. 304. For the crucial distinction between "autobiographical" and "useful" memory, see particularly pp. 286–304.

18. Quoted by Martin Jay, "Anamnestic Totalization: Reflections on Marcuse's Theory of Remembrance," *Theory and Society*, 11, 1 (January 1982), 5. See also Max Horkheimer and Theodor W. Adorno, *Dialectic of Enlightenment*, p. 230.

19. Herbert Marcuse writes: "This ability to forget – itself the result of a long and terrible education by experience – is an indispensable requirement of mental and physical hygiene without which civilized life would be unbearable; but it is also the mental faculty which sustains submissiveness and renunciation. To forget is also to forgive what should not be forgiven if justice and freedom are to prevail. Such forgiveness reproduces the conditions which reproduce injustice and enslavement: to forget past suffering is to forgive the forces that caused it – without defeating these forces. The wounds that heal in time are also the wounds that contain the poison. Against this surrender to time, the restoration of remembrance to its rights, as a vehicle of liberation, is one of the noblest tasks of thought.... Without release of the repressed content of memory, without release of its liberating power, non-repressive sublimation is unimaginable" (Herbert Marcuse, *Eros and Civilization: A Philosophical Inquiry into Freud* [New York: Vintage, 1962], pp. 212–13). Frank Hearn similarly emphasizes: "When remembrance is replaced by forgetfulness, when imagination is suppressed and play is trivialized, the past becomes invalid, emptied of meaning. In these circumstances, trans-systemic criteria of assessment and action disappear, and people either consent to the legitimating standards supplied by society as it is ... or, because there are no alternatives, resign themselves to the present." (Frank Hearn, "Remembrance and Critique: The Uses of the Past for Discrediting the Present and Anticipating the Future," *Politics and Society*, 5, 2 [1975], 223).

20. Rockwell Gray, "Autobiography Now," 50.

21. Sigmund Freud, "Remembering, Repeating and Working-Through," trans. James Strachey, *The Standard Edition of the Complete Psychological Works of Sigmund Freud* (London: Hogarth P., 1958), 12, 147–56.

22. Hans-Jürgen Syberberg, "Introduction," *Hitler—A Film from Germany*, trans. Joachim Neugroschel (New York: Farrar, Straus and Giroux, 1982), p. 9. See also his *Die freudlose Gesellschaft, passim.*

23. See, e.g., Paula Heimann, "Bemerkungen zum Arbeitsbegriff in der Psychoanalyse," *Psyche*, 21, 5 (1966), 323–60; Theodor W. Adorno, "Was bedeutet: Aufarbeitung der Vergangenheit"; also Alexander und Margarete Mitscherlich, *The Inability to Mourn: Principles of Collective Behavior*, trans. Beverley R. Placzek (New York: Grove Press, 1975), *passim.*

24. In his study *The Active Society: A Theory of Societal and Political Processes* (New York: Free Press, 1968), Amitai Etzioni discusses how personal, collective, and societal projects – the dialectical autobiographical project could be seen to be a personal one and thus "only" the first step on the road to social change – can reduce inauthenticity and alienation (pp. 647–55).

25. Theodor W. Adorno, *Negative Dialectics*, trans. E.B. Ashton (New York: Seabury Press, 1973), p. 171. Contrary to Adorno's endeavour, structuralist and post-structuralist critics again, instead of attempting to emancipate, that is, to de-alienate, the subject (at least on the theoretical plane), try to get rid of it altogether and thus hypostatize its estrangement and non-identity. Subjective experience being subordinated to and subsumed into measurable discursive structures, the human being is entirely instrumentalized and nullified (see, e.g., Tzvetan Todorov's *Grammaire du Décaméron* [The Hague: Mouton, 1969] in which the author [sic!] reduces the world of the *Decameron* into a purely grammatical one, the characters being nouns, their attributes adjectives, and their actions verbs). The total effacement of the individual is made into a programme. Having dismissed what he calls " 'an ideology of alienation,' "

Alain Finkielkraut, e.g., writes: "The end term of liberation is not the presence of the self to the self. On the contrary, to let oneself become invested by writing is not only to consent to the de-subjectivizing of the subject, but to establish from the beginning of the game (in order that the game may actually take place) that the mastery of the self is excluded" ("Desire in Autobiography," 229).

26. Russell Jacoby, *Social Amnesia: A Critique of Contemporary Psychology from Adler to Laing* (Boston: Beacon Press, 1975), p. 80.

27. Dieter Wellershoff, "Zu privat: Über eine Kategorie der Verdrängung," *Literatur und Veränderung* (Köln: Kiepenheuer & Witsch, 1969), p. 34 (my translation).

28. Ernst Bloch, *Philosophische Aufsätze zur Objektiven Phantasie* (Frankfurt: Suhrkamp, 1969), p. 18 (my translation).

29. Ernst Herhaus, *Notizen während der Abschaffung des Denkens* (Frankfurt: März, 1970), p. 106 (my translation). English excerpts of this collection are in "Notes during the Abolition of Thinking," trans. Michael Mundhenk and Shelley Wong, *Telos*, No. 52 (Summer 1982), 178–85.

30. Herhaus, pp. 120–1.

31. Herhaus' criticism obviously applies to this study as well; however, time limitations made it impossible for me to write a life-historical essay on the question of contemporary autobiography. For a glimpse at the gap between theory and practice in my own life, see my autobiographical "Notes during the Sublimation of Libido," *Paunch*, Nos. 57–8 (January 1984), 31–52.

32. Jean-Paul Sartre, in André Gorz, *The Traitor*, trans. Richard Howard (New York: Simon and Schuster, 1959), p. 7 (the English edition [London: John Calder, 1960] has identical pagination). Page references (which appear in the body of the essay) are to these editions, although I have corrected Richard Howard's at times rather careless and faulty translation wherever necessary. The French version I worked with is *Le traître* (Paris: Editions du Seuil, 1978) [Collection Points 87].

33. André Gorz, *Fondements pour une morale* (Paris: Editions galilée, 1977), p. 18 (my translation).

34. Peter Sloterdijk, *Literatur und Organisation von Lebenserfahrung*, p. 113 (my translation).

35. Erik Erikson, "'Identity Crisis' in Autobiographic Perspective," *Life History and the Historical Moment* (New York: Norton, 1975), p. 21.

36. After only a few pages of this new kind of writing in which he does not disavow his own existence, Gorz realizes that *The Traitor*, even in its embryonic form, is already more important to him than his life-work *Fondements pour une morale* (63).

37. The concept of the subject–object dialectic proceeds from the Hegelian principle that the self and the world are always in reciprocal dependence on each other, that there is a nexus between these antithetical concepts (*Begriffsdialektik*) and the antagonistic reality (*Realdialektik*) to which they refer and from which they are derived (Arnold Hauser, *The Sociology of Art*, trans. Kenneth J. Northcott [Chicago/London: U. of Chicago Press, 1982], p. 337). Subject and object, then, are not mutually exclusive; instead "the decisive moment of [their] dialectic" is the fact that "the constitutive function of the one moment [is] the genesis of the other" (Hauser, p. 340). The essence of the subject–object dialectic consists, then, in a dialogical interpenetration of its two antithetical components.

38. Russell Jacoby, *Social Amnesia*, p. 79.

39. Theodor W. Adorno, "Society," trans. F. R. Jameson, *Salmagundi*, Nos. 10–11 (Fall 1969–Winter 1970), 152.

40. For a discussion of the relationship between the principle of exchange and the principle of identification, see Theodor W. Adorno, *Negative Dialectics*, p. 146.

41. On the essay as form see, e.g., Theodor W. Adorno, "The Essay as Form," trans. Bob Hullot-Kentor and Frederic Will, *New German Critique*, No. 32 (1984), 151–71.

42. Theodor W. Adorno, "Standort des Erzählers im zeitgenössischen Roman," *Noten zur Literatur* (Frankfurt: Suhrkamp, 1981), p. 42 (my translation).

43. Adorno, "Standort des Erzählers im zeitgenössischen Roman," p. 45. Here Adorno denounces a one-dimensional language which, uncritical of itself, fails to negate and

undercut itself, simply reproduces the façade of contemporary society (rather than reflectingly appropriating and therefore producing reality), and thus becomes assimilated by mass culture. To avoid this disappropriation, non-identity and alienation must be allowed to enter language itself; only then can writing become truly critical of that which is because in an unreconciled and estranged world a linguistic "reconciliation of the reality and the subject" (Theodore W. Adorno, "Voraussetzungen: Aus Anlass einer Lesung von Hans G. Helms," *Noten zur Literatur*, p.438 [my translation]) would be but a treasonous ideological sham. André Gorz, however, displays no doubts whatsoever as to the representational faculty of language. He writes his autobiographical essay as if the relationship between language/literature and reality were not in the least problematical, as if the reality of his life-story constituted itself in a one-to-one transcription of the reality of his life-history rather than in the refractive process of constructing and reflecting the tentative possibility of its verbal presentation. This deeply uncritical and uncontemporary use of language is Gorz's blind spot: his own experiences of non-identity and alienation do not find entry into the linguistic substance of his autobiographical work. The form of Gorz's writing, then, that is, the dialectical montage of abstract analyses and concrete life-historical prose narratives, is multi-dimensional, dynamic, self-conscious, and self-critical; the language of his work is not. The form of *The Traitor* dialectically turns against itself and is non-identical; the language of Gorz's reconstruction of his complex of non-identification progresses straightforwardly and is identical. The only breach in the wall of this identical language is made at the very location where form and content converge: in the person of the non-identical narrator who autobiographically searches for self-hood.

44. He uses "he" in both the present and the past on pages 38–42, 65–8, 71–2, 75, 90–5, 183; he employs "I" in both these tenses on pages 39, 41, 178–9, 183–4, 187, 231–2, 239, 259, 261.

45. See pages 38–42, 47–51, 65–79, 90–5, 179–89, 231–9, 256–61.

46. The life-historical urgency for Gorz to regain a sense of reality and to establish meaning in his life suggests, then, that the narrative alternation between the perspectives of the third and the first person singular is more than just a "game of figures" and "focalization," as Philippe Lejeune claims ("Autobiography in the Third Person," trans. Annette and Edward Tomarken, *New Literary History*, 9, 1 [Autumn 1977], 32 and 40). Reducing Gorz's deep-rooted identity crisis to a linguistic, narrative amusement, Lejeune fails to understand that this act of continually splitting asunder one's own grammatical referent is set in the background of contemporary social atomization and alienation, a background he only mentions in passing. The formalist ontological reduction of human beings to grammatical categories and functions, symptomatic of the structuralist and post-structuralist *Weltanschauung* in general, totally disregards and, in fact, discards the human realities that authors like Gorz are attempting to confront and work through by means of autobiographical writing. Thus Paul L. Jay, e.g., claims that the autobiographical subject's identity is primarily disappropriated by language and that writing in general and autobiography in particular is pure discourse in which "the idea of 'self-hood' [is] disengaged from biography, the past, and history" ("Being in the Text: Autobiography and the Problem of the Subject," *MLN*, 97, 5 [December 1982], 1046). See also Rudolphe Gasché, "Foreword," *MLN*, 93, 4 (May 1978), 574, as well as the essays by Michael Sprinkler and Alain Finkielkraut mentioned above.

47. Gorz's work on *The Traitor* produces, in fact, a subject able to say not only, "This is I," but also, tentatively, "This is we" – the life-story of a traitor to humanity ends with the words: "... it is my reality in the eyes of those who are on the same side as I which is important to me. Not to bow humbly beneath their verdict, not to make myself their instrument, but to play according to the rules that we have in common and in the determination of which it must be possible for a dialogue to get under way. While waiting for something better" (304). This "we" (faintly hinted at as a potential), as opposed to the "we" of the first section of *The Traitor*, will not be an "abstract universality" or the "anonymity of the generic" (95), but rather the embodiment of a concrete community of individual human beings who act in solidarity with each other in order to achieve the same historical aims.

48. Christa Wolf, "The Reader and the Writer," in *The Reader and the Writer*, trans. Joan Becker (New York: International Publishers, 1977), p. 212. The preceding is my translation of Wolf's phrase "das Subjektwerden des Menschen". Wolf has followed her own advice most explicitly in her dialectical autobiographical narrative *A Model Childhood*, trans. Ursule Molinaro and Hedwig Rappolt (New York: Farrar, Straus and Giroux, 1980).
49. Sigmund Freud, "New Introductory Lectures on Psycho-Analysis," trans. James Strachey, in *Standard Edition of the Complete Psychological Works of Sigmund Freud* (London: Hogarth Press, 1964), Vol. 22, p. 80 (the preceding is my literal translation of Freud's famous axiom: "Wo Es war, soll Ich werden").
50. Christa Wolf, "The Reader and the Writer," p. 212.
51. Kate Millett, *Flying*, p. 165.
52. See, e.g., Wolfgang Müller-Funk, "Das Exil ist eine Krankheit: Autobiographie als ein Mittel sich zu behaupten," *Merkur*, 36 (1982), 1231–6, and Rainer Zimmer, "Die Autobiographik des Exils 1933–45: Verarbeitung und Vermittlung geschichtlicher Erfahrung," in *Faschismuskritik und Deutschlandbild im Exilroman*, eds. Christian Fritsch and Lutz Winckler (Berlin: Argumente, 1981), pp. 214–27.
53. Herbert Marcuse, *The Aesthetic Dimension*, p. 50.
54. Sigmund Freud, "New Introductory Lectures on Psycho-Analysis," p. 57.
55. Theodor W. Adorno, "Was bedeutet: Aufarbeitung der Vergangenheit," p. 13 (my translation).
56. Ernest G. Schachtel, *Metamorphosis*, p. 289, see also p. 288 and p. 304.
57. Paolo Freire, "Conscientisation," in *Conversion: Perspectives on Personal and Social Transformation*, ed. Walter E. Conn (New York: Alba House, 1978), pp. 297–306. Freire's conscientisation would be a collective and/or societal project in Amitai Etzioni's *Active Society* (pp. 649–52).
58. André Gorz, *Fondements pour une morale*, p. 23.

The Politics of
Edwin Muir's Autobiographies

On publication, Edwin Muir's *The Story and the Fable*[1] was hailed as "a book of outstanding delicacy and integrity."[2] Michael Hamburger described *An Autobiography* as a "singularly honest and lucid account,"[3] while Rex Warner almost ran out of adjectives in gushing that these writings should be labelled "gentle and wise, modest, vivid and illuminating."[4] Alfred Kazin referred to Muir as "a giver of testimony"; and Stephen Spender, with a note of meekly resigned puzzlement, commented that "it is difficult to criticise a work which gives a single-minded impression of integrity."[5] No less an authority than T.S. Eliot sought to stress Muir's "unmistakable integrity";[6] but even this tribute is less revealing than that paid by Richard Hoggart.

Hoggart's 1965 lecture on autobiography to the Royal Society of Literature draws upon his established sensitivity to ideological bias in writings from and about the working classes; yet, having neatly dispatched the sentimentalities of a clutch of unmemorable memoirs, he too falls back on the matter of Muir's "integrity." Autobiography depends, he argues, on "questions of tone or voice," and he continues:

> For myself, I would like to find a voice which would carry a wide and deep range of attributes and emotions without being socially self-conscious or derivatively literary. Among modern autobiographers I know hardly anyone who has found this tone, this clarity which seems almost like talking to oneself, since no one is being wooed. Edwin Muir's autobiography has this quality, and about it one can properly use terms like 'sensitive integrity'. He was a poet, and he used his poetic skills here in a disciplined way.[7]

Hoggart's use of quotation marks here seems to suggest a certain disquiet underlying the apparent approbation; but he remains incapable of breaking through the confusion of the earlier reviewers. He knows that the tone which convinces him of Muir's "sensitive integrity" can only be a product of the "poetic skills" to which he makes obeisance; he knows that he is dealing not with a natural object found by chance but with a literary text deliberately fashioned for publication and carefully constructed to make a certain impression on the reader: and yet part of that impression is the conviction that no impression whatever had been intended at all. At the end of a most intricately and cleverly patterned work, Muir's autobiographical persona writes, "I cannot bring life into a neat pattern" – and the critics believe him! If we were to continue Hoggart's metaphor, we might say that he has not been wooed by Muir's text so much as raped. This essay outlines some of the arguments which support a less ingenuous reading of Muir's prose, and which help reveal the complex of ideological pressures which determined its character.

If Muir is transported from England to Scotland, his autobiographies cease to be seen as the stronghold of purity and integrity which the persona was designed to make them seem. In Scotland, Muir is not simply the latest in a long line of English mystical writers that stretches from Traherne and Vaughan to Eliot;[8] he is primarily seen as a political writer, author of *Scott and Scotland* (1936), the major attack on the Scottish Literary Renaissance and the most cogent defence of the Unionist ideology to be written this century. In this context, *The Story and the Fable* is the representation of what Chris Grieve/Hugh MacDiarmid described as Muir's "own little personal Whipsnade,"[9] a self-indulgent self-examination by which he attempted to exclude from history the political and cultural debate which the initial reaction to *Scott and Scotland* suggested that he had lost. And exclude it Muir most certainly did. If the autobiographies are Muir's rewriting of his personal history, created to compensate for the apparent failure of his attempted rewriting of Scotland's history, then they work simply by denying space – by denying time – to those elements of his earlier commitments which were no longer compatible with his new devotion to the role of religious and "apolitical" mystic. This is the great success of the writer Edwin Muir: that he has triumphed in determining which aspects of the totality of his work are to be seen as constituting his oeuvre and as bearing the development of his ideology. The extent of Muir's victory is seen, for example, in Peter Butter's biographical study where he writes of the *New Age* material that "Muir would not wish much attention to be paid to this early work," and then himself dispenses with it in a superficial account which condemns the writing of four or five years in a page and a half.[10] Such naivety not only accepts Muir's self-image unquestioningly: it also underestimates the degree of literary ability which Muir employed in constructing that image.

I

In an important article on "History and the Scottish Novel," Cairns Craig began with W.B. Gallie's argument in *Philosophy and the Historical Understanding* that "all history [is] founded upon the processes of narrative: history is the construction of story out of the amorphous, fragmented, hypothetical totality of what has happened to occur." Narrative, however, is essentially teleological:

> "it is chiefly in terms of conclusion – eagerly awaited as we read forward and accepted at the story's end – that we feel and appreciate the unity of a story"; and the ultimate teleology of the historical story is the present.[11]

If the skills Muir uses in producing his autobiographies are seen not as "poetic" (in Hoggart's phrase) but as those of a novelist (and Muir had already made "stories" out of his life in writing two – arguably, three – autobiographical novels in *The Marionette* [1927], *The Three Brothers* [1931] and *Poor Tom* [1932]), then an analysis of them reveals a literary methodology of selection and presentation which remains notable for its skill and cleverness, but which can no longer be shielded from investigation by the claim that the autobiographies simply represent intuitions of essential mystery.

Gallie claims that it is the ending of the story, the present, which makes sense of the past by explaining the final position of the writer. The clue to Muir's ideological terminus in his autobiographies is first apparent in the conclusion to *The Story and the Fable*. The narrative which he constructs in 1940 out of the events of his life goes only so far as the removal to Dresden in 1922: but there is a concluding section headed "Extracts from a Diary, 1937–39." The passages themselves are a miscellaneous collection. Although they do admit of political reflection in a more direct manner than *An Autobiography* was to do, these reactions are placed within a discourse primarily preoccupied with varieties of religious and transcendental experience (dreams, visions, aphorisms).

An Autobiography, distanced by eighteen years from the storm surrounding *Scott and Scotland*, and produced by a Muir who had given up almost entirely his engagement with Scottish and socialist concerns, shows a much greater confidence in the explanatory role of transcendental mysticism. It is significant that here again he returns to the form of the diary, from which he now takes just one extract:

> It was the last day of February 1939 – when I saw some schoolboys playing at marbles on the pavement; the old game had 'come round' again in its own time, known only to children, and it seemed a simple little rehearsal for a resurrection, promising a timeless renewal of life. I wrote in my diary next day:
>
>> Last night, going to bed alone, I suddenly found myself (I was taking off my waistcoat) reciting the Lord's Prayer in a loud, emphatic voice – a thing I had not done for many years – with deep urgency and profound disturbed emotion. While I went on I grew more composed; as if I had been empty and craving and were being replenished, my soul stood still; every word had a strange fullness of meaning which astonished and delighted me. It was late; I had sat up reading; I was sleepy; but as I stood in the middle of the floor half-undressed, saying the prayer over and over, meaning after meaning sprang from it, overcoming me with joyful surprise; and I realized that this simple petition was always universal and always inexhaustible, and day by day sanctified human life.

I had believed for many years in God and the immortality of the soul. (A, 246).

As soon as Muir has given the diary account of his conversion, his first impulse is, as always, to redefine the past in its light, again replacing change with discovery: he had "believed *for many years* in God." And this is the process that is repeated throughout the autobiographies, so that all his life is shown only in its relation to this transcendentalist faith of the late thirties. Consequently, he announces quite early in the work,

> I shall attend and listen to a class of experiences which the dis-believer in immortality ignores or dismisses as irrelevant to temporal life. The experiences I mean are of little practical use and have no particular economic or political interest. (*A*, 54)

As we have seen from Butter, this claim to have selected material for these books according to its relevance to other-worldly concerns has been widely welcomed by Muir's critics. Only Q.D. Leavis dared publicly to suggest that something had been lost in his decision not to write "that invaluable account of the central literary world in the formative post-war years, the era of *The Calendar of Modern Letters* and *The Athenaeum*, Eliot's poetry and the early Virginia Woolf and all the rest"; but she too put this heretical thought aside in admitting that Muir remained "notable for his integrity" and conceding that he could "hardly be blamed for writing his own book and not the one we wanted."[12] "Blamed," no: but this compliance in reading Muir only in the context in which he chose to direct us to read it leads directly to the kind of intellectual bullying of which Roger Knight is guilty when he attempts to warn off the sceptic:

> The directive to the reader of Muir's own work is clear: if it does not exercise his 'capacity for admiration', he had better leave it alone.[13]

The irony is that in seeking for literary gossip (albeit of the higher order) Mrs Leavis had identified one of the prime absences in Muir's work, one of the silences in the text: his life as a literary critic.

But as already mentioned, Scottish critics and historians make much of the events of the twenties and thirties, of the literary and critical battles which Muir omits. To Grieve, Muir was less the man of integrity and the private individual than the collaborator who had sold out his country's culture to become the "leader of the white-mouse faction of the Anglo-Scottish literati."[14] Yet such attacks came from the same Grieve who in 1925 had hailed Muir as "incontestably in the first flight of contemporary critics of *weltliteratur*" [*sic*].[15] The source of the rupture was, of course, *Scott and Scotland*. In that work the argument depends on the premise that Scotland has somehow dropped out of History, and that Scott consequently lived in "a temporal Nothing ... dotted with a few disconnected figures arranged at abrupt intervals" (2). Since Scotland is not part of the historical process, it follows that there can be no change which will bring her out of the cultural malaise which Muir defines: and so this narrative leads inexorably to the conclusion that "Scotland can only create a national literature by writing in English" (111). Such a version of the past, justifying such prognosis, gives the lie to the autobiographies' contention that spiritual issues had always taken precedence in Muir's life, and opens the way to other moments being seen as the determining crisis – or crises – in his story. And the paradox remains that, whereas the autobiographies claim overtly to be rebuttals of the kind of political interest displayed in *Scott and Scotland*, both the two studies of self and the examination of Scott share the denial of historical progress ("some kind of development, I suppose, should be expected to emerge, but I am very doubtful of such things" [*A*, 280]) which makes them, at a deeper level, part of the project of rewriting Scottish history that lay at the heart of the Renaissance Movement. Muir's versions may come to conclusions quite different from those of the *Scottish Chapbook*, *Albyn* or the *Drunk Man*: but the burden of his works is identical.

By analysing the ways in which the autobiographies deny significance to the history of Muir's political development, selecting and shaping his story to highlight and propagandise the religiose conservatism which the failure of those politics had brought about, it is possible to give an alternative reading of *The Story and the Fable* and *An Autobiography* as narrative constructions, in such a way as to open up access to a wider and deeper understanding of the historical constraints within which Muir wrote.

II

In an article published shortly after *The Story and the Fable* appeared, Muir wrote:

> I tried to make clear the pattern of my life as a human being existing in space and moving through time, environed by mystery. After I had finished, I went over the manuscript many times, seeking to make the pattern clearer, and felt like a man with an inefficient torch stumbling through a labyrinth, having forgotten where he entered and not knowing where he would come out.[16]

Here, the concession that the autobiography is a deliberate literary creation, a manuscript actively worked over many times to stress *the* pattern, is defused by the persona's only being allowed to work "to make the pattern *clearer*"; and the image of the professional writer is quite overshadowed by that of the clumsy, forgetful persona's inefficiency. The reader's attention is directed away from the process of writing which is the ostensible subject of this text, and towards the progress of the narrator, that innocent "environed by mystery" but bravely coping with the maze. Such language is typical of the later Muir's strategy: "environed," for instance, implies that being surrounded by "mystery" is man's natural habitat, and it encourages the acceptance of Muir's anti-intellectual philosophy.

The pattern to which Muir refers is, naturally, defined as being inaccessible to intellectual investigation:

> It is clear that no autobiography can begin with a man's birth, that

we extend far beyond any boundary line which we can set for ourselves in the past or the future, and that the life of every man is an endlessly repeated performance of the life of man.... In themselves our conscious lives may not be particularly interesting. But what we are not and never can be, our fable, seems to me inconceivably interesting. I should like to write that fable, but I cannot even live it; and all I could do if I related the outward course of my life would be to show how I have deviated from it; though even that is impossible, since I do not know the fable or anybody who knows it. One or two stages in it I can recognize: the age of innocence and the Fall and all the dramatic consequences which issue from the Fall. But these lie behind experience, not on its surface; they are not historical events; they are stages in the fable. (*S & F*, 55)

But Muir's art is that of the bluff. He tells us that he cannot make the pattern clear so that we do not investigate too closely its inconsistencies, do not suspect him of propagandising: yet the work in which he tells us this is itself structured in such a way as to present an image of the Fable which takes a religious form as reflected here in the references to the Fall. And this form is in turn validated by Muir's offering of his own conversion to Christianity as the climax of the familiar structure of the *Bildungsroman*.

The autobiographies logically cannot be the investigative exercise which the imagery of the man with the dim torch would seek to suggest. After 1939, Muir could not step outside of his religious commitment in order to examine it "objectively"; he necessarily and consistently wrote from within it. Consequently, the notion that there is an independent, objective pattern to which Muir fits his own poor experience as best he can must be seen not as an account of his progress towards the theory of the story and the fable, but as an instance of that theory's operation.

The values which structure this pattern are slowly brought together in the opening chapters of the book, long before their theoretical significance – for Muir or for the reader – is expounded. The most consistent element – not surprisingly – is religion itself. Often, the touch is very light indeed: St Magnus's cathedral, for instance, is said to be "the most beautiful thing within sight" of the Bu farm (*A*, 16); but this apparently descriptive fact is turned into a point of a very different order when the narrator adds that "it rose every day against the sky until it seemed to become a sign of the fable in our lives," anachronistically attributing to his childhood (and to all his family – and all the residents of Orkney?) the belief held by the man of 1940. Again, although he claims to remember nothing of the routine of his first seven years (*A*, 19), he nonetheless displays almost total recall of his baptism. Family prayers are singled out as being among his "happiest memories," creating "a feeling of complete security and union among us as we sat reading about David or Elijah" (*A*, 26): as in *Scott and Scotland*, where the ideal unified sensibility is located only in pre-Reformation Scotland, religious harmony here creates a community which Muir depicts – through the use of the first person plural – as unified. Organised religion, however, is tainted with Calvinism even so late as the 1890s, and it meets little approval: Muir's participation in revivalist meetings is attributed to a child's fear of exclusion – but this too takes on a more narrowly political force when the feelings of distaste established here are invoked to disparage his later Socialist convictions: "my conversion to Socialism," he needs only say, "was a recapitulation of my first conversion at fourteen" (*A*, 113).

The Orcadian routine of the late nineteenth century is quickly established as the good life, and one prefiguring that of his later beliefs. This life becomes the touchstone against which all later experience is measured. For example, the speakers at the Clarion Scout meetings which Muir attended in Glasgow are presented as self-seeking charlatans (*A*, 112), but their political engagement is also denigrated by being contrasted with the quietism on Orkney. The landlord whose exactions drove the family from farm to farm and finally into Glasgow is discussed only in the context of a single shooting trip to the islands, and the terms of that description – "a mere picture" (*A*, 115) – suggests that this role in the capitalist system is parallel with his activity as a hunter of game birds: that it may not be a particularly pleasant role is conceded, but on the grounds that it belongs to a larger pattern which transcends its apparent evil it is allowed to pass unquestioned.

There is another emblematic distinction in the contrast of prevalent attitudes to beggars in Orkney and on the mainland. In the islands, men such as John Simpson – regarded almost as blessed fools, being "not right in the mind" – are "always taken in and given food" (*A*, 82); one of the first things the reader is told about the adjustment to city life is that

> beggars were perpetually ringing the bell, and we did not learn for weeks that you must not take a beggar in and give him something to eat, but must slam the door at once in his face. (*A*, 91)

Glasgow is cast throughout as the antithesis of Orkney, presaged by such bad omens as his father's cold, the dark and windy day of travel and the dirty train awaiting the family when they had docked (*A*, 90). Leading into the chaos of family deaths, personal illness and the degradation of the bone factory, Glasgow is opposed to the rural idyll which it replaces.

In reading the presentation of Muir's pre-literary life, then, it is possible to discern the elements of the structures which underpin the autobiographies' ideological purpose as a whole. The country is seen as being intrinsically better than the city because it is depicted as having "natural" links with a religious (Christian) faith that is expressed in the terms of the "organic" peasant community. It is a fairly conventional mixture of Rousseau, Wordsworth and T.S. Eliot, though none the less potent for that.

But the project of deconstructing these images of his life can only be properly tackled when the independent evidence about Muir's life becomes available with which to challenge his own version of his past. Such evidence becomes available when we turn to the time Mrs Leavis longed to know about, his years in London in the early 1920s, and to the writing that he did for *The New Age* in that period.

III

Most of those who have researched the intellectual history of Britain in the first decades of this century will agree on at least one thing: that the full significance of *The New Age* has yet to be realised by the majority of readers. Edited by A.R. Orage, it was undoubtedly the most wide-ranging of contemporary magazines in that heyday of periodical journalism, seeking to keep its readers abreast of the latest developments in every field of thought, from psychoanalysis and philosophy to physics, as well as fulfilling the functions of a more conventional literary and cultural review. Above all, much work remains to be done on the journal's politics, and on the role of the journal from 1919 (starting a few months before Muir joined the staff as assistant editor) as propagator of Major Douglas' Social Credit economics. Certainly, by early in 1920, even a cursory reading of the paper would show that those writing for the periodical regarded working for the success of what had become "the Douglas–*New Age* Scheme" as their *raison d'être*.

Shortage of space prevents a full analysis here: but it is important to note that the columns which Muir regularly contributed to *The New Age* during these years show little sign of the Guild Socialist or Nietzschean ideas which had originally attracted his attention, and are entirely in keeping with the new ethos. And it is particularly important, in relation to the strategy of the autobiographies, that at this early date the use of a literary persona is signalled by the use of a precisely anglicised pseudonym, "Edward Moore."

The major part of Muir's contributions in this period involved the production of "Our Generation," ninety-six articles which were published almost weekly from November 1920 to September 1922, and which consist of comments on three or four topical issues or events of the week. The point of view is that of someone overtly committed to social credit and completely lacking in any doubts or fears about tackling the most sensitive political or cultural problems, from the miners' strike and unemployment to the role of the Anglican bishops.

These columns, however, were not just simple occasional pieces: they sought to fulfil a mission. It was not until 1934 that Lewis Grassic Gibbon wrote off the Scheme as a "bourgeois funk-fantasy";[17] in the 1920s and early '30s, many (including Eliot, Grieve, Lewis, Pound and Gunn) saw it as the only salvation from the alternatives of Communist or Fascist totalitarianism. Muir's problem was to devise a literary strategy by which he, as a writer whose ideology had been most strongly determined by being a working-class Scot, could persuade his largely English, middle-class audience of the virtues of Douglasism. Consequently, "Moore"'s chief characteristics are his blunt common sense, his lack of arrogance, and his persistent belief that the truth is perfectly clear and easy for men of goodwill to discern if only they will disabuse themselves of the conventions of capitalist ideology, the "superstitions" against which his co-propagandist Pound would rail in adjacent columns. And just to be on the safe side, "Moore" shows a marked predilection to talk in the first person plural, and to make explicit contrasts between the habits of "we English" as opposed to the mores of the Scots! Yet the reader of the autobiographical accounts of these years would get a completely different impression from that derived from the primary sources.

After their London wedding in June 1919, Muir returned to Glasgow and Willa Anderson set about finding a place where they might live. Having rented and furnished rooms in Guilford Street, she was astonished to find on her arrival in Scotland that her husband had yet to resign his job in a Renfrew office. "But you said you didn't want to be a clerk all your life, and that you wanted to get out of Glasgow," she protested. "But I'm earning three pounds seventeen and six *a week*," he replied.[18] In Willa's memoir, this anecdote performs several roles. Showing how little she knew of her husband and emphasising her greater adventurousness, it also supports the image of his unworldliness: by 1968, the date of the publication of *Belonging*, with knowledge of his success and with inflation having made the security of his wage seem negligible, his appeal to an economic argument seems slightly ridiculous, an excuse for his timidity and a result of his inability to discuss his neuroses. But the fact that Muir was concerned about his earnings is at least discernible in his wife's autobiography: his own autobiography suggests that at the time the matter was of no interest whatsoever. Implying that they were infected by their surroundings with a Peter Pan-like insouciance, he claims that he and his wife existed

> in a suspended state, waiting for work, not really apprehensive, for we could not imagine the possibility of not finding it: the work was there, invisible for the present, and one day it would appear. When we were tired of looking for it we went to Kensington Gardens, and in complete idleness dreamt through the afternoon. (*A*, 155)

Once again, like all good things, work is depicted as simply waiting to be discovered. But since Muir's psychological difficulties continued in London and beyond, despite several months of psychoanalysis, the discrepancy between the anguished protestations recalled by Willa and the confident ease of Edwin's account cannot be explained simply by the fact of their having left Glasgow. The *Autobiography*'s description re-inforces the impression that Muir – seen here as too interested in "dreams" to be "really apprehensive" about diurnal economic realities – had *always* acknowledged the dominance of the transcendental.

In fact, Willa had lost her job in a ladies' college on her marriage, and was able to find only less well-paid work at a crammer's, so when Muir accepted Orage's offer of £3 for three days work each week, the loss of nearly a quarter of his income must have imposed the kind of difficulties he had anticipated from Scotland. The autobiography discounts this entirely, slanting the image of the past to help create the feeling that the supremacy of transcendentalism in the autobiographical persona is the inevitable realisation of his "true" self. And this strategy of selecting the aspects of the period which can be turned to congruence with his later concerns is followed throughout the description of his time in London and his continuing association with *The New Age*.

The account of his career during these years, for example, is very thin. Having mentioned that reviewing for *The Athenaeum* and providing drama criticism for *The Scotsman* boosted his income to an acceptable level (*A*, 157), he makes no comment on the manner in which this new work was approached nor on its relationship with his contemporary editorial training. Instead, emphasis is placed on his personal life. Having arranged for Muir to join the paper, Orage's first role in the "London" chapter is not as editor of *The New Age* but, surprisingly, as the provider of Muir's introduction to psychoanalysis through his friendship with Maurice Nicoll and his colleagues (*A*, 157). Moreover, having chosen to ignore the interest possibly inherent in a description of the Jungian analytic method he underwent in the early 1920s, Muir concentrates exclusively on his subjective experiences. The five-page account of a particularly vivid "waking dream" details such religious images as Muir and his wife rising on angels' wings to sit on the shoulders of "a gigantic figure clad in antique armour, sitting on a throne with a naked sword at his side" (*A*, 162); and although other dreams are left in comparative obscurity, the cumulative effect of their description is to suggest that the spiritual – and, tangentially, the poetic – development they signify is what is most important about the period. Further, the similarly protracted account of his friendship with John Holms (*A*, 177–81) also stresses the personal side of this stage of his life at the expense of his public and literary development.

The autobiography does give some space to his association with *The New Age*, but this is largely taken up by a discussion not of the paper itself but of the personalities surrounding it. Orage's influence is not discussed in terms of his writings, but in the impressionistic terms of Muir's interpretation of his character, and this derives from the autobiographical persona's transcendental Christianity. Consequently, passages apparently praising Orage resolve themselves into indictment, on the grounds of his failing to achieve the kind of spirituality held to be the standard within the autobiography. For example, his skill as an editor is seen as a gift for clarifying thought, but only at the expense of altering its essential character: "his mind," says Muir,

> was peculiarly lucid and sinuous, and could flow round any object, touching it, defining it, laving it, and leaving it with a new clarity in the mind. From a few stammering words he could divine a thought you were struggling to express, and, as if his mind were an objective

clarifying element, in a few minutes he could return it to you cleansed of its impurities and expressed in better words than you could have found yourself. This power was so uncanny that at first it disconcerted me, as if it were a new kind of thought-reading. Sometimes the thought was not quite the thought that I had had in mind, and then I was reassured; perhaps, indeed, it was never quite the same thought, though it came surprisingly close to it. He was a born collaborator, a born midwife of ideas, and consequently a born editor. His mind went out with an active sympathy to meet everything that was presented to it, whether trifling or serious; and his mere consideration of it, the fact that his intelligence had worked on it, robbed it of its triviality and raised it to the level of rational discourse. (*A*, 172)

Consistent with the anti-intellectual bias of the autobiography, Orage's intuitive qualities are praised – his ability to "divine" a thought, his attitude of "active sympathy" – while his skill in objective expression is referred to as "uncanny," as if it were the cheap trickery of "a new kind of thought-reading." His seriousness of approach and generalist orientation are turned into a lack of discrimination as he deals equally with the (undefinedly) "significant" and "trivial," and his major success is described as an ambiguous talent for elevating unimportant matters to the level of rational discourse.

Having undermined his intellectual career, the autobiography goes on to attack Orage's spiritual interests by implying an ineradicable dilettantism. "Ever since his youth," it is claimed, Orage

had taken up and followed creeds which seemed to provide a shortcut to intellectual and spiritual power. He had been a theosophist, a member of a magic circle which included Yeats, a Nietzschean, and a student of Hindu religion and philosophy. He was convinced that there was a secret knowledge behind the knowledge given to the famous prophets and philosophers.... It was this that made him throw up *The New Age* a few months after I had left it, and put himself under Gurdjieff's directions at Fontainebleau. (*A*, 173)

The derogatory suggestion that for all his self-discipline Orage was seeking only a shortcut cancels out the tribute paid in acknowledging that he was prepared to "sacrifice everything and take upon him any labour, no matter how humble or wearisome or abstruse" (*A*, 173–4), in the interests of his quest. Enthusiasm untempered by discrimination is shown to lead to an unreliable lack of constancy. (Muir's own enthusiasms could form a list at least as long and perhaps less adventurous: but, of course, by this stage the reader is aware that Muir's true religious core was always safely hovering in the background, waiting its cue in St Andrews.) There is real cruelty in giving the pretentious yoga mantra which Orage recommended to the Muirs ("Brighter than the sun, purer than the snow, subtler than the air is the self, the spirit within my heart. I am that self, that self am I", *A*, 173); and an account of a book he gave them cataloguing "all the spiritual dominations, principalities and powers giving the exact numbers and functions of each" (*A*, 173) emphasises further the tendency to crankiness in such matters. This eccentricity is not even seen as being original: rather, it is a given characteristic of the *New Age* circle as a whole, as represented by Mitrinović.

The decision to introduce Mitrinović at this point was not arbitrary. That he and Orage are analogous figures is suggested by using an account of a book which he lent to Muir, to imply the absurdity of his ideas. Noting that it was a French volume and that it described "the history of man since his birth in Atlantis, when he was a headless emanation with flames shooting from his open neck" (*A*, 175) is sufficient to complete the impression of his oddity derived from the account of his thought:

> He was a man for whom only the vast processes of time existed. He did not look a few centuries ahead like Shaw and Wells, but to distant milleniums, which to his apocalyptic mind were as near and vivid as to-morrow. He flung out the wildest and deepest thoughts pell-mell, seeing whole tracts of history in a flash, the flash of an axe with which he hewed a way for himself through them, sending dynasties and civilizations flying.... He would arrive with a large bottle of beer under each arm and talk endlessly about the universe, the creation of the animals, the destiny of man, the nature of Adam Kadmon, the influence of the stars, the objective science of criticism (for he held that it was possible to determine the exact greatness of every poet, painter and musician and set it down in mathematical terms), and a host of things which I have since forgotten. (*A*, 174–5)

The hint of violent apocalypse in the image of Mitrinović wielding a flashing axe against the centuries seems out of joint with the list of his rather abstract interests and mildly silly convictions such as the project of a mathematically formulaic aesthetic; but this is because what Muir claims to have "forgotten" is that the column Mitrinović largely wrote for *The New Age* under the joint name "M.M. Cosmoi," "in an English of his own, filled with energy but difficult to understand" (*A*, 174), was savagely anti-semitic, and that, whatever its unspecified influence on Orage, Muir himself had found it deeply attractive. "Our Generation" would appeal to its precepts as authority in discussion of contemporary events, as for example when it was suggested that an English Jew should be appointed Indian Viceroy:

> There is no question of impugning the qualities of the Jewish people. Their tact, ability and character it is impossible not to admire; but as the writers of World Affairs have insisted, they are not members of the Aryan race, and cannot undiluted be made the instruments for the Aryanisation of the world. Yet the Press talks of sending Lord

> Reading to India as the representative of Aryandom, and only a few
> have made any protest against it. Nevertheless, everyone would feel
> it was wrong if Lord Reading were called Sir Rufus Isaacs. (*The
> New Age*, 13 Jan. 1921, 124–5)

There are several reasons why Muir might wish to hide this allegiance,
including the disgust at anti-semitism aroused by his experiences in
Europe between the wars and the possibility that the views expressed by
"Moore" were not necessarily held with absolute conviction by Muir
even in 1921. Whichever took precedence in 1940, the autobiography's
intention is clearly to suggest that Muir in the early 1920s observed the
follies of his fellow contributors and even of his editor from a secure
position within his own ideology.

That the ideology involved an apolitical stance is made clear when Muir
refers to Orage's attempts to persuade him to write the weekly editorial of
the paper. His efforts are said to have met with an uncompromising
integrity:

> I was capable of doing only one thing, which was to write what I
> thought in my own way. I did not have Orage's intense interest in
> politics. I did not possess real political intelligence, and although in
> Orage himself this would merely have inspired him to acquire an
> interest in politics and create in himself a political intelligence, in
> me it had the opposite effect; I thought that if I yielded I should be
> unfaithful to what talent I had. Orage at last gave up his attempt to
> get me to write the 'Notes of the Week' and uncomplainingly
> continued them himself. (*A*, p. 171)

Orage is here made to serve as the political figure against which Muir's
apolitical stance may claim to be defined. There is a curious movement, if
the passage is read in context, whereby apparent self-depreciation resolves itself as self-congratulation. Muir describes himself negatively in
relation to Orage – he was "capable of doing only one thing" in contrast
to the polymathic editor; he could only "write what I thought in my own
way" whereas Orage could articulate, albeit with alterations, another's
ideas for him; he "did not possess real political intelligence" and was not
inspired by this absence as he says Orage would have been – but within
the autobiography's rhetoric, the episode takes the cast of the denial of a
temptation to which Muir refuses to "yield" for fear of being "unfaithful"
to his true, transcendentalist self. By this choice of vocabulary and use of
negative syntactic structures, that which appears in terms of the ideology
of the *New Age* as churlish inadequacy is read in terms of transcendental
Christianity as heroic steadfastness; and one more indictment, that of
attempting to entice Muir into the foreign world of politics against his
natural inclination, is added to the charges of intellectual confusion and
spiritual dilettantism against the *New Age* circle and its political ethos.

Conspicuous by its absence from the autobiographies is any discussion
of the nature of that political ethos: the attempt is rather to condemn by

association, using the crankiness of its adherents to blacken the ideology they espoused. The critics have drawn from this the conclusion Muir had designed concerning his own articles: Butter's dismissal of the *New Age* material is not based on any inherent quality of the articles themselves, but justified because in them

> he [Muir] was sometimes uncharacteristically ill-tempered and carping, sometimes too confident on matters of which he was ignorant. He adopted the stance, distasteful to him later, of a prophet denouncing his contemporaries for spiritual impotence while himself having nothing very precise or securely-held to offer.[19]

The complaint is not that the writings are "uncharacteristic," but that Muir was behaving "uncharacteristically" in producing them, and this again reveals the depth of the conviction that criticism of his works should be determined solely by the degree to which they conform to the image created in the autobiography – the picture of a man whose spirituality lifted him above or beyond such evidence of temporal fallibility as being impatient or poorly informed. Butter can see that in "Our Generation" Muir was "adopting a stance": but he is blind to the idea that some or all of his later writings may have used the same strategy. Assuming that the autobiography is true to the *real* Muir and that everything else must thereby be false, he moves on, unconcerned with the reasons for this uncharacteristic mendacity. For Butter, Muir becomes interesting only after he has achieved spiritual calm and has something "precise or securely held to offer"; the processes which determined the nature of that special knowledge are regarded as irrelevant.

In his account of his interest in Nietzsche's writings, Muir says that the "infatuation" was unnaturally prolonged "since they gave me exactly what I wanted: a last desperate foothold on my dying dream of the future" (*A*, 126). Apart from fostering the political pessimism of the 1940s, this suggests that his Nietzscheanism, passing by 1919, was the final manifestation of his political concerns and commitments. Yet "Our Generation" begins in 1920 as the most politically optimistic gesture of his literary career, reflecting his confidence in his ability to infiltrate a foreign cultural formation (the operation of the English literary periodical) and to choose a sector of that formation, *The New Age*, which would offer the opportunity to direct his writings towards changing the entire economic, political and cultural workings of capitalism.

It was, of course a misplaced faith. He may have left the paper in 1922, but he did not leave social credit ideology behind, as his pamphlet *Social Credit and the Labour Party: An Appeal* (1935) shows. In itself, this argument only proves that Muir was not very clever at politics: Pound's reading of Douglas led him to Mussolini's fascism, after all. But the irony is that the price Muir paid for admission to Orage's circle was an anglicisation which denied exactly those Scottish and working-class elements of his experience which had first brought him to engage with the political system. It was this idea of an English "core" culture which he then used to deny Scottishness, before he retreated into a religious denial of all temporal reality.

IV

Considerations of space prevent my detailing all the ramifications of such a reading for studies of Muir's works, and from even beginning an examination of his writings which would seek to integrate the other biographical and non-biographical determinants of his ideology, such as the movement towards high Anglicanism and Anglo-Catholicism among the English literati of the 1930s and '40s, the effects of the market for autobiography on the style, form and techniques used, even the influence of the publisher of the two autobiographies: the Hogarth Press. Nonetheless, I would hope that the outline of such a reading at least points out that there is an interpretation of Muir's life that reveals a pattern of recurrent crises and revaluations, and that this thoroughly denies the structure whereby a single, significant moment of revelation dominates all. That instant may have been chosen to determine the representation of the life in the writing: but that is a subject of quite a different order.

SHEILA LODGE

NOTES

All works published in London unless otherwise stated.

1. Muir's autobiography appeared in two forms, *The Story and the Fable* (1940) being revised for republication as *An Autobiography* in 1955. For a detailed account of the differences between the two, see the appendix to this article. Where the distinctions are not of consequence, references are to *An Autobiography*, since this was reprinted in 1980 and is much more widely available.
2. Unsigned review, *TLS* (1 June 1940), 268.
3. "Connections Everywhere," *The Spectator*, CCXIV (18 June 1965), 791.
4. *London Magazine*, I (Dec. 1954), 80.
5. "A Dream-Haunted Giver of Testimony," *New York Times Book Review* (13 March 1955), 4; "Being Alive," *New Statesman and Nation* (22 June 1940), 778.
6. Introduction to *Selected Poems of Edwin Muir*, (London: Faber, 1965), p. 4.
7. *Essays in Diverse Hands, Being the Transactions of the Royal Society of Literature*, XXXIII (1965), pp. 28–9.
8. There are many English and American critics who see Muir in this way; the most recent advocate of this approach is Roger Knight, *Edwin Muir: An Introduction to his Work* (London: Longman, 1980).
9. "On Making Beasts of Ourselves" (1949): reprinted in *The Uncanny Scot*, ed. Kenneth Buthlay (London: MacGibbon and Grey, 1968), p. 149.
10. Peter Butter, *Edwin Muir: Man and Poet* (London & Edinburgh: Oliver & Boyd, 1966), pp. 73–4.
11. Cairns Craig, "The Body in the Kitbag: History and the Scottish Novel," *Cencrastus* 1 (1979), 18.
12. "The Literary Life Respectable," *Scrutiny*, IX (1940–1), 170–1.

13. Knight, p. 5.
14. *Lucky Poet* (London: Methuen, 1943), p. 21.
15. "Edwin Muir," *The Scottish Educational Journal* (4 Sept. 1925).
16. "Yesterday's Mirror: Afterthoughts to an Autobiography," *The Scots Magazine*, n.s. XXXIII, 5 (Aug. 1940), 404.
17. *A Scots Quair: Grey Granite* (London: Jarrolds, 1934), p. 101.
18. Willa Muir, *Belonging: A Memoir* (London: Hogarth Press, 1968), pp. 30–1.
19. Butter, p. 73.

APPENDIX

The significance of Muir's revisions to *The Story and the Fable* (1940) for republication as *An Autobiography* (1954)

Although Muir's ideology underwent no major revision after 1939, it did continue to develop, and the differences between the two published versions of his life – *The Story and the Fable* and *An Autobiography* – show a distinct movement over the intervening fourteen years towards a deeper distrust of the remnant of his early political idealism, and a greater confidence in his handling of tone and persona as propagandist devices against that ideology. I can find no evidence of editorial influence on either version of the autobiography, and indeed Muir's comments in contemporary letters on struggling with revisions support the supposition that the texts were fashioned by him alone.

Some of the alterations are, of course, merely a matter of bringing facts up to date. For example, the death of his sister Elizabeth leads him to change the single paragraph which refers to his relationships with her and his other sister, Clara. After his assertion that she had "an eager mind and a spirit equal to anything" he omits the phrase "and still has," and he amends "she died some years ago" (of Clara) to "both are now dead" (94/80). More interesting are those changes which relate to the dominant areas of conflict within his ideology (notably, as so often with Muir, concerning his socialism and his Scottishness) and those which embody his response to that conflict in the creation of a literary persona. In each of these cases Muir can be seen to be reinforcing his transcendentalism.

Muir wrote *The Story and the Fable* around the time of his religious conversion in 1939, so it is not surprising that it should carry vestigial traces of the socialist interpretation of society which he had been expounding – albeit in the version diluted for middle-class taste implicit in Social Credit philosophy – as recently as 1935, in *Social Credit and the Labour Party*. But for the persona of *An Autobiography*, even these remnants are unacceptable: the changes he makes here suggest that he finds such references too overtly concerned with temporal and political reality. For example, in discussing the Scottish Enlightenment philosophers' thesis that the human personality is distorted by modern society's demand for specialisation, he had originally written:

> These things are of enormous importance, and we shall never settle
> them until the miner can live a civilized life and the stockbroker has
> disappeared. (57)

Echoes of the concept of class struggle, with the ultimate victory of the
proletarian over the bourgeois, are resolutely stripped from this sentence
in the 1954 version:

> These things are of enormous importance, and we shall never settle
> them until the miner and the stockbroker live a civilized life. (*A*, 51)

Similarly, in condemning the conditions in which he had lived in the
slums of Glasgow, Muir first makes specific attacks on those who have
become complacent about their social origins since they managed to
escape from them: "successful business men and Labour leaders who
wear their youth as if they were flaunting a dingy decoration" clearly
worry the old member of the I.L.P., as is emphasised by his naming them
again ("Members of Parliament or business magnates or trade-union
leaders") within the same paragraph (*S & F*, 12). In *An Autobiography*,
this attack is turned into a more general observation when he complains
of any "successful men" (*A*, 110), thus reducing the sense of the precise
phenomenon of upward social mobility eroding class consciousness and
political radicalism. He actually goes further, inserting at the end of this
section a new sentence which convicts him of a complacency perhaps
different in kind but nonetheless arising from the same causes and
equivalent in significance to that which he has just condemned:

> There has been a great improvement in the lot of the poor since the
> time I am speaking of, and that is one of the entirely good achieve-
> ments of our century. (*A*, 110)

This implies that all social problems existed only in the past, and thus
political activity in the present could carry no humanistic justification.

In the account Muir gives of his stay in Prague in the early 1920s, he
devotes a paragraph in *The Story and the Fable* to the destruction by the
Nazi invaders of the communal, organic life he claims to have sensed in
Czechoslovakia:

> Karel Capek died shortly after the seizure of his country by Ger-
> many, whether of his illness or of a broken heart I do not know.
> After the Prague in which he was 'Karlicku' to everyone and where
> he could walk about as he liked, the new Prague must have seemed
> like a prison-yard. We met many other Czech writers. I dread to
> think what may have happened to them now; even if no physical
> harm has come to them their life has been snatched away, and their
> Prague no longer exists. We spent many evenings in their houses;
> we were taken into their lives. We had no premonition then that
> history, to use Oswald Spengler's words, 'would take them by the
> throat and do with them what must be done'. The idea of history
> taking people by the throat pleased Spengler. (*S & F*, 229)

By omitting this section from *An Autobiography* (189), Muir implies that
the only danger to social life in Prague comes from the later repression of
the Communist regime. To have actively decided to cut from the text his
earlier condemnation of Fascism implies at least that by 1954 he regarded
repression inspired by right-wing convictions as being less contemptible
than that resulting from left-wing dogmas. While the Communist takeover which he witnessed when working for the British Council must
understandably have been most vivid in his mind in 1954, this excision
reveals, if nothing else, a propagandist thrust out of keeping with the
notion of the apolitical but generally compassionate persona.

There is a further set of such political examples to be noted in the final
section of *The Story and the Fable*, "Extracts from a Diary, 1937–39."
The omission of these pieces from the revised version of the book was
obviously caused by the general restructuring of the work; yet it is
pertinent to note that cutting these passages altogether rather than
working them into the new pattern changes the overall effect of the
writing and helps create the different tones of the two autobiographies.
Significantly, among the most interesting passages from the "Extracts"
are the one that asks: since "the rich live on the poor: why should they
sneer at them as well?" (242), and that which defines Nazism as the
inevitable extension of nineteenth-century materialism, industrialism
and ideals of "progress" (257). Again, the loss of these passages greatly
reduces the impression of any political interest on the part of "Moore"'s
persona.

In *The Story and the Fable*, references to the problematic status of
Scotland and to his own Scottishness are less numerous than political
observations, perhaps because the quarrel over *Scott and Scotland* was
barely three years old in 1939. However, there are two significant
alterations to passages dealing with Scottish Nationalism. The first comes
in relation, again, to his affection for pre-war Prague. In 1939 he had
written admiringly of Capek's popularity with all sections of the popu-
lation:

> This warm, easy-going contact could only have been possible in a
> small town, and it was the first thing that made me wish that
> Edinburgh might become a similar place and that Scotland might be
> a nation again. (*S & F*, 228)

The 1954 version ends simply with the pious hope "that Edinburgh might
become a similar place" (*A*, 189), and the question of how that happy
result is to be achieved is completely ignored, thereby rendering the
matter of political nationalism irrelevant.

The second consideration of nationalism is another of the "Diary"
extracts omitted from the 1954 version. Arguing against imperialism on
the grounds that "mankind has never managed to do anything as it should
be done" due to the impossibility of achieving full knowledge of all
circumstances from within the temporal world, he continues:

> Because of this I believe that men are capable of organising them-
> selves only in relatively small communities, and that even then they
> need custom, tradition and memory to guide them. For this reason I
> believe in Scottish Nationalism, and should like to see Scotland a
> self-governing nation. In great empires the quality of individual life
> declines: it becomes plain and commonplace. The little tribal
> community of Israel, the little city state of Athens, the relatively
> small England of Elizabeth's time, mean far more in the history of
> civilization than the British Empire. I am for small nations as
> against large ones, because I am for a kind of society where men
> have some real practical control of their lives. I am for a Scottish
> nation, because I am a Scotsman. (*S & F*, 260)

It seems incontrovertible that this passage was originally a reply to
MacDiarmid's contemporary attacks on *Scott and Scotland*; albeit implicitly, it certainly puts paid to the insistence of many Muir critics that he
never deigned to respond to Grieve's invective, even if only by showing
his continuing confusion on the subject! While the Eliotesque cast of
thought here is perfectly in keeping with the notion of the small, organic
community which *An Autobiography* resolutely propagandises, Muir
chooses to exorcise its specific application to his own background from
the later publication.

Other changes are further instances of the increased conservatism of
the older Muir. For example, in writing of the rise from the slums of
successful business men and Labour leaders, he had earlier felt it necessary that he should deny that he had himself shared any such ambition:

> I have never had any social ambition, nor do I have any literary
> ambition beyond the wish to write well; I am not much concerned
> whether I have or lack a reputation. To be a Member of Parliament
> would not excite me, and if I were one I should not look back on my
> youth in self-approval and think that I have done a great thing by
> rising from fourteen shillings a week to six hundred pounds a year.
> (*S & F*, 129–30)

Contemporary letters which show Muir's keenness to make his mark in
the literary world of the twenties ("even a column ... done regularly and
conscientiously, should waken a little respect. And it is only a beginning."; "I want primarily to get some kind of hearing in England.")
reveal that this vaunted humility is part of his creation of the other-
worldly persona. The omission of the passage from *An Autobiography*
(110) shows Muir exercising a greater degree of subtlety than fourteen
years previously.

Again, he cuts almost a full page from his description of his friendship
with John Holms (*S & F*, 213/ A, 178), referring specifically to their
shared love of argumentative debate. This may be because he no longer
wishes it to be recorded that he once contended that, had he been Christ,
he would not have consented to be crucified: such opinions don't quite fit

with the non-contentious orthodoxy of the *Autobiography's* persona. Alternatively, the cut may have been made because the passage acknowledges the fact that Willa seems deeply to have disliked Holms, and to have had grave misgivings about the nature of the friendship. The notion of Muir experiencing domestic disharmony is as inappropriate to the persona as the experience of political activism. The general effect of this deletion is to intensify the sense that Muir sits in judgement on his friend, and finds him (like Mitrinovič and Orage and the political discussion group in St Andrews) to have fallen short of the transcendentalism he had later espoused himself.

If most of the changes charted here show the greater confidence and subtlety of *An Autobiography* over *The Story and the Fable*, there is also one example which reveals a greater degree of caution to have been characteristic of the writing of the older Muir. Having quoted in the first version of his life an excerpt from his article "Impressions of Prague," he comments: "These reflections were set down when my impressions of Prague were fresh; they were sincere, on the whole, though romantically touched up" (*S & F*, 226). All that follows the semi-colon here is omitted from *An Autobiography* (187): to admit that he was a professional writer, that he did not always remain more than "on the whole" sincere, and that he was capable of literary manipulation by having "touched up" what purported to be direct recording of autobiographical fact, was too near to admitting the nature of his current practice to be allowed to stand.

However, for all the significance of these instances, the greatest difference of *An Autobiography* from *The Story and the Fable* is, of course, in the structural development of the work. Like Muir's two Scottish novels, *The Three Brothers* (1931) and *Poor Tom* (1932), *The Story and the Fable* ends with a series of extracts from a diary. The sense of open-endedness in *The Story and the Fable* is an illusion worked by the form, since the final section is an unflinching exposition of Muir's faith in the order of the "mediaeval communal feeling," and, following from the impossibility of its realisation in the modern world ("I do not think there is anything admirable in being up to date, apart from the fact that it is necessary" [263]), his implicit transcendentalism. *An Autobiography*, on the other hand, is more conventionally shaped, with no pretence at openness of ending: here Muir, having asserted that "I cannot bring life into a neat pattern" (280), has the nerve to bring his book – which in terms of the literary artefact precisely constitutes his "life" – to a perfectly neat ending, with all the satisfaction of the happy ending of a novel, and of a completed and successful pattern of development. And here the Christianity is explicitly avowed:

> As I look back on the part of the mystery which is my own life, my own fable, what I am most aware of is that we receive more than we can ever give; we receive it from the past, on which we draw with every breath, but also — and this is a point of faith — from the Source of the mystery itself, by the means which religious people call Grace. (*A*, 282)

Emphasising the personal again and again ("I look back," "my own life," "I am most aware"), yet talking in the plural voice ("we receive," "we can ever give," "we draw"), he creates a balance that suggests the image of the impartial writer unwilling to foist his own opinions upon the reader while constantly impressing on him or her the need to do so. And by suggesting that "Grace" is a term he cannot bring himself to use he implies an entirely undogmatic faith that is nonetheless held with the absoluteness of any theologian. Such techniques show Muir to have developed between 1940 and 1954 a surer conviction in his own ideas, a stronger confidence in his ability to propagandise them through the medium of his autobiography, and a greater willingness to define and control the ideological context in which all his writing, poetry and prose, was to be read.

Autobiography, Epistemology and the Irish Tradition: The Example of Denis Johnston

I

The Irish autobiographer of Denis Johnston's generation writes in a tradition of powerful precursors. George Moore, W.B. Yeats, Sean O'Casey, Oliver St. John Gogarty: each either published volume upon volume to tell the story of his life, or returned to the same events in repeated retellings.[1] Despite striking differences of style and tone, these autobiographers of the Irish Literary Renaissance converge in a number of their preoccupations.

Each, especially in treating of adulthood, foregrounds his intellectual life while allowing much of his emotional life to remain in the shadows.[2] George Moore provides the pattern, particularly in *Hail and Farewell*: reconstructed (and often fanciful) conversations, reveries, and interior monologues chronicle his initial enchantment and subsequent disenchantment with the Gaelic cause and his "conversion" to Protestantism. But self is in some ways the least of the concerns of these Irish autobiographers. Each has used a narrative version of the self to present his relation to Irish nationalism; the very Ireland from which each feels more or less estranged figures centrally in one or more of his autobiographies. The autobiography begins to seem allied to the multi-volumed chronicle novel of the nineteenth century, for each autobiographer consciously tells the story of his society and his country through the story of his own life. In his specifically Irish content, each is busily concerned to set literary and nationalist records straight. Moore concludes that Ireland is incapable of great literature; Yeats writes *Dramatis Personae* so as to discredit Moore's judgement of him; in numerous anecdotes, Gogarty jibes at Moore's affectations and gives us an alternate version of how Buck Mulligan to Sandymount Tower came; O'Casey points to the Abbey Theatre as a priest-ridden clique, portrays every critic except Nathan as a fool, and characterises Denis Johnston (among others) as the type of the precious and simpering English-educated Irishman. Rising above personal scores, they often become Messianic. Moore and Yeats in all seriousness, Gogarty more ironically, O'Casey implicitly in set pieces that are scorching sermons, present themselves as the Messiah Ireland needs but doesn't have the good sense to welcome.[3]

Denis Johnston belongs to the next generation. Born in 1901, he was educated in Dublin, Edinburgh and Cambridge, and Harvard Law School.

From his call to the Irish Bar in 1925 until 1936, when he began a career in broadcasting, he combined law practice with playwriting. After spending 1942 to 1945 as a BBC War Correspondent, he moved in 1947 to the United States where he did scriptwriting for stage and film and taught English and Theatre in several colleges until his return to Dublin in 1973. But 1947 was significant to him for more than emigration. That year saw him well into a war autobiography he titled *Dionysia*. Although Johnston rewrote this autobiography several times, he never published it, contenting himself with depositing the manuscript in the British Museum so as to prevent his tinkering further with it. Still rewriting, however, he did publish a later version of the war autobiography in 1954 under the title of *Nine Rivers from Jordan*. That publication was the first notice of Johnston's quest for an explanation of the universe, an explanation which, when given in an extension of the autobiography titled *The Brazen Horn*,[4] proved to rival in complexity and totality Yeats's *A Vision*.

Johnston did write plays after his emigration to the States (though his critics have complained that they are too few), but his autobiography and its theoretical and philosophical extension in *The Brazen Horn* are his major literary work from the last thirty-five years of his career. It is a work that stands in obvious relation to the autobiographies of the Irish Literary Renaissance. It relies heavily on the reconstructed conversations, reveries, and pastiches which Moore, Gogarty and O'Casey all used and it has something of the aggressive flippancy and occasional facetiousness of style (masking complete seriousness) of Gogarty. Like Yeats Johnston is a system maker, one writing against death not only in the ontological sense by which the autobiographer writes himself into history and, he hopes, literary immortality, but in the sense that he constructs an explanation of the universe by which death dies.

But Johnston's divergences from his predecessors are equally marked and more significant. He is, to begin with, not the least concerned with Irish nationalism; unlike many of his predecessors, he refuses to make his departure from Ireland an exile and speaks of his country with neither bitterness nor longing. He prefers the viewpoint of a citizen of the world to the more narrowly Irish one. A Protestant, he structures his autobiography as a Mass, finding an analogy for his knowledge of himself and of the world in one of the received rituals by which we have expressed our collective wisdom. The result is an autobiography the end of which is no longer knowledge of the self, of Denis Johnston, but of the universe in which he lives. Nowhere is Johnston's confrontation of the conventions of the genre and of its Irish Literary Renaissance tradition, nowhere is his use of autobiography as a form of epistemology, more evident than in his treatment of death.

II

Whether they are elegantly malicious or messianically nationalist, Johnston's Irish predecessors enact that deepest and most futile of autobiographical motivations, the desire to outwit death. For death is the (unwritable) ending nature and logic demand to the story of a life. The impossibility of this ending to autobiography (so frequently remarked by critics and not the least lamented by autobiographers) means that Death becomes the figure on the other side of the horizon, the autobiography a monument designed to keep a representation of its author before those of us who remain behind. Death becomes a powerful ontological presence in autobiography,[5] the event against which the author writes and in view of which he chooses the postures (a misunderstood Messiah, for example) by which he will limn himself for posterity. But as actual presence, Death enters autobiography only through displacement onto someone other than the author/protagonist. These autobiographers, writing of an Ireland where poverty and civil war kill as surely as the usual diseases of mankind, give us the deaths of Synge, of Susan and Ella O'Casey, of Michael Collins and Arthur Griffith, of Stella and Mrs Moore. As for Yeats and O'Casey, Gogarty and Moore, they aim at forestalling the rigor mortis symbolized by the biographer's laying out of their lives. Ireland may kill their hopes for Cathleen Ni Houlihan, but, they would have us believe, they live on. In the absence of religious belief, this pattern becomes a simple affirmation of life over death; watching sunset and evening star, O'Casey and Gogarty still drink to "Life."[6] Or death becomes a symbolic event which, in the future to be sure, will effect the transition of the writer to an immortal world where his fame will be more enduring than even that his autobiography can give him: Gogarty imagines himself in the context of Celtic mythology "dreaming back" to his youth; Yeats constructs a Platonic and hermetic philosophy to prove that all things both do and do not exist; even George Moore can imagine himself, recycled and re-evolved, thousands of years hence sitting in the same room and writing the same words with which he ends his memoirs.[7] Symbolic deaths, afterlifes of many sorts, are imaginable by the autobiographer, but never literal death. Should an autobiographer be so unnatural and illogical as to narrate the actual event of his own death, we read it as "symbolic," not "real." And if he insists that his is a *literal* death, he affronts our common sense and we explain the anomaly as whimsey or insanity, as a miracle or the deception of a ghostwriter.

Without whimsey, insanity, belief in miracles, or deception, Denis Johnston ends his war autobiography, *Nine Rivers from Jordan*, with his own death, narrated in the most matter-of-fact manner. As a War Correspondent for the BBC, he had followed (and sometimes nearly preceded) the Allied Armies from Egypt, through Italy, France, Belgium and Germany and had finally reached the Brenner Pass. In a series of events he would later label "Take One," he spoke with a Nazi officer named Otto Suder who, wounded and trapped in his saloon car in the Brenner Pass on the Italian side of the frontier with Austria, borrowed Johnston's Luger to (he said) commit suicide; instead, he fatally shot Johnston with his own gun. In each of *Dionysia, Nine Rivers from Jordan*, and *The Brazen Horn* Johnston describes with great care the events leading to his death.

All three tellings begin with his seeing a woman D.P. bent, like a pietà, over the half-naked body of a man. In *Dionysia* and *Nine Rivers*, in the "Take One" version of events, this happens in a village on the road into Innsbruck, immediately after Johnston's conversation with a German schoolteacher who wants to know why American soldiers have looted her home. He answers her out of the rage of his new belief in Absolute Good and Evil, a belief which is the result of his tour of Buchenwald, telling her, "The only thing to do is to kill as quickly and as cleanly as possible." He also terms Pity "a trap to ensnare fools and lead them to their own destruction" (NR, 426; a judgement borne out by the gesture of pity in which he gives his gun to Suder), and tells the Fräulein that, if he does not blame Pity, then he must "blame God." As he leaves, she calls after him the words that become the crux of his dilemma in the autobiography: "Then you must learn to forgive God" (427). Walking across the street, he sees the woman D.P. but does not speak to her. The sight, and his failure to respond, are their own comment on the preceding conversation.

Johnston's autobiographical method, as he acknowledges it in both *Dionysia* and *Nine Rivers*, is one of selection and compression by which he "condenses" several events and conversations in order to "'produce,'" as in a theatre, an "honest picture" (NR, 294). This usual, though not usually acknowledged, practice is especially prominent in Irish autobiography, particularly in the reconstituted reveries and conversations of Moore and Gogarty, and as the springboard in O'Casey to both childhood imagination and the polemical essays of his later volumes. Johnston supplements the "production" method with a more documentary account in *The Brazen Horn*. There he tells us he sees the woman D.P. not on the way into Innsbruck but early on the morning he dies, just before crossing his last river. Hearing trucks starting up and realizing the army is about to move up the Brenner, he does not speak to her in this account either, and he also abandons his plan to go up to the Hafelekar.

In *Dionysia* and *Nine Rivers*, beginning with his arrival at the Brenner, Johnston becomes uncharacteristically precise about the time of the events that end in his death by the hand of Otto Suder: he leaves with a small military convoy from the summit "at about a quarter to eleven" (NR, 433), notes the man sitting in his car, travels ten miles into Italy where the meeting between the occupying armies of Italy and of Germany and Austria is effected, and returns to the summit to meet General McAuliffe and the Corps Commander, who are "due about noon" (434). On their return, *Dionysia* tells us, they find the generals have already arrived; Johnston has his picture taken with them (it is printed in *The Brazen Horn*), then re-crosses the border into Italy to investigate the man sitting in the car and is shot. In *Nine Rivers* he stops at the car on the way back from Italy, is shot, and so never meets the generals. In both accounts, however, Johnston insists that he is *literally* dead, no matter how much this affronts autobiographical conventions or our assumptions about the physical universe. And he still insists on it in *The Brazen Horn* which he published some twenty-seven years after his initial account of the event in *Dionysia* and which is an exegetical appendix to the two earlier narratives that takes the form of a scientific and theological inquiry developed from the question of how he could die and live to write about it.

The trigger pressed, Johnston writes, in both *Dionysia* and *Nine Rivers*, a short chapter that has elements of a funeral oration and of a last testament and that concludes with the words, "Ite Missa Est" ("Go, the Mass is over"; NR, 441), words which in ancient Ritual ended the Mass immediately after Communion and without the Benediction of the contemporary Ritual. Given that, standing by the Dead Sea at the beginning of his journey, Johnston has heard a voice telling him he will be safe only so long as he goes unarmed, and that, on the way out of Buchenwald, deciding that "there is no answer to this, except bloody murder" (NR, 397), he has picked up a Luger, the less comforting form of the earlier Ritual is appropriate. Not only does Johnston imply, however, that his life has been a Mass which ends with his death, but the final section of both *Dionysia* and *Nine Rivers* is titled "Epiklesis" after those words that follow immediately upon the consecration of the Host and that invoke the Holy Spirit that it might change bread and wine into body and blood. The frequent allusions to the Mass as the dominant structure of *Nine Rivers* (allusions even more pronounced in *Dionysia*) intimate that what began as "an Autobiography, strictly realistic in all its facts and characters, in the course of which I was going to have a lot of rather malicious amusement in debunking the official pomposities of war" (D, 3–4), has been transformed into Sacred and Revealed Word. "Epiklesis" to title the section of an autobiography in which the author dies implies his transubstantiation.

III

"Ite Missa Est," Johnston dismisses his communicants, and then demands in sprightly tones, "Or would you prefer a different ending?" (NR, 441).[8] Not only does he offer us an autobiography that narrates his own death, but he asks us to believe that two alternative endings both occurred. Hardly conventional autobiography, and even less so when we realize that the facts of these two endings, documented in *The Brazen Horn* as two "takes," differ from each other in three significant ways. In the "different ending" or "Take Two," Johnston sees the woman D.P. before dawn on the morning of his journey up the Brenner, he *does* speak to her, and is reminded by her both of Michelangelo's *Pietà* and of a German girl, Annaliese, whose photograph, along with her letters to a German soldier, he had found in an abandoned jeep in the Egyptian desert. The resemblances evoke stages on his journey, for in Rome he had still been the Irish neutral, but enquiries after Annaliese had led him to Buchenwald, the conviction of Absolute Right and Wrong, and the Luger. In this "take" he *does* go up the Hafelekar, where, in the silence and snow, he is moved to "a conversation with Heaven" (BH, 207) and to throw away his gun, the symbol of his new Knowledge of Evil. He redescends and, as in "Take One," accompanies the army up the Brenner (with a certain sense of *déjà vu* along the road), past the German officer (whose name he never knows) sitting in his car at the Austrian/Italian frontier, and into Italy. On his return, however, he goes on to meet the generals and has the photograph to prove it.[9] That is, in "Take Two" of both *Nine Rivers* and *The Brazen Horn*, he never goes near the saloon car. Instead, he is told by P.R. personnel that a Nazi officer has shot himself, an event he uncharacteristically refuses to investigate at closer quarters, having "somehow seen him already" and having "no wish to see him again (or anything else that might have been in that car)" (BH, 211).

To summarize these alternative endings: in "Take One" Johnston does not speak to the D.P., carries his gun up the Brenner, speaks to Suder, and is killed. In "Take Two" he does speak to the D.P., throws the gun away, and does not speak to a Nazi officer who kills himself while Johnston goes on living. Two later attempts, reported in *The Brazen Horn*, to ascertain the existence of Suder and if, when, and how he died, neither prove nor disprove either "take." Johnston learns in 1974 that Suder's official duties had indeed made him a representative of that Absolute Evil confronted at Buchenwald: "Herr Suder war Obersekretär bei der Kriminal-polizei in Luxemburg und im Kriege SS-Oberschar-führer beim Chef der Zivilverwaltung für das Land Luxemburg" (BH, 212).[10] Officially, he is a Missing Person, known to have been alive on 1 April 1945 and to have been called up after that date for military duty in the Brenner Pass. And that is all. Johnston, or a Nazi officer, died on 4 May 1945.

In *Nine Rivers*, Johnston presents "Take Two" in two parts. The second part briefly narrates his refusal to look at the dead Nazi and his recognition of what he takes as a punning sign from heaven that his journey is ended (a sign that *Dionysia* names as the "Benediction" missing from the first ending). Its tone is matter-of-fact and even slightly sardonic, as is his account of his death. But the first part is as symbolic as this second is literal: it gives us the Canon of an unknown Mass, which puts into the mouths of four "characters" – an Acolyte ("Johnston"), the Pietà, a (Divine) Voice and an Antiphon (whose responses are motifs from the journey) – the "conversation with Heaven" that "actually" took place at Hafelekar and here is taking place in the context of Johnston's death. In it, the questions Johnston has asked with increasing insistence as he journeyed through the War and reread his Bible are raised: is there Absolute Good and Evil? what is the nature of Evil? why are we plagued with Pity for what we must destroy? what must we do with our Knowledge of Evil? how can we forgive God for that Evil, for our Knowledge?

Answered, the Acolyte is returned to life with a new Credo. Thus where the "first" ending to *Nine Rivers* stresses literal death as the end of the journey, the "second" stresses revelation, symbolically expressed. Where the "first" pushes Johnston into the study of physics and the construction of a scientific theory (of which more later) to explain his experience of having both died and not died, the "second" demands of him a poetry of "fluid exaggerations – the changing identities of the living and the dead – the voices speaking through the lips of others" (BH, 206). In the unpublished *Dionysia* he attempted that poetry in an earlier version of the Canon, a version in which the Acolyte speaks, at different moments, in the voices of "The Man," "The Bleeding Nazi," "The Dead," "Dion–Dead," "Adam" and "Job," as well as in that of "The Acolyte." *Dionysia*, with its Acolyte's multiple roles, makes even more obvious than does *Nine Rivers* the extent to which Johnston has come to see his experience as representative of his generation. And both versions, while insisting on the full shock of the protagonist's literal death, stress the revelation of the Canon; Johnston descending from the Hafelekar with a new Credo becomes a new Moses bringing the Tables of the Law down from Pisgah.

IV

Never one to trust his reader too far, Johnston has embedded in *Dionysia* and in *Nine Rivers from Jordan* a good many directives for interpreting his double ending and his characterization of himself as representative and prophet of his generation. "I died one Spring morning in the Brenner," the "Introit" of *Nine Rivers* closes, "Or maybe I only dreamed my death on the night before I went up. Yet dreamed or not, I remember it, and all memories are one, interwoven into the fabric of a more subtle tapestry than we can apprehend from this abyss of five senses in which we are fettered" (3). That he dreamed his death is a notion that allows his readers to pull *Nine Rivers from Jordan* back into line with autobiographical conventions and with our shared assumptions about the workings of Nature; it is the notion Johnston's critics have usually adopted.[11] However, Johnston himself repudiates this notion, both at the end of *Nine Rivers* (439) and in his reconsideration of the matter in *The Brazen Horn* (210). The burden of the "Introit" rests, as *The Brazen Horn* attempts to prove, not on the scraps of a dream thrown to the sceptical but on the notion of a "more subtle tapestry" than that known to our five senses.

An interpolation at the opening of "Epiklesis" gives more specific directives. In *Dionysia* this takes the form of an "Offertory and Announcement" in which Johnston, signing himself the " 'Inconstant Reader,' " describes himself as "one of the 'oldest and closest friends' " (603) of the author in whose favour he remarks that "so painstaking and unspectacular an intelligence may qualify him in his ... modest claim to represent the norm of his day and generation" (605). Calling himself "The

First Editor," Johnston had already drawn attention to his omission of his name from *Dionysia* on the grounds that "the actual name and genealogy of the Traveller have nothing to do with the issues that are raised" (5; *Dionysia* is also illustrated by snapshots of those who figure in its pages but Johnston is identified in none of them). In *Nine Rivers* one E.W. Tocher, a pseudonym Johnston had used before the War to separate his dramatic from his legal career, reiterates this self-effacement in a parodic "Critical Exagamen." Tocher describes the autobiographer as "a Norm of his generation" and an "Everyman" (297), and as a "Quest-Hero" (294) whose "journey" is an "Orphic day, proceeding ... from noon to noon" (295). "Tocher," quoting the " 'Inconstant Reader' " of *Dionysia*, also points out that Johnston often uses comedy when he is most serious, an observation borne out by Johnston's plays. And if "Tocher's" assertion that Denis Johnston, War Correspondent, never existed as an individual but was "created by the parthenogenic processes of group representation" (295) is pompously expressed, it should nonetheless make us ask ourselves to what extent the autobiographer is "Norm" as well as individual.

Beginning with Georges Gusdorf's argument that autobiography as we know it is a product of the value Western culture in general and Christian doctrine in particular have attached to the individual, most critics have argued that autobiography privileges the individual, the unique self. But a less discussed strain in autobiography holds that the narrative of the individual life is of value as that life is representative or illustrative of the spiritual condition of mankind. In that strain, the autobiographer presents himself, either explicitly or implicitly, as an Everyman,[12] and he often structures his story around the most ancient metaphors for the spiritual life, the journey and the search. Until Johnston reaches the just-liberated Buchenwald, the crucial encounters on his journey – the prophecy of the dragoman, the voice by the Dead Sea, two conversations with priests in Italy[13] – are experiences particular to himself. But the metaphors of the journey and the search which control the narrative already gesture towards the autobiographer as Everyman. And Johnston strengthens that gesture by associating himself with the Gospel of a suffering and a prophetic Christ.

Johnston is too good a lawyer not to know he will be laughed out of court and into an asylum if he insists his experience makes him Christ; moreover all three books of his autobiography make clear his impatience with those who claim the historicity of Jesus. For practical as well as literary reasons, then, he chooses to establish mythic analogies rather than to make literal assertions. To begin with the autobiographer/narrator as suffering Christ: immediately before he baptises himself in the Jordan, for example, Johnston is guest of honour at an Arab Legion banquet. The occasion, the first of several in which he is advised to re-read the Bible to find out what the Book really says (as opposed to what the Church says it says), is twice compared to the Last Supper (NR, 56, 58). More morbidly, as he prepares to go on his first bombing mission, nicknamed " 'dicing with death,' " his mates play soldiers-at-the-foot-of-the-cross, quarrelling over the division of his property should he fail to return (65–6). These allusions to *la via dolorosa* reappear several times in the autobiographies, as does Johnston's association of the mass de-humanization of the concentration camps with the Passion; seeing the "Pietà" of the woman D.P. and her companion, for example, he identifies with Christ crucified, telling us he was struck "with a cold shudder of recognition" by "the fact that the face of the dead man seemed very like my own" (BH, 206). As prophet, he writes *Nine Rivers* in 1947 from "the Dome of the Rock" as the "Proconsuls" (1) prepare to leave Palestine. But he also subverts the identification with Christ as scapegoat and as prophet which he has so painstakingly established by telling us he is not a Christian, by bluntly asserting that "Nobody rises from the dead" (BH, 12), by proposing a Fourth order of Saint Francis "open only to Pro-testants, Sceptics, the Unbaptised" (NR, 289) and other Undesirables, by writing the Papal Bull creating the Order (D, 601), and by finally acknowledging only an unnamed and unaffiliated Ultimate Observer who exists in an infinite and changeless sixth Dimension.

Johnston's decision to use the Christian myth and the structure of the Mass in his autobiography is clearly not a matter of Belief or of failure to imagine other symbols; it is a decision to present his experience in terms of mankind's most powerful story of its shared experience. He had early in his career[14] used the unicorn as symbol of "Man, himself – . . . a creature that is born, that struggles for its right to Be, that grows old and dies . . . that spends his life seeking for what he conceives to be his Fulfillment, while at the same time professing his fears for the natural denouement of Death."[15] In *Nine Rivers*, he paints the image of the unicorn on his windshield and finds a statue of it in Saverne, symbolically linking French to German territory as he journeys northwards; in *The Brazen Horn* it stands emblematically on the dust-jacket. The values Denis Johnston attaches to the Christian myth and to the unicorn are of the same sort; his decision to structure his autobiography around the imagery of the *via dolorosa* and the Mass is a choice of the public myth over the more personal symbol. He refuses to believe in Christ as God's only begotten Son because he too is His son. Walking the Way of the Cross in Jerusalem where he gets lost – unable "to follow the Christian all the way to Calvary" (NR, 62) – he ends up at the YMCA drinking tea. But still he recognizes in Christianity the mythic expression of "the accumulated wisdom," the "accumulated errors" (NR, 285) of mankind. For Johnston, whose search for he-knew-not-what unexpectedly ended at Buchenwald the day after its liberation, where he was escorted past truckloads of emaciated corpses and between tiers on which were shelved the skeletal and filthy barely-living, so weak their cheers sounded like wailing, every man has been Christ-like in his suffering and in the necessity to forgive both God and man for that suffering. Thus to intimate analogies between himself and Christ is also to intimate that he is a "Norm" of the generation that faced Buchenwald. But it is to do so in a manner opposite to the way in which analogies with Christ usually function in spiritual autobiography. In Quaker and Puritan spiritual autobiography, for example, comparisons of the life of the autobiographer with the life of Christ, even conscious imitation of the life of Christ, valorize the particular experience as a testimonial to the Christian teaching. Johnston is not bringing his widow's mite of experience to illuminate the greater glory of God; he is asserting that in autobiography, as in other forms of knowledge, the shape we give our experience in our telling overrides the particularity of our experience. He is valorizing myth, the shared archetypal patterns into which we cast our experience, over the self.

V

As "Tocher" continues his list of mythic "analogies" in *Nine Rivers*, he emphasizes "Take Two" and the Canon of the unknown Mass. The journey of "Take One" ends in death at the Brenner at noon, of "Take Two" in revelation at Hafelekar at dawn; "Tocher" cites Hafelekar and dawn. This is in fact to emphasize that man has a choice of journeys and that some forms of heroism are preferable to others; it is also to stress Johnston's autobiographical role as prophet. Johnston, dead in "Take One" as the consequence of the desire for revenge which has made him carry a gun, leaves as testament his "translation" of the opening passage of *The Odyssey*, which he casts as a dialogue between the critic and Odysseus. The Greek has the last word on the contagion of Evil which has killed Johnston, the questing protagonist:

> How vain your hope
> For all your bitter tongue,
> For fools who slay the Oxen of the Sun
> To feed their anger or to ease their dread
> Shall eat Damnation as their daily bread. (NR, 441)

But in the Canon of "Take Two," the gun, symbol of Knowledge of Evil, thrown away, the Voice turns God's challenge to Job[16] into a promise of preservation:

> I have harnessed the Unicorn to the plough.
> The range of mountains was his pasturage
> But now he shall bend his back to the furrow.
> In Famine he shall save you from starvation
> And in War from the power of the sword.

But, lest the promise breed complacency, the Voice adds a warning to man (the unicorn) using the words of Job weighing his grief for his earlier unthinking acceptance of good fortune:

> But keep him hungry till his work is done.
> Will the wild ass bray while he has grass? (NR, 455)

Johnston seems to be telling us that Everyman, now as always, can choose to descend to the Underworld and to stop there; he can follow the army of liberation to Buchenwald and devote himself to slaying the Oxen of the Sun in revenge on man and the gods for the Evil he finds there. That possibility is intimated early when Johnston is given a copy of Dante's *Inferno* without the *Purgatorio* or *Paradiso*; he reads it on his first long-distance bombing mission. The real possibility of this journey for Johnston/Everyman is also implicit in the play on the Greek form of *Denis*: *Dion, Dioniad, Dionysia, Dionysus*, link him with the infernal regions. In *The Brazen Horn*, Denis Johnston will describe the decision to take this journey as the expression of man's Death Wish, leading him, lemming-like, to dehumanization and to an Otto Suder or, now, to the Ultimate Weapon.

Or Everyman may choose the journey that "Tocher" emphasizes, a cyclical rather than a terminal journey, enacted for us by the quest-hero who, as Joseph Campbell has shown us, travels from life to death to life, from light to dark to light, from consciousness to unconsciousness to consciousness, from this world to the underworld and back to this world. The quest-hero is a hero not because he descends into the Underworld, but because he returns, re-emerging from the place of Death, *and* because in the full noon of his return, he is able to share the knowledge of *both* descent *and* return with his tribe. He expresses that knowledge in the forms and motifs of the myths of his tribe. Independent of our individual belief or disbelief, the dominant myth of our tribe, the expression of our "accumulated wisdom," is the Christ-story. So Johnston, who declares himself non-Christian, who describes his "deity" as a Voice or as an Ultimate Observer rather than as God, expresses his knowledge in the forms of the Mass, in the equation of every man with Christ. So too he takes care to set one ending at sunrise, hour of return from the Under-world, but the second ending at noon, hour at which, the cycle completed, the hero speaks his knowledge: "So now I speak at high noon, and from the Dome of the Rock," the "Introit" opens (NR, 1). The auto-biography's double ending also represents the quest-hero's double knowledge: knowledge of death, the consequence of the contagion of evil; knowledge of life, the consequence of putting evil behind him. For the hero, the two exist simultaneously, one the positive image of the other; the Dioniad into the infernal regions finds its positive double in the "Fides Dionis" (NR, 416). "I am Dion that bringeth good tidings" (NR, 454), Johnston announces this transformation; the Canon of *Nine Rivers* and *The Brazen Horn* are the gospel and the epistle of those tidings.

VI

Johnston *seems* well within a tradition in which, as Vivian Mercier has noted, Irish writers are anxious to put themselves forward as Messiahs for their country.[17] That Ireland consistently refuses the sacrifice accounts for much of the satire and the bitterness we find in the autobiographies of George Moore, Sean O'Casey and W.B. Yeats. Johnston, however, has too much common sense to offer himself as a Messiah for the country he thought ideal to grow up in and retire to. As the tone of plays like *The Old Lady Says "No!"* and *The Scythe and the Sunset* make clear, Johnston retained a caustic awareness that a lot of Irish hero-worship was blarney and that, if all the codgers who, by 1925, were claiming to have been with Pearse in the Post Office actually had been there, instead of displaying "intense hostility"[18] to the Easter Uprising, all of Dublin, let alone the Post Office, could scarcely have contained their legions. If Johnston's "messianic" ambitions touch those of other Irish autobiographers, it is where these go far beyond Irish borders: like Yeats in *A Vision*, he is offering an explanation of this life and the life to come. Where Yeats encountered Madame Blavatsky at an impressionable age, Johnston clearly encountered the new physics opened up by the work of Einstein and Bohr. Yeats wanted to explain man's spiritual life in terms of an occult tradition, more ancient than and alternative to the Christian myth, and constructed his own System, based on that tradition, in *A Vision*. Johnston wants to account for his death in the Brenner in terms of scientific explanation of the physical universe, and constructs his own System, based on physics and geometry, in *The Brazen Horn*. As *A Vision* is the philosophy in terms of which Yeats wrote *The Trembling of the Veil* and all his later autobiographies, so *The Brazen Horn* presents the scientific explanation in terms of which Johnston wrote *Nine Rivers*. As Yeats, armed with an occult tradition but lacking, he said, philosophy, shaped his system around what he knew, and studied philosophy during the seventeen years he wrote and revised *A Vision*, so Johnston, armed with spiritual knowledge and some skill in geometry, shaped his science out of what he knew and studied physics and borrowed mathematical explanations over the approximately twenty-seven years (from *Dionysia* to *The Brazen Horn*) during which he elaborated his system of thought.

That the three volumes – *Dionysia*, *Nine Rivers from Jordan*, and *The Brazen Horn* – form a single enterprise, and that Johnston's scientific explanation of his experience of having both died and lived informs even the earliest of the three narratives is plain in the "second" ending of *Dionysia*. Introducing the "Canon," Johnston cites "a school of philosophy that tells us that all possibilities have a real existence" and that he is about "to go back and pick another of the possibilities from the bag" (D, 883). And the "Canon" ended, he asks:

> You see what I mean?
>
> What we are faced with is quite a job – nothing more or less than a re-statement of such of the facts of religion that matter, and the affirmation of a belief that will give us once again a moral positiveness and the chance to have a really good time – a creed that is violent and yet compassionate, that will re-admit the supernatural in terms of modern science – a religion that does not ask us to

believe the unbelievable, and yet recognizes the incomprehensible as the only thing that man can really understand – a faith that does not preach Peace (for the only true Peace is Death) but will reconcile the exhilarating fact of Conflict with the Godlike grace of Pity – a yardstick of This Life (and not of another one) that tells us we are not strangers here, that teaches us not to seek the end before its time, nor to fear it when it does come, and that inspires us neither to submit to Evil nor to punish it. (D, 904)

In *Dionysia* he begins to put this programme into effect first by a studied and courteous salute to a Luftwaffe officer he has just been interrogating, then by a concluding address "To the Recipient" which he will later revise as the Credo or "An Approach to an Absolute Statement" that concludes *The Brazen Horn*.

I do not know why Johnston chose to remove this programme for "re-statement" when he revised this ending for *Nine Rivers*. However, the example of Yeats, whose *A Vision*, in 1953, was still being treated as an embarrassment best not mentioned, suggests that his explanation of what had happened to him might have met with considerable derision when *Nine Rivers* was first published, and this likelihood may have been a factor in the decision. It may also have determined the revision between *Dionysia* and *Nine Rivers* to make the hospital scene in which the essence of that explanation is given more disarmingly comic. During an interlude in a Paris hospital, Johnston reads Mary Frances Cleugh's *Time and Its Importance in Modern Thought* (1937), which he treats rather flippantly as "girlish chatter" (NR, 322). A query about one of her references, however, gets an emphatic answer from the Provost Officer in the next bed: "There's a lot of crap being written about Time these days. There's no great mystery about it. The really interesting thing is Observation – the thing that appears to put an arrow on Time, and makes us imagine that we move from a definite Past to an indefinite Future" (NR, 322). This new Virgil to Johnston's Dante then gallops him through a description of a seven-dimensional universe which, he claims, is the explanation in the physical world for a Platonic theory of "parallel Continua" (NR, 323). A highly "produced" scene, with its reconstructed conversation between the enthusiast tumbling through his frenetic explanation and a sceptical, slightly naive, and uninterested Johnston, it is also a rough précis of the theory of *The Brazen Horn*. The Observer as the figure on whom the theory depends is intimated in the references to astronomy which link *Nine Rivers* to *The Brazen Horn*. "Tocher" reminds us that the Orphic day, from noon to noon, is the day as measured by astronomers, in contradistinction to the day, from midnight to midnight, measured by Church and State. Consistent with this, Johnston crosses the last of his nine rivers, each linked with one of the Muses, and goes to meet (or not meet) Otto Suder and his death at noon under the inspiration of Urania, Muse of Astronomy. And the deliberations and "non-answers" of a conference of astronomers open the scientific inquiry of *The Brazen Horn*.

What Johnston does there is to assert the pre-eminence, on a universal scale, of the observer and his motion: in everyday terms, the train actually moves, the landscape only seems to move, or: the location of the astronomer determines what he sees of the heavens and the angle at which he sees it. Velocity, he concludes, is "a dimensional Effect caused by our own Procession" (BH, 241) or movement through Space. Johnston, however, is no follower of Bishop Berkeley; he hypothesizes an objective reality which persists apart from our observation, but its persistence is not a phenomenon involving change, and, therefore, not a question of Time: "The difference between one Moment and the next is not one of change in the physical world, but of change in Observation," the Provost Officer explains (NR, 322), or: something happens because we observe it.

Johnston posits six dimensions. The conventional three dimensions he uses to explain the world of appearances – of length, breadth and depth that give objects their solidity, their presence in Space to the observer. 4D accounts for "objective Reality" (BH, 242), the persistence of these "objects" when we do not observe them. 5D introduces the subjective element, produced by the observer's Procession, and, therefore, by changes in what is observed. It is this Procession that, Johnston claims, we erroneously label Time[19] and it is this Procession, productive of changes in the angle of our observation, that gives the "Effect" of velocity. In fact, all motion is the observer's; the universe itself is static. But since a multitude of observers can exist in the many Nows of their observation, and since they can observe each other observing, the system, if it is to be coherent and not merely infinitely regressing, demands a principle encompassing them all (a principle mathematics and physics, as well as theology, make necessary). To meet the demand, Johnston posits a Sixth Dimension, "the realm of the unchangeable and only Infinity, which is 'X' " (BH, 88), a realm "where all Times are Now and all Places are Here" (BH, 79).

With a fifth dimension and the geometry of curvature, Johnston re-theorizes some of the galactic phenomena physicists have explained in terms of dynamics. These theories Johnston offers by way of providing an alternative explanation of the physicists' data and of making his system credible in terms of that data. But most significant for this theory is that 4D and 5D allow for the Platonic theory of "parallel Continua" proposed by the Provost Officer. For if there can be persistence in 4D independent of observation, then what is never observed, as well as what is observed, possibilities as well as "actions," exist. Applied to man, Johnston terms these possibilities "World Lines" which exist in parallel Nows. While each of these possibilities is determined in 6D Infinity, we have free will in the matter of observation, for, by an awareness of the *simultaneous* existence of parallel continua, we can choose in which one we will live

while the others persist as possibilities. Looking forward, this means that
death marks the end of one "World Line" but not of all; this body dies,
but the "élan" persists elsewhere, *The Brazen Horn* suggests. Looking
backwards, it means that the past as well as the future is "open," is a
number of possibilities of which one has been/or will be chosen.[20]

Johnston derives this theory from the experience of his own death and
uses it to explain the seemingly impossible. His final explanation of the
two "Takes" of the end of his journey is that they belong to two parallel
and simultaneous "World Lines." The only thing he claims as unusual in
his experience is his *awareness* of the two continua, an awareness he urges
as a useful mutation for the race to undergo since it in fact made it possible
for him to choose against the Death Wish: "This present *corpus in-
delictum* of mine is in a common continuum with the Reader. It never met
Otto Suder, and that is why I cannot remember what he looked like,
although I am aware, in ways other than by means of memory, of what
took place at a meeting, more Elsewhere than is commonly accepted"
(BH, 144). But that *this* body never met Suder does not make Johnston's
death in another 4D continuum any less real by his theory; this body's not
going to the deadly encounter is simply a function of the direction of
observation along which Johnston chose to proceed at a critical juncture.

Faced with this re-visionism of contemporary theories about the
universe, some of Johnston's readers have declared it "too soon" to
discuss *The Brazen Horn*. Others choose to believe his death in the
Brenner a dream despite his statements to the contrary and the elaborate
theoretical edifice he has erected to prove them. To insist on the "dream"
theory because, after all, Johnston continued for many years to walk
among us, is simply to agree with him that we and he are observing this
Now in a shared continuum. It no more refutes his theory that in another
and parallel continuum he died than Dr Johnson refuted Bishop Berkeley
by kicking a stone. Obviously, if we have philosophy or physics enough,
we can undertake to disprove the Systems of a Yeats or a Johnston in
order to uphold more received views or even to advance a System of our
own. But we cannot simply deny their systems of thought nor, as literary
critics, can we fully understand the visions shaping their poetry, plays,
autobiographies and criticism without the context of those systems.

VII

For it is to the larger theological and epistemological questions of belief
and vision, to the acts "of faith" (NR, 455) and of knowledge that the
writer's work professes, that these systems lead us and which they are
designed to support. Having raised these questions after presenting his
arguments about the nature of the physical universe, Johnston deals with
them sketchily in *The Brazen Horn*. For this is a "non-book" not only
because it stands as an alternative to the explanations and belief of the
Bible, but because it does not stand independently of *Nine Rivers from*

Jordan but is an appendix to it: the moral and theological imperatives of his System are, as Johnston notes, largely dealt with in the Canon of an unknown Mass that concludes the autobiography.

This canon is divided into two scenes, each one roughly corresponding to one of the two endings of *Nine Rivers*. The first scene takes place before the Pietà, reminiscent of the D.Ps and of Annaliese, but also reminiscent of all the myths by which we express our suffering – the Antiphon names the dead man as Adonis, not Christ. In the ensuing dialogue, the Acolyte advances Johnston's conviction, after his knowledge of Buchenwald, that "All guilt must be avenged on earth" (NR, 442). But the Pietà distinguishes between refusing to submit to evil and punishing it, between fighting it and catching its contagion by avenging it: "Fight evil if you will/But – oh – do not admit the Knowledge of it" (NR, 443) for that Knowledge "is the poison of the seed of Adam" (NR, 444) which infects its knower. In the careful parallelism and balance of *Nine Rivers*, the Acolyte in this scene expresses the righteous anger and determination upon revenge that, in the earlier dramatized trial of "The High Court on the Brocken," has put all of infected humanity into the dock. And, just as humanity, condemned, can be released from the services of the hangman for its own "Death Wish" will lead it to carry out the court's sentence, so the Acolyte's participation in the evil will lead to his death at the Brenner.

That this is his *choice* the Pietà makes plain by answering the most serious of Johnston's persistent questions on his journey: How can we believe in a God of Good and Evil? The Pietà confirms his conviction that we cannot by relocating Evil; there is no Evil, she tells him, "Except that which the poison in your blood creates" (NR, 445). Evil is the choice and not the necessary burden of man; while the "one and nameless Infinite" remains the "Author of Good and Evil" (BH, 201), man does not inherit Evil but chooses to exercise it. While the Pietà's answer repudiates the doctrine of Original Sin (as Johnston himself does in *The Brazen Horn*) hers is not an argument for primal innocence, but an argument against guilt and atonement:

> Can you not be wiser than our Father, Adam?
> Is there not an innocence that lies beyond maturity?
> Some day will come a generation,
> A generation that has been tempered in the furnace,
> A generation that knows – yet cannot be killed by knowledge,
> A generation that needs no redemption
> And has nothing against the Creator of Night and Day. (NR, 445)

At this point, the revisionism of Johnston's identification of himself as Everyman through the figure of Christ becomes apparent. For even if the sufferings of Johnston/Everyman have been Christ-like, even if he too must refuse revenge, Johnston cannot follow Christ all the way to Calvary. He does *not* offer his death as a redemption for himself and the

allied armies; he offers it as a cautionary tale, as a self-inflicted punishment brought on by participation in the contagion of Evil. For in
refusing to follow Christ all the way to Calvary, Johnston refuses, as his
Pietà would have him do, the myth of Adam and of Christ, of guilt and of
atonement. Knowing Evil, having seen Buchenwald, Johnston tells us,
man cannot undo his Knowledge. *The Brazen Horn* closes with the
confession that, having thrown away the Luger, he went back next day
and found it; it opens with the Luger, having been abandoned a second
time, being restored to Johnston in 1956 and subsequently redisposed of.
The Pietà does not argue that Knowledge of Evil can be undone; she
argues that it must not be used, that man must "Spit out the fruit of the
tree" (NR, 445), must not carry a gun up the Brenner in an avenging
spirit.

The second part of the Canon balances the first just as the entire Canon
balances the drama of "The High Court" scene. Titled "Epiklesis," it
enacts the "conversation with Heaven" of the second ending. In the
symbolic and biblical language of this scene, God is less clear than was the
Pietà. However, He seems to suggest that man has created Him in his own
image: "In whose image have you created God?/If you hate Pity, why do
you not cast it out?" he demands (NR, 448). Having so created Him, this
God suggests, man can accuse and forgive Him as he accuses and forgives
himself. By firing his Luger into the sky, the Acolyte symbolically
challenges the Evil that is part of His creation, symbolically accuses Him,
and can "leave the human race in peace" (NR, 454).

The Acolyte also discovers the second use of Pity. A trap it can be,
especially when fools bent on revenge are moved by it to hand their guns
over to the Otto Suders of the world. But without the contagion of Evil, it
can be life-giving, as Johnston himself proved without thinking when he
disobeyed non-fraternization orders by offering chocolate to a child and
showed no hostility when that child refused to take the gift or to speak to
him. That act of pity is cited by the Voice of the Canon as His justification
for a similar mercy which releases the Acolyte back into the garden.
There, with the unicorn (whom Johnston has defined as man without the
contagion of Evil) harnessed to the plough (and protecting him when the
ploughshares become swords), he can "reject the inheritance of ...
Adam" (NR, 454) and live in the natural world of Night and Day,
forgetting Good and Evil. He becomes an Everyman who saves himself,
as the Antiphon intimates when he recites from the Irish "saga" of
Johnston's marriage, the life-continuing event which, preceding and
contrasting with the Buchenwald scene, is one of its alternatives in *Nine
Rivers*:

> I am a City that is not forgotten
> I am the first to come into Czernowitz.
> A Mirror am I to you who perceive me.
> I am Dion that bringeth good tidings. (NR, 45)

VIII

Johnston uses autobiography as a vehicle to inquire into the nature and uses of Knowledge itself. As *The Brazen Horn* points out, any observer can observe other observers within his range of vision. But if A can observe B observing, he cannot observe precisely *what* B observes for he cannot share *exactly* B's angle of observation. To this extent all epistemological statements are subjective and to use autobiography as the vehicle of epistemology is to acknowledge this. But observation, as Johnston also points out, is a function of scale as well as of angle of vision. If our scale becomes the cosmos, then man, for all practical purposes, shares a common angle of observation; one autobiography, one epistemology, tells us something about all men and women.

Johnston invokes that scale when he structures *Nine Rivers from Jordan* as a Mass, the journey as successive encounters with each of the Muses, when he prefaces each of its sections with a song cycle for the seasons and incorporates plays and learned articles into his autobiography. That our knowledge takes representative forms becomes a didactic point in *The Brazen Horn*. There, twelve chapters conclude with "An Approach to an Absolute Statement," a Credo that is the consequence of the science the book argues. That "Approach" also has twelve parts and each one, in order and in Latin (language as another analogous knowing), serves as an epigraph to one of the twelve chapters where it shares a page with a woodcut, taken from the *Poetica astronomica* (1482), of one of the zodiacal signs. These signs mime a complete noon-to-noon cycle as well as relate to the chapters they head. Cancer, for example, the sign which marks the beginning of summer (noon), opens the book and a chapter in which Johnston recalls the double ending of his journey and advances the idea of the "Open Past" (in Orphic teaching Cancer signifies a threshold between incarnations), while Johnston's own sign, Gemini, which ends at the summer equinox, completes the cycle and the book by bringing noon around again.

Through such structures, autobiography becomes the manipulation of myths through which the returned quest-hero can communicate his knowledge. In its record of an individual journey and an individual knowledge, it addresses itself to us as also representative of our collective journey and our collective knowledge. It functions as myth, creed, and epistemology or, as Johnston would have it, as gospel and epistle.

It is as gospel and epistle that Johnston's autobiographies break covenant with previous Irish (and most contemporary) autobiography. Since Rousseau, autobiography has stressed psychological, social and political man over epistemology, the individual over Everyman, and nowhere more so than in Ireland. Johnston can seem deceptively consistent with this tradition. For example, his reliance on symbol and allusion, on interior monologue, pastiche, and "produced" scenes (what Gogarty summed up as "Phantasy in Fact"), and his stylistic shifts from lyricism to bravura, from dogmatism to satire, are part of a tradition that runs from Moore, through Yeats, Gogarty, and O'Casey, to Francis Stuart in his *Black List Section H* (1975). Irish writers have exacerbated the tendency of autobiography since Rousseau to blur "fact" and "fiction" in order to recreate the "reality" of an individual, but they have remained firmly within a tradition which sees the genre as self-revealing (or self-justifying). Even Johnston's systematizing is not enough in itself to take him beyond that tradition; Yeats, after all, used his philosophical system to explain his life and this is generically no different than more common appeals to Christian values as a principle of autobiographical explanation.

Just here, however, in the difference of Johnston's and Yeats's use of their philosophies, Johnston's reversal of the aims of his fellow Irish autobiographers becomes evident. For where Yeats uses his philosophy to explain his life, as other autobiographers use psychology, sociology, politics, or fiction, Johnston makes an event in his life (the War and, specifically, his death in the Brenner) simply the occasion from which he derives an explanation for the workings of all life. Where epistemology is generally put to the service of autobiography, he puts autobiography to the service of epistemology. His epistemological method is at least as old as Augustine's *Confessions*. But in taking up that older tradition of autobiography as an occasion for epistemology, and in adapting it to the exigencies of twentieth century conflict and twentieth century science, Johnston moves Irish autobiography beyond its personal and parochial concerns; he writes as Everyman.

SHIRLEY NEUMAN

NOTES

1. George Moore, *Confessions of a Young Man* (first published 1888); *Memoirs of My Dead Life* (1906); *Ave* (1911), *Salve* (1912), and *Vale* (1914), collected as *Hail and Farewell* (1925).

   W.B. Yeats, *Reveries over Childhood and Youth* (1916), *The Trembling of the Veil* (1922), *Dramatis Personae* (1936), *Estrangement* (1926), *The Death of Synge* (1928), and *The Bounty of Sweden* (1925), collected in the order given above as *The Autobiography of W.B. Yeats* (1938).

   Sean O'Casey, *I Knock at the Door* (1939), *Pictures in the Hallway* (1942), *Drums under the Windows* (1946), *Inishfallen Fare Thee Well* (1949), *Rose and Crown* (1952), and *Sunset and Evening Star* (1954), collected as *Mirror in My House* (1956).

   Oliver St John Gogarty, *As I Was Going Down Sackville Street* (1937); *It Isn't This Time of Year at All!* (1954).

2. In the case of George Moore, this generalisation applies only to his "Irish" autobiography, *Hail and Farewell*.

3. Oliver St John Gogarty, *As I Was Going Down Sackville Street* (N.Y.: Reynal & Hitchcock, 1937), p.6; George Moore, *Hail and Farewell* (Gerrards Cross: Colin Smythe, 1976), pp.257, 609; W. B. Yeats, *Autobiographies* (London: Macmillan, 1955), p.379. Herbert Howarth draws attention to Irish writers' willingness to become Messiahs in *The Irish Writers 1880–1940: Literature Under Parnell's Star* (London: Rockliff, 1958), cited by Vivian Mercier, "Perfection of the Life, or of the Work?", *Denis Johnston: A Retrospective*, ed. Joseph Ronsley (Gerrards Cross: Colin Smythe;

Totowa: Barnes and Noble, 1981), p. 228.

4. [Denis Johnston], *Dionysia: The Mass of the Nine Nereids*. Unpublished ts., mimeographed and "abandon[ed] ... in a few semi-public places" (*Dionysia*, 5) in 1949. I have consulted the copy deposited in the British Museum; references to it are identified by "D." Where the texts of *Dionysia* and *Nine Rivers from Jordan* are identical or very similar, I have quoted from *Nine Rivers*.

   Denis Johnston, *Nine Rivers from Jordan: A Chronicle of a Journey and a Search* (London: Derek Verschoyle, 1953); references to *Nine Rivers* are identified by "NR."

   Denis Johnston, *The Brazen Horn: A Non-Book for Those Who, in Revolt Today, Could be in Command Tomorrow* (Ireland: Dolmen Press, 1976); references to *The Brazen Horn* are identified by "BH." An earlier version was privately printed: Alderney, 1968.

5. See particularly G. Thomas Couser, "The Shape of Death in American Autobiography," *The Hudson Review*, 31, 1 (Spring 1978), 53–66; and Barrett John Mandel, " 'Basting the Image with a Certain Liquor': Death in Autobiography," *Soundings*, 57, 2 (Summer 1974), 175–88.

6. Sean O'Casey, *Sunset and Evening Star*, in *Mirror in My House* (N.Y.: Macmillan, 1956), II, 339; Gogarty, *As I Was Going Down Sackville Street*, p. 341.

7. Oliver St John Gogarty, *It Isn't This Time of Year At All! An Unpremeditated Autobiography* (N.Y.: Doubleday, 1954), p. 256; George Moore, *Memoirs of My Dead Life* (11th rev. ed; London: Heinemann, 1928), pp. 269–70.

8. This ending was omitted from the American edition (Boston: Little, Brown & Company, 1955), an omission Johnston attributes to the publisher rather than himself. Here too *Nine Rivers* shows some divergence (of which more later) from *Dionysia*, although both offer a second ending in the form of the Canon with its two "scenes."

9. The existence of this photograph doubtless led Johnston in *Dionysia* to combine the events of "Take One," as he reports them in both *Nine Rivers* and *The Brazen Horn*, in which he first stops at the car, with those of "Take Two" in which he first goes to meet the generals.

10. Before receiving this information, Johnston had already fictionalized Suder as a guard at the gate of Buchenwald in his libretto for Hugo Weisgall's opera, *Nine Rivers from Jordan* (first produced, 1968).

11. See especially Mercier, p. 241.

12. Georges Gusdorf, "Conditions and Limits of Autobiography," trans. James Olney, in *Autobiography: Essays Theoretical and Critical*, ed. James Olney (Princeton: Princeton U.P., 1980). Gusdorf's essay first appeared in 1956. The tradition of autobiography he describes has been most fully elaborated by Karl Joachim Weintraub, *The Value of the Individual: Self and Circumstance in Autobiography* (Chicago: U. of Chicago Press, 1978). Stephen A. Shapiro, "The Dark Continent of Literature: Autobiography," *Comparative Literature Studies*, 5 (1968), 421–54, discusses the autobiographer as Everyman, the genre as traditionally epistemological.

13. These and later stages of Johnston's "quest" have been the focus of nearly all the discussion of *Nine Rivers*. See Mercier, pp. 233–39; and Gene A. Barnett, *Denis Johnston* (Boston: Twayne, 1978), pp. 107–23.

14. In *A Bride for the Unicorn*. Mercier, pp. 230–1, discusses Johnston's use of an Everyman figure in this play and his "Everyman" attributes as husband, father, divorced man, child, etc. in *Nine Rivers*. Barnett, p. 123, alludes to the concept of the "Open Past" as already present in *A Bride for the Unicorn*.

15. Denis Johnston, "Concerning the Unicorn," in *The Dramatic Works of Denis Johnston* (Gerrards Cross: Colin Smythe, 1979), II, 13–14.

16. Canst thou bind the unicorn with his band in the furrow?
    Or will he harrow the valleys after thee?

17. Mercier, pp. 228–9, situates Johnston in this tradition of the writer's offering himself "as an alternative Messiah for Ireland."

18. Denis Johnston, "Up the Rebels!", in *The Dramatic Works of Denis Johnston*, I, 90.

19. At this point many readers will find themselves unable to go along with Johnston, either out of a conviction that it takes more than physics to account fully for our experience of

Time, or out of a conviction that his explanation of Time does not account for what we often call "mental time."

20. In Johnston's Sixth Dimension, the reader will recognise aspects of the time theories of J.W. Dunne (*An Experiment with Time*, 1927). However, Johnston's theory of simultaneous Nows is distinct from Dunne's pre-vision and is closer to the tradition of Platonism.

In Search of Himselves:
The Autobiographical Writings of
Graham Greene

In the 'thirties Graham Greene reviewed Somerset Maugham's auto-biography, *The Summing Up* (1938). It represented, he said, "an excellent example of his hard-won style at its best, clear, colloquial, honest."[1] The comment suggests interesting correspondences with the problems Greene encountered in his own autobiographical writings. Above all, one senses his striving, sometimes to the point of masochism, to achieve a similar "honesty" while at the same time avoiding what he described in Maugham's other work as the "deadening" effect of a too-easily paraded "humility and self-distrust."[2] Greene's apparent intimacy with his reader is somehow unembarrassing, severely controlled as it is by an obsessive modesty and reticence.

Greene's "frame of mind" is one of persistent doubt. Behind his accounts of personal and theological uncertainties, though, lies a problem which is particularly distressing for a writer: his awareness of the impossibility of ever rendering in words an "honest" impression of his confusion of spiritual and temporal experience. The elliptical, enigmatic style of these writings is, surely, a deliberate reflection of this. He wishes both to recount certain memories and to call into question the reliability of any recorded account. Dream and "reality" are frequently inter-changeable; mystical or "magical" experience walks hand in hand with precise empirical description. Ultimately we are left less with a "portrait" of the author than with reflections upon the nature of time and memory of which he is as much a victim as his reader.

Greene published *A Sort of Life*[3] in 1971, late in his career. It is the only work which he has presented to the public as "autobiography" and it is a slim volume, barely 150 pages. But he has written, or collaborated in, three other books which offer autobiographical information: *In Search of a Character. Two African Journals* (1961),[4] *Ways of Escape* (1980),[5] and Marie-Françoise Allain's *The Other Man. Conversations With Graham Greene* (1983).[6] Read in isolation *A Sort of Life* appears as a brilliant *tour de force* of Freudian self-analysis which unsettles the reader from the outset: there seems to be no distinction made between the rhetoric of fiction and that of autobiography. We tend to assume that the latter form draws on evidence rather than invention. The honest autobiographer is, rather too easily, supposed to be the most reliable narrator of his subject's life, being closest to what Greene calls " 'the documents in the case' ."[7] *A Sort of Life*, however, sets out to subvert these expectations. When wishing to establish the objective truth of an incident he often has recourse to third parties whose understanding of the "documents" varies from his own. We are presented with an autobiography which seems to be "honest" but which is simultaneously, and unrepentantly, evasive. The apparent paradox here is, I believe, to some extent resolved by reading *A Sort of Life* alongside Greene's three other "autobiographical" books. (For the purposes of this essay I shall exclude discussion of the travel books as a separate *genre* whose first-person narrator is far less intimate than that of autobiography.)

A comparison of the four works, very different in style and approach, reveals two common factors: all these accounts are fragmentary and all appear to divide Greene's history into a public and a private life. "Public" and "private" lives, though, do not simply connote an alternation of social roles: the distinction suggests two fundamentally opposed ways of re-ceiving and de-coding information. The "public" life is associated with his business as a professional writer, the mechanics of his aesthetic, his political views and actions as *agent provocateur*; his understanding and description of this life rely on empirical evidence. The private life is not the intimacy of domesticity, fireside and children. Nor is it the discussion of his various affairs since leaving his wife. It is rather that intangible nether-world of the imagination hinted at in "Under the Garden,"[8] the world of religious faith, magic, dream, romance, where the apparently incontrovertible truths of empirical data are called into question, re-ordered, given new meaning. As we shall see, Greene makes the dis-tinction when discussing his Catholicism between belief and faith: belief belongs to the intellect, faith to the imaginative, instinctive impulses. We might add that belief, that unimpassioned intellectual conviction with which he was received into the Church in 1926, belongs to the public life and that faith belongs to the private.

The more closely we examine these rather simple categories, however, the more we find the distinctions between them breaking down. When he is writing about his private history we often find that he is discussing a character he does not recognise as himself but has reconstructed from an unreliable memory. The "author" of *A Sort of Life* seems to present himself as someone else, and his reticence in refusing to use the word "autobiography" in the title is, surely, significant. Conversely, in writing about writing he is using a coded and formalised language of intimate revelation. The problems of literary presentation become to Greene exactly equivalent to the problems of self-knowledge.

In short, he finds it almost impossible to distinguish between his public and private lives. His intellectual attachment to the material world, to common sense, to empirical evidence is strong but is persistently sub-verted by his irrational imaginative faculty which draws him away from the boredom of the quotidian towards fantasy, magic and faith. He does not know which approach comes closest to the "truth" and he does not wish to choose. We can never be certain, any more than Greene can, that the events described in *A Sort of Life* "actually happened" but, however we interpret this ambivalence, it has one crucial function for the author: by disestablishing the solid basis of "fact" it serves, in an odd way, to protect his privacy. The "honesty" of Greene's autobiographical writings is not equivalent to a shared intimacy with the reader.

It would seem clear that the brevity of *A Sort of Life*, and its elliptical nature, reflect these (and other) personal and aesthetic difficulties presented by the form. Autobiography is, perhaps by definition, the most narcissistic of literary genres. It often represents a modest display of pride in its subject's success. *The Diary of a Nobody* conversely derives its humour from the received idea that it is absurd for a person of no importance to render public account of his life. Where Pooter records the trivia of bourgeois routine, the "successful" autobiographer often recalls anecdotes of those unusual people whose lives he has shared. Greene, however, refuses to play this game. The essay on *The Summing Up* notes with admiration that "even in this personal book the author is unwilling to communicate more than belongs to his authorship; he does not, like a professional autobiographer, take us with commercial promptitude into his confidence."[9]

The remarks might apply directly to *A Sort of Life* and an interesting distinction arises here between Greene's use of the words "honesty" and "confidence." His honesty, his public self-castigation, is unsparing; his confidence is reserved for those friends protected by anonymity in these writings. Anecdotal material rarely deals with "the great" but usually serves either to support a compound impression of his own life (the dead dog in the pram, the man cutting his throat at a window, the journal's account of his period as an Air Raid Warden) or to suggest the absurdity of human behaviour (the sacks of gold from wartime Norway, the ludicrous Selznick, the whimsical Sir Robert Scott placing bananas in a grand piano). When we compile the list of Greene's close friends who make an appearance we find that only two are substantially fleshed out as "characters": Alexander Korda and Evelyn Waugh. As for the rest – Tooter and Barbara (his cousins), Claud Cockburn and Peter Quennell (school and Oxford friends), Kenneth Richmond (his psychoanalyst), Robert Scott and George Whitmore (undergraduate friends), Kenneth Bell (his Oxford tutor), Trevor Wilson (Consul in Hanoi), and Herbert Read – very little is said. The crucial relationship of the period covered by *A Sort of Life* – with his wife Vivienne (née Dayrell) – is barely touched upon. We have no idea of her appearance, of the details of their marital difficulties, even of the date of their separation. Greene studiously avoids naming any of his subsequent lovers. When Mlle. Allain rather clumsily tried to press him to "reveal" more about one of these he firmly deflected the question. "I took advantage of [*Life*'s commission to cover the Malayan troubles in 1951] to escape from certain private worries." "What kind of worries?" "I can't say. There are some things I can't talk about because they also concern other people." "1951 coincides with *The End of the Affair*." "More or less. Perhaps we can get back to the real questions?"[10] The " 'real questions,' " it would appear, relate in Greene's mind to the general "experience" of his life rather than to its specific events.

The same reticence applies equally to his close family. Of his father all we learn is that Greene "had no feelings about him,"[11] that he was reserved and kindly, that he caned Greene once for truancy, awakening sexual feelings in the boy, and that Greene regrets rejecting his attempts at intimacy. His mother, we are told, he associates "with a remoteness, which I did not at all resent, and with a smell of eau-de-cologne."[12] His brothers and sisters are equally mysterious figures. We find, then, not an account of family and close friends spiced with anecdotes of the great, but a memoir from which all intimate acquaintance has been either excluded or barely sketched in. *A Sort of Life* is a story with one character – Greene – or rather, the many Greenes he recognizes in himself through memory. The supporting figures – Selznick, Dupont, Mlle. André de Jongue, for instance – are acquaintances rather than friends and those friends to whom he allows space – Nordahl Grieg and Robert Scott, for instance – are no longer public figures. The famous flit through his autobiographical works as mere names (Ernest Bevin, Elizabeth Bowen). If one knew nothing of Greene's life beyond his own records, one might assume him to have known almost no one of importance rather than to have been a senior figure of English Letters since the 'thirties.

In one sense, of course, this is true. It was not that he "knew no one," but that he coveted anonymity and loathed the trappings of literary success.[13] "Fame" was necessary to supply financial support for his obsessive desire to write, but this obsession paradoxically sprang from a persistent inability to settle to any fixed pattern of life. "Unhappiness," he remarks in *A Sort of Life*, "is a daily routine";[14] and referring to his mental collapse at the age of sixteen: "I think it may have been the interminable repetitions in my life which finally broke me down."[15] Throughout these writings there is a recurrent theme: boredom. And this is no trivial *ennui*, but a crushing manic-depressive tendency which verges on madness and insists on Greene's "escape" from the public life to the private.

On the simplest level, this is escape from the Pooters. There are frequent, if oblique, suggestions of distaste for bourgeois conformism. Of his forebears he says that he now feels "closest"[16] to his father's father, the man who ran away to St. Kitts at the age of fourteen. "He wasn't made for the family life in Bedford," he notes and wryly adds:

> He wasn't much missed, judging from Alice's letters to her brother Graham in London. Life in Bedford was as exciting as ever, with birthday treats and excursions and tea in the garden and walks by moonlight and the seductive behaviour on a tricycle at Barford of my other grandfather's curate, Mr. Humble, and a further visit from

the alarming Mr. Rust ('He is so utterly inscrutable in his looks, words and deeds, that I know no more what his feelings are than if he were the Sphynx').[17]

No commentary is offered, but the irony is unmistakable. Greene's attitude to the *frissons* of provincial existence is derisory; the breathless haste of the passage mocks Alice's stupidity. Narrow-mindedness is something he particularly associates with England and what he terms elsewhere its "parish-pump mentality."[18] But this approach extends much further to a distaste for the secure self-confidence of all such societies in the face of what he takes to be the world's intrinsic disorder. As such, it colours his political views causing him to sympathise with the underdogs who must battle against the great world powers. He now looks back on his brief membership of the Communist Party at Oxford as a puerile aberration and has no faith in "socialist realism,"[19] yet his loathing for the United States is unremitting. His travels to Indo-China, Cuba and Central America have only confirmed his horror of American imperialism: "The terrifying weight of this consumer society," he remarks in *The Other Man*, "oppresses me."[20]

On a deeper level, however, this need to escape from the "public" life is intimately connected with his most fundamental psychological difficulties and with the act of writing itself. He roots his manic-depressive tendency and his desire to write in his schooldays. The depression, indeed, is directly productive of his art: "Writing is a form of therapy," he says in *Ways of Escape*; "sometimes I wonder how all those who do not write, compose or paint can manage to escape the madness, the melancholia, the panic fear which is inherent in the human situation."[21] He learnt his lessons in "madness" and "melancholia" early, at his public school, Berkhampstead, where his father was headmaster.

The language in which he deals with this experience offers a coherent analogue with the world of espionage. At Berkhampstead he discovered a profound confusion of "public" and "private" identities. On the school side of the green baize door his sense of privacy and aesthetic delicacy were outraged: "no moment of the night was free from noise, a cough, a snore, a fart."[22] On Sunday hikes in the surrounding countryside "no one, under any circumstances, would ever walk dangerously alone."[23] From his days in the school O.T.C. he developed "a permanent dislike of uniforms"[24] and of uniformity. Carrying the analogy a stage further, he sees himself less as a soldier in the regular army of society than as a member of the Maquis subverting the forces of occupation. It was something deeply imprinted upon him by the alienation and humiliations of his schooldays. "I had friends, a few, but I was also my father's son – and they disliked my father," he told Mlle. Allain. "I belonged to neither side. I couldn't side with the boys without betraying my father, and they regarded me like a collaborator in occupied territory. I made obvious use of these divided loyalties in the person of the priest in *The Power And The Glory*."[25] It is significant, surely, that Greene, a man who dislikes being interviewed, should submit to the (often banal) interrogation of Mlle. Allain. Why did he make this exception? Because she is the daughter of a former close friend, a prominent member of the Maquis during the Second World War who had been abducted and assassinated in Morocco. It was Greene's memorial to a fellow traveller.

This *leit motif* – the " 'dangerous edge of things' ... the narrow boundary between loyalty and disloyalty ... the paradox one carries within oneself"[26] – is, of course, the obsessive concern of his fiction. But it is not to our purpose to pursue this here other than to note its congruence with the image Greene constructs of his earlier self and to argue that this idea of the writer as double agent is crucial to an understanding of the particular problems facing him in writing autobiography. Again, discussing his schooldays he suggests that his horror of "the total absence of solitude"[27] led him to a schizophrenic (and potentially self-destructive) frame of mind: on the one hand, he was tortured by rejection; on the other, he thirsted for isolation. In retrospect, he sees this mental conflict as crucial to the nascent writer. The writer, he says, cannot afford to be partisan:

> a novelist is a creature without scruples, which is tiring. The novelist's station is on the ambiguous borderline between the just and the unjust, between doubt and clarity. But he has to be unscrupulous.... I would take Mauriac as an example not to follow. I'm a great admirer of some of his books. But his loyalty to the Catholic Church has made him rather too 'scrupulous' a writer – in the theological rather than in the moral sense.... A writer must be able to cross over, to 'change sides at the drop of a hat. He stands for the victims and the victims change.'[28]

In Greene's autobiographical writings, however, the victim–hero is Greene himself and the oppressors "real" people. His normal pose as "unscrupulous" double agent faces him with a particularly delicate problem here where his charity refuses to invade the privacy of these friends and acquaintances. He partially solves it, as suggested earlier, by omitting them from the story. But this leaves him both with enormous gaps in his history and with the dual difficulty of avoiding egotistical self-congratulation and maintaining that crucial anonymity. The first difficulty is resolved by the presentation of his life as the history of a series of "selves" and the second by the stylistic dexterity of producing what is effectively an "impressionist" text, deliberately rendering the visible universe through a series of arbitrarily related sense impressions and a disruption of the unities of time, place and action.

A persistently reiterated theme is that, finding himself faced with potential mental breakdown, Greene sought through danger (Russian roulette, travel), heightened sensual experience and art to escape the crippling constrictions of "civilized" life. "I write not to be read," he told Mlle. Allain, "but for my own relief. My only readership is me."[29] He consistently refers to the importance of the unconscious mind in the act of writing. "Memory," if by this we signify accurate recollection, is in many ways seen to be the enemy of art. "Perhaps a novelist has a greater ability to forget than other men –," he writes in *A Sort of Life*; "he has to forget or become sterile. What he forgets is the compost of the imagination."[30] This naturally presents a particular problem to the autobiographer. Looking back, even at his own writings, Greene finds small correspondence between his contemporary accounts of events and his present memory of them:

> It is a curious experience to read an account of one's own past written by – whom? Surely not by myself. The self of forty years ago is not the self of today and I read my own book, *The Lawless Roads*,[31] as a stranger would. So many incidents in my story have been buried completely in my subconscious: so many I now recall only faintly like moments in a novel which I once read when I was young. And yet *The Lawless Roads* is not a novel, only a personal impression of a small part of Mexico at a particular time.... These are all facts, I tell myself. These things really happened to me – in 1937–8 – or at least to that long-dead man who bore the same names on his passport as I do.[32]

Like so many of Greene's statements in these writings, its lucidity is deceptive. What appears almost as an elaboration of the obvious – "people forget things" – suggests, on further consideration, a whole vista of receding complexities.

Memory, as has been said, is a particular problem for a writer like Greene who relies so heavily on the unconscious mind: he *needs* to forget. But there are two further, quite specific, obstacles to accurate recollection. The first is that, as a writer, he has spent more time with imaginary characters than with "real" ones. "No wonder ... a novelist often makes a bad husband or an unstable lover," he says. "There is something in his character of the actor who continues to play Othello when he is off the stage, but he is an actor who has lived far too many parts during far too many long runs. He is encrusted with characters."[33] The second is that during this intimate involvement with the imaginary and the subconscious, the book changes the author: "With a novel, which perhaps takes years to write, the author is not the same man at the end of the book as he was at the beginning. It is not only that his characters have developed – he has developed with them."[34] Beyond all this, of course, lies the minefield of mystical or "magical" experience which colours so much of Greene's view of the visible universe: intimations of predestination, dream, *déja vu* ("I have been here before") and the Catholic faith. It is no wonder, then, that autobiography, which traditionally purports to describe a single developing self, should prove such a profoundly difficult genre for Greene. Whereas, in fiction, he writes to escape his "self" through a search for others' characters, in autobiography he must use his therapeutic art for precisely the reverse purpose and attempt to confront those earlier "selves" which he has been burying since the age of sixteen. *A Sort of Life* began literally as a therapeutic exercise. On the verge of another mental breakdown, he had approached a psychoanalyst requesting electric shock treatment. The analyst had refused and instead asked Greene to record his early life.[35] In a sense, he is forcing himself in his autobiography to name those deliberately unlabelled, deep-seated horrors rendered anonymous by his conscious mind.

Again, Greene's aesthetic notions are directly relevant here; to repeat myself, the problems of literary presentation are exactly equivalent to the problems of self-knowledge. "One simply forgets one's own existence," he told Mlle. Allain about his process of composition. "It's not so much a question of taking leave of oneself . . . : it's more a case of taking leave of one's conscious 'I'. Telling one's dreams to a psycho-analyst every day gives one the same sensation: while the dreams are a part of oneself, in reciting them one has the illusion of their being part of quite another life. Books and dreams have that much in common, I suppose."[36]

If we place this statement beside two images of Greene encountering difficulties in fictional composition, an interesting reciprocity emerges between "forgetting" and "naming." In the first, we see him struggling with Querry's character in his African journal: "How few letters there are one can use in place of a name. . . . Can I avoid names altogether for the principals as I did in *The Power and The Glory*?"[37] The second comes from *Ways of Escape* and refers to *The Human Factor*. Chant, Chase and Crane had been leading figures in unsuccessful books. He was superstitious about the letter "C": "I tried my best to give [Castle] another name, but there is a magic quality in names – to change the name is to change the character. Castle it had to be, but I went ahead with a sense of almost certain failure."[38] The three phrases: "in reciting [dreams] one has the illusion of their being part of quite another life"; "Can I avoid names altogether?"; and "there is a magic quality in names," suggest that Greene has two interdependent senses of reality: that belonging to the "conscious" and that to the "unconscious 'I'." The word "illusion" does not so much establish that the world of dreams, of mystical experience, is false, as that we have no choice but to live in the material world.

Greene is famous for his relish of ecclesiastical paradox. Here we have a psychological one: man escapes the regularity, embarrassments and degradation of the material world through dreams. Yet it is only through dreams, through the unconscious, that Greene finds a path back to the "real" world. Staring straight at it, without this intermediary imaginative process, he sees nothing more than what Waugh termed "the knockabout farce of people's outward behaviour."[39] To name a character locates and locks him or her in the material world, limits and fixes possibility. Hence he defers this until the last possible moment, as he prefers his figures to develop autonomously. He prefers to feel uncertain as to what they will do next, just as he prefers to forget in order to imagine.

In autobiography, we might think this need not be a problem or, at least, it is a problem already solved. He *knows* what happened next. But does he? Or, perhaps more relevant, does he want to? These are questions repeatedly suggested by the fragmentary nature of *A Sort of Life*. He knows, of course, an outline of the "facts" – the dates, the places, the crucial meetings and partings – but somehow this historical "knowledge" does nothing to elucidate the character of Graham Greene. It belongs to the material (public) world, the "conscious 'I'." It does nothing to explain how things happened "to that long-dead man who bore the same names on his passport." "It is a disadvantage to have an 'I' who is not a fictional figure," he notes in *Ways of Escape*, "and the only way to deal with 'I' was to make him [in *Journey Without Maps* (1934)] an abstraction. To all intents I eliminated my companion of the journey and supported the uneventful record with memories, dreams, world-associations."[40] "To all intents" this is precisely what he does in all his autobiographical writings. His "companions" are largely "eliminated," not egotistically to concentrate attention upon himself as a more substantial figure, but for precisely the reverse reason: to render "himself" an abstraction.

When he comes to recount his personal history, then, Greene is unwilling to present his account as a sequence of empirical data. "I sometimes wonder" is a typical prefix to some rumination on the mystical dimension (or, simply, the intangible nature) of human experience:

> I sometimes wonder whether [Nordahl Grieg] didn't also leave spells in far places which drew me there long afterwards. Why did I take a solitary holiday in Estonia in the thirties? Was it because I was following in his footsteps? And Moscow in the fifties?[41]

Throughout these accounts mystery, magic, *déja vu*, coincidence, religious belief combine to create a trance-like atmosphere in which the central figure floats in a sea of forces beyond rational comprehension. He describes himself in 1931, after the commercial failure of two novels, as suffering from "the desolate isolation of defeat, like a casualty who has been left behind and forgotten."[42] Grieg's arrival at this point "down a muddy Gloucestershire lane ... seemed unaccountable, dreamlike and oddly encouraging. Like the appearance of three crows on a gate, [he] was an omen or a myth, and he remained a myth. Even his death was to prove legendary...."[43]

The act of reminiscence is in itself painful:

> The further back we research the past, the more the 'documents in the case' accumulate and the more reluctant we feel to open their pages, to disturb the dust.... one is never certain what vivid memory may not revive, and the longer life goes on, the more surely one finds that old memories will be painful.[44]

But there seem to be other reasons, apart from the gentlemanly reticence already noted, for his unwillingness to present us with a coherent, sequential account of the "documents in the case." One is that to present such a dossier might wreck that precious anonymity vital to his function as the "double-agent" novelist. Another is that he does not believe such an account possible: first because, like the hardened spy, he has lived so long with so many alternative identities that he can no longer distinguish the truth from the fiction; and second, because he does not believe either in the Victorian concept of linear progression in historical accounts, or in the naturalist notion of the direct transference of empirical data to writing.

For those who know Greene's early essay on Mauriac,[45] the last point may seem straightforwardly inaccurate. There, Greene appears to stand for the "objective" novel, for "reality" as something quite separate from any individual perception of it, and for the material presence of the "visible universe." We cannot, however, take that essay as representative of his current critical position. In the first place, Greene's defence of realism is not, as he pretends, based on the separate vitality of the material world, but is unrepentantly rooted in his belief in the supernatural (and, to muddle things further, he has consistently subscribed to the "point of view" technique developed by James, Ford and Conrad). Second, as he stresses in his autobiographical writings, he is not the man he was. Greene's religious position today is substantially changed. Whereas he entered the Church in 1926, unemotionally convinced by the arguments for the existence of God, today the balance has shifted. He makes the distinction between belief and faith. Belief is based upon argument; faith is an irrational acceptance of the tenets of his Church: "If I don't believe in X or Y, faith intervenes telling me that I'm wrong not to believe. Faith is above belief. One can say that it's a gift of God, while belief is not. Belief is founded on reason. On the whole I keep my faith while enduring long periods of disbelief."[46]

Greene's frankness about his religious doubts is one of the more startling aspects of his rigorous "honesty." He confesses to advocating birth control; he loses no opportunity to mock priests for their human failings; he has "small belief in the doctrine of eternal punishment";[47] he dislikes the term "sin";[48] he sympathises with "the agnostic reader";[49] and he can even begin a proposition with the blunt reservation: "if God exists – I'm not convinced He does …".[50] In short, he is an "odd" Catholic, though a Catholic he remains. His basic position (and personal torment) is clearly revealed in the short story "A Visit to Morin."[51]

As Greene has grown older, then, his faith in the power of the intellect to resolve any of life's contradictions has diminished. His belief in the tractable nature of the "visible universe" has slackened, it seems, at the same rate as his belief in God. We do not find him supporting Mauriac today with the assurance of 1945. Mauriac, as we have seen, considers a writer "not to follow" because he is too "scrupulous" in his religious allegiance; his Catholicism pre-judges all situations and places him perpetually on the side of the establishment (the "public" world), whether the establishment defends or persecutes "the victims."

It is crucial to Greene's image of himself as a writer that he should remain a "victim." One of Mlle. Allain's prefatory remarks pinpoints this paradox: "After so many years of success, Graham Greene is still soliciting a sort of failure – without obtaining it."[52] Greene's belief in his personal failure is, of course, perfectly genuine. He recognises unsentimentally that he has been a "bad husband and a fickle lover";[53] he compares his life's work to the great masters' and despairs at his "flawed intention." Just as the priest cannot hope to become a saint, so Greene acknowledges that he cannot compete with Tolstoy, Balzac, or Dickens: "for a writer as much as a priest, there is no such thing as success."[54] But he grows restive when critics talk of "Greenland" as an invention of his morbid, self-castigating imagination:

> [Greene-ian] is a term I can't stand, any more than the word 'Greenland'. I don't believe in it, I can't make it out. So don't go asking me to explain myself. I don't know myself, and I don't want to. Don't try to trap me with some sentence I wrote thirty to fifty years ago, expecting me to think the same way today. I am, remember, someone who changes. Each year I feel different.[55]

This may appear to be simply evasive. But success for a writer, as he says in *A Sort of Life*, "is only a delayed failure" (156). He chooses to present this composite image of his disparate earlier selves – the atheist and the convert, the fearful schoolboy and pugnacious under-graduate, the political radical and supporter of the Establishment during the General Strike, the bachelor and the married man – as an elaboration of a central theme: failure as a condition of life. None of these identities satisfactorily accommodates his "curiosity" or his "desire to reduce the chaos of experience to some sort of order" (9). Writing can provide a substitute, aesthetic, control over the phantasmagoria of events. Analytical reasoning, however, appears to him to be more or less irrelevant. He can no longer remember the arguments for the existence of God (190). "The experience of a long life may possibly increase one's intuition of human character, but the mass of memories and associations which we drag round with us like an over-full suitcase on our interminable journey would weary me now at the start with all such arguments as we indulged in then. I cannot be bothered to remember – I accept" (121). Even the first statement here is qualified by "possibly."

A Sort of Life is the story of a "successful" writer who wishes to depict himself as the reverse. "Success" connotes contentment in the popular imagination and Greene is a melancholy man – sympathetic, modest, temperamentally inclined towards a relentless search for sensation, but a self-confessed manic-depressive. The essence of this depression, it seems, lies in his profound sense of failure – of loss. The "scraps of the past" which he selects for *A Sort of Life* end "prematurely" "with the years of failure which followed the acceptance of my first novel" (9). As such his history of early disappointment is emblematic of the rest of his career as well. Essentially it comes down to a failure to accommodate himself to "public" life.

Various techniques are used which he has learnt from his early masters, Ford, Conrad and James: a range of "voices," all framed by the sceptical authorial rhetoric of an older man who refuses to pretend to omniscience;

chronological distortion circling outwards from the focal "present" to connect events by association rather than historical contingency; the juxtaposition of apparently irrelevant detailed observations of the physical environment to suggest images of that failure and degradation which is his subject:

> And then there remains to be set reluctantly on my personal map the School – part rosy Tudor, part hideous modern brick the colour of dolls'-house plaster homes – where the misery of life started, and the burial ground, long disused, which lay opposite our windows, separated from our flower-beds by an invisible line, so that every year the gardener would turn up a few scraps of human bone in remaking the herbaceous border. Further off, to the north, on the green spaces of a map empty as Africa, by the wastes of gorse and bracken of the great Common which extended to Ashridge Park, and to the south the small Brickhill Common and the park of Ashlyns, where once I saw a Jack in the Green covered with spring leaves, dancing cumbrously among his attendants like the devils I met later in Liberia.[56]

Chronologically this moves from Tudor times to Greene's mature manhood. In tone it varies from depicting the school as a place of repulsive bourgeois stagnation ("part hideous modern brick ... plaster homes") to offering an image of this dull institution as the focus of dark and mysterious forces. Beyond lies the Common and its associations of freedom and danger. The Jack in the Green acts as a metaphor for this thinly-buried and tempting primitivism, just as the "invisible line" between the tidy herbaceous borders and those wild forces is reflective of that borderline on which the double-agent novelist was to live his uncertain life. Even the phrase "turn up a few scraps" suggests association with his "And the motive for recording these scraps of the past?" one page earlier. Greene is, surely, self-referential here, aligning himself with the gardener, unearthing odd pieces of human remains, in this case his own.

In general, the technique of the book, while purporting to offer an ordered sequential account of empirical data, works towards the subversion of such an account. *A Sort of Life* is full of playfully irrelevant footnotes. The passage quoted above has the surface rhetoric of the comfortable "scene-setting" of a Bennett or Galsworthy, yet tends rather to unsettle the reader's assumptions about the literal nature of the description. As dream and "reality" merge ("But how could I have imagined Miranda?" [49–50]), Greene attacks our complacency. The ending of the book is thoroughly in keeping with this. He depicts himself as middle-aged in Siam, sadder but not wiser, smoking opium with an old Oxford friend who has "accepted the idea of failure" (156). Instead of a constructed climax or conclusion to this history we have a casual conversation mellowed by years and narcotic reverie. The concluding words are simple, arbitrary and inconclusive. Even the distinction between the apparent "success" of Greene's career and the failure of his friend's is blurred: if anything, Greene's sense of his own inadequacy is seen to be the greater by virtue of his chosen profession.

Greene's observations about writing, then, are studded with self-questioning about a series of related aesthetic problems: serious attention is paid to the use of narrators, the "point of view," chronological distortion, "free association."[57] The difficulty he faces in his 1959 journal, for instance, is typical: "Through whose eyes shall I tell my story?"[58] When Mlle. Allain confronted him with: "In *Under the Garden* you say that there are two important things in life, 'laughter and fear' " he quickly retorted: "It's not I who say so – it's the narrator, Wilditch. At that time, 1962–3, I probably shared his view, for I was Wilditch as I wrote. Today – I don't know. I'm no longer in the same situation as he was in."[59]

The distinction between life and its literary reconstruction, between the raw material of experience captured by memory, and its author's selective presentation is of crucial importance to Greene. The first can belong to the "conscious 'I'," the public life, empirical evidence, depending on the proximity of the author's to the narrator's point of view. With the passage of time, however, that correspondence inevitably decays to become part of the "unconscious 'I' " 's perspective, the private life, the unconscious, something belonging to the ambiguous past reclaimable only through fragmentary and partial recollection. Greene is only too well aware that as Peter Berger puts it, "memory itself is a re-iterated act of interpretation."[60] He consistently denies writing *romans à clef* for the simple reason that he can "know" a fictional character far better than he could ever know an acquaintance. In writing autobiography, though, this escape route to fictional omniscience is blocked: the "character" is himself and he is, at least notionally, refused the liberty of invention.

Mlle. Allain noticed in her *Conversations* Greene's reluctance to use the first person singular. "You say 'one', not 'I'. Why is that?" "Yes, I know; it's a habit," he replied:

> one of those tics I often have to suppress when I'm writing. I suppose I don't like being too personal. In ... *Ways of Escape*, I never wanted to use the first person; as a result, in my new version I have had to suppress all the *ones* even though they're more precise than *we*, with its connotation of several individuals sharing an identical view of things. *One* presupposes a single individual – a more abstract one, I'll grant you. I'll admit, too, that it's a way of escaping from myself.[61]

In *A Sort of Life* he has no such choice: the "I" of autobiography is unavoidable. But he solves the problem by presenting the "conscious 'I' " as an abstraction, a plurality of selves, and its memories as relative.

To support this image of self, the narrative style of all his autobiographical writing is deliberately digressive and his remarks on the nature of memory confirm the notion that the "self" is constantly making and un-making its own image. In a footnote to his "Congo Journal" he says: "I do not apologise for such digressions. Memories are a form of simile: when we say something is 'like' we are remembering."[62] By the same token, when Greene says that he is "remembering" he is offering not an accurate account of the "facts" but a simile for, an image of, them. "Memory," he says in *A Sort of Life*, "is like a long broken night. As I write, it is as though I am waking from sleep continually to grasp at an image which I hope may drag in its wake a whole intact dream, but the fragments remain fragments, the complete story always escapes."[63] Speaking of his fiction, he said to Mlle. Allain, "Only God and the author are omniscient, not the one who says 'I'."[64] But in *A Sort of Life*, inescapably the one saying "I" *and* the author, he is faced with an unusual problem as a writer: he cannot know his central character. In the world of his autobiography, only God can be omniscient and Greene is no longer certain of his existence.

"I see myself now," he wrote at the beginning of *Ways of Escape*, "as a character in an historical novel writing the first words of an historical novel."[65] His "memories" in these writings are presented not so much as "facts" belonging to a sequential development as incidents which may or may not have involved another "long-dead" man, a fictional figure carrying the same name as Graham Greene:

> The first thing I remember is sitting in a pram at the top of a hill with a dead dog lying at my feet.... The memory may well be a true one as my mother once told me how surprised she had been months later by some reference which I made to the 'poor dog'.[66]

The second statement undercuts the factual validity of the first. It shifts the emphasis from our need to attach significance to empirical data towards the crucial importance of the memory, the perception, of the individual in reconstructing experience. It is irrelevant to Greene whether there be any correspondence between the two and central to his construction of his own "character" that he should be seen as a "victim" of historical process.

As such, these fragmentary memories present a consistent and, in one sense, wholly "unreliable" series of recollections. If we are to believe Greene, his childhood was nothing but a series of macabre events – dead dogs, the white mouse which ate its partner and died of loneliness, the tin jerry full of blood, the man cutting his throat at a window. These images create a profound impression of loneliness, alienation, suffering. But it matters nothing whether we believe them to be an accurate record of his early years. It matters greatly that we should believe them to be an honest recollection of the selective memory available to quite another person recalling them.

A Sort of Life is arguably a fiction presented by the "conscious 'I'" describing the "unconscious 'I.'" It offers no guarantee, any more than does the hero of one of Greene's favourite novels, *The Good Soldier*, that we can make sense of it all. It is a book which analyses fear and failure as the recurrent *leit motifs* of Greene's life, but suggests a profounder terror: that of discovering the "truth" about himself. And from this he always backs away: "I've no wish to present any image of myself," he told Mlle. Allain. And when she pursued the idea – "So there does exist somewhere or other a true image?" – he replied:

> That's for others to discover, not me. I expect you're familiar with Henry James's words about 'the pattern in the carpet'. In any body of work there's always a pattern to be found. Well, *I* don't want to see it. When a critic discovers certain keynotes, that's fine and may be of interest, but I don't want to be steeped in his discoveries, I want to remain unaware of them. Otherwise I think my imagination would dry up.[67]

This is neither moral cowardice nor a failure to maintain that scrupulous honesty mentioned earlier: it is a brutal acknowledgement of the terror of self-confrontation.

One is reminded of other themes noted in this essay: his unwillingness to attach names, his desire for anonymity, his need to forget, to divorce the conscious and unconscious self. *A Sort of Life* is an extraordinary autobiography in that it is written by a man who admits to a fear of extensive self-knowledge. He sympathises with Rilke who "was afraid of psycho-analysis. He said he was frightened that it might clear everything up, to the detriment of his unconscious mind – the part of the mind which nourishes creativity."[68] For all its honest probing at delicate nerves – the phobias, the embarrassments, the failures – *A Sort of Life* is a book which ultimately seeks to protect his fears rather than to exorcise them. Greene, it seems, requires the stimulus of fear as other people need the security of conformism. At the end of his life the saddest note is struck by the approach of the ultimate horror: "I'm not afraid any more – that's the real bore."[69]

It is significant, surely, that he should conclude *Ways of Escape* with a chapter called "The Other." It documents his fascination with the man (or men?) who for many years has been masquerading as "Graham Greene." Newspaper reports and photographs, those agencies of the public world of "fact," present another person assuming Greene's identity. He relishes the phenomenon – probably a perfectly straightforward confidence trick – as near-supernatural, deliciously absurd, mysterious, frightening. He pictures the shadowy figure as a *Doppelgänger*. On one occasion he was informed that the other Graham Greene had been arrested in India and was imprisoned in Assam. Greene arranged a commission with *Picture Post* to take him there and confront "Other." But before he could set off, Other had broken bail. One senses a certain unspoken relief on Greene's part. The Edward Thomas poem from which he derives his *Doppelgänger*'s soubriquet is quoted at the beginning of the chapter, the ending selected for special attention:

> He goes: I follow: no release
> Until he ceases. Then I shall cease.[73]

Can there be any doubt, in the light of his other statements, that, despite
his ostensible determination to track down his persecutor, he would not,
ultimately, wish to find him? It would represent a confrontation of
Greene's private and public lives, of imagination and empirical data, faith
and belief. Were he to meet Other, his mystery would be killed and with it
would disappear a source of fantasy and fear, a powerful emblem of the
intractable nature of the visible universe. Just as Greene fears that
psychoanalysis might unravel those mysteries in his unconscious mind
which are so productive of imaginative thought, so he fears in his
autobiography the resolution of the conundrum of his selves. If there be a
pattern in the carpet he doesn't want to know about it; if there be a
"correct" preference for either the empirical or the subjective mode of
thought, he prefers not to make it. But this very hesitation implies that
the decision has already been made: he has moved away from belief
towards faith; he prefers mystery to "fact." The Other needs to remain
anonymous. To name him would be to imprison him permanently in the
material world.

MARTIN STANNARD

NOTES

1. Graham Greene, *Collected Essays* (London: Bodley Head, 1969; repr. Harmondsworth: Penguin Books, 1970), p. 153.
2. *Ibid.*, p. 149.
3. Graham Greene, *A Sort of Life* (London: Bodley Head, 1971; repr. Harmondsworth:
   Penguin Books, 1972 and 1974).
4. Graham Greene, *In Search of a Character. Two African Journals* (London: Bodley
   Head, 1961). The second "journal," "Convoy to West Africa," first appeared in *The
   Mint* in 1946.
5. Graham Greene, *Ways of Escape* (London: Bodley Head, 1980).
6. Marie-Françoise Allain ed., *The Other Man. Conversations With Graham Greene*
   (London: Bodley Head, 1983); originally published as "L'Autre et Son Double"
   (Belfond, 1981).
7. *Ways of Escape*, p. 45.
8. Graham Greene, "Under the Garden," *A Sense of Reality* (London: Bodley Head,
   1963; repr. Harmondsworth: Penguin Books, 1968), pp. 9–64.
9. *Collected Essays*, pp. 153–4.
10. *The Other Man*, pp. 113–14.
11. *Ibid.*, p. 32.
12. *A Sort of Life*, p. 15.
13. In a talk given to the Leicester University Literary Society Greene stated that: "I think
    the trouble is that it becomes more and more difficult to be anonymous ... when one is a
    young writer one can pass through the jungle with protective colouring.... You know
    it's a question of a novelist being able to hide like a tiger from the media."
14. *Ibid.*, p. 59.
15. *Ibid.*, p. 64.
16. *Ibid.*, p. 69.
17. *Ibid.*, p. 71.
18. *The Other Man*, pp. 108–9.
19. *Ibid.*, p. 83.
20. *Ibid.*, p. 94.

21. *Ways of Escape*, p. 275.
22. *A Sort of Life*, p. 54.
23. *Ibid.*, p. 58.
24. *Ibid.*, p. 63.
25. *The Other Man*, pp. 25–6. See also *A Sort of Life*, pp. 54–5: "Was my father not the headmaster? I was like the son of a quisling in a country under occupation. My elder brother Raymond was a school prefect and head of the house – in other words one of Quisling's collaborators. I was surrounded by the forces of resistance, and yet I couldn't join them without betraying my father and my brother."
26. *The Other Man*, p. 19.
27. *Ibid.*, p. 34.
28. *Ibid.*, p. 82.
29. *Ibid.*, p. 121.
30. *A Sort of Life*, p. 132.
31. Graham Greene, *The Lawless Roads* (London: Heinemann, 1939).
32. *Ways of Escape*, p. 81.
33. *Ibid.*, p. 273.
34. *Ibid.*, pp. 272–3.
35. Information reiterated in the talk at the Leicester University Literary Society; see note 13 above.
36. *The Other Man*, pp. 137–8.
37. *In Search of a Character*, p. 74.
38. *Ways of Escape*, p. 20.
39. "Fan-Fare," *Life* (International: Chicago), 8 April, 1946, pp. 53–60; re-printed Donat Gallagher ed., *Evelyn Waugh. A Little Order* (London: Eyre Methuen, 1977), p. 32.
40. *Ways of Escape*, p. 48.
41. *Ways of Escape*, p. 21.
42. *Ibid.*, p. 20.
43. *Ibid.*, pp. 20–1.
44. *Ways of Escape*, p. 45.
45. Graham Greene, "François Mauriac," *Collected Essays*, pp. 91–6.
46. *The Other Man*, p. 173.
47. *Ways of Escape*, p. 121.
48. *The Other Man*, p. 158.
49. *Ways of Escape*, p. 137.
50. *The Other Man*, p. 161.
51. Graham Greene, *A Sense of Reality*, *op. cit.*, pp. 65–79.
52. *The Other Man*, p. 175.
53. *Ibid.*, p. 142.
54. *Collected Essays*, p. 345.
55. *The Other Man*, p. 18.
56. *A Sort of Life*, pp. 11–12.
57. Cf. *The Other Man*, pp. 125, 129, 131, 137.
58. *In Search of a Character*, p. 21.
59. *The Other Man*, p. 129.
60. Peter L. Berger, *Invitation to Sociology. A Humanist Perspective* (New York: Doubleday, 1963; repr. Harmondsworth: Pelican Books, 1966), p. 70.
61. *Ibid.*, p. 21.
62. *In Search of a Character*, p. 49.
63. *A Sort of Life*, p. 25.
64. *The Other Man*, p. 131.
65. *Ways of Escape*, p. 11.
66. *A Sort of Life*, p. 13.
67. *The Other Man*, p. 22.
68. *Ibid.*, p. 15.
69. *Ibid.*, p. 183.
70. Edward Thomas, "The Other," quoted in *Ways of Escape*, p. 301.

Autobiography and Fiction

I

The writing of a diary can be attributed to various promptings – curiosity, vanity, anxiety, a need for self-expression; but underlying all of them is the desire, implicit in any imaginative literary undertaking, to record what for the writer is "the truth," by describing, and to that extent controlling, the flux of daily sensations and impressions. To keep a diary not only nails time down, it assumes the diarist's power to set time in order. But, through the substantiation of some memories and the correction of others, a diary is a reminder that this ordering of time is only provisional. Memory has editors; social conditioning, heredity and temperament all determine what is recalled. Yet just as the process of recollection can be opened up through psychoanalysis, or modulated through religious conversion, so it can, through the impulse towards autobiography, attain to the objective status of an art.

The authors of diaries and autobiographies are engaged on the impossible task of objectifying something that remains elusive; they aspire to a knowledge of themselves that would be synonomous with writers' knowledge of their artefacts.

In their finite and selective nature the diary and the autobiography are akin to the novel, though the objective truthfulness of the first two is based on particulars, of the novel on generalities. But whereas the material that does not find its way into the final draft of a novel is irrelevant to the text as it stands, a knowledge of the rejected aspects of an autobiography or published diary can affect its credibility. The great autobiographies and diaries, however, are independent of such exactions: they have the self-sufficiency of a novel, their authority depending on the quality of the imagination that has shaped them.

When an imaginative writer turns to autobiography or keeps a journal, the result is likely to be not only a record of events but also an exploration of the origins and formation of the personality of the recorder. The work both narrates what memory selected and attempts to account for that selection. The diaries of Virginia Woolf are a case in point. While genuinely private, and not, like those of André Gide or Julian Green, designed to be read by others (still less designed to look as if designed to be read, as in the case of Cyril Connolly's *The Unquiet Grave*), they are written in the knowledge that the self is not fixed or solid, is not simply an observer or an agent, but that it can change, can react to what it sees and records in the moment of recording it, and can be object as well as subject in the transitive process of analysing its experience. This is why the Woolf diaries reveal the nature of their keeper more consistently than do her letters, letters being the product of the recipient as well as of the sender, even when the sender is (as was, for instance, D.H. Lawrence) egoistical. The mere fact of the other person's presence conditions what is being said. We are all each other's fictional creations, not only in how we see each other, but in how we induce others to see us.

Autobiography is one method of seeking to halt this process of endless relativity: it proffers, as it were, a final version, a definitive reading of a text, authenticated by an intimate and even exclusive knowledge of that text's origins (and a more provisional one of its motivations). And yet the attempt is inevitably doomed; each text absorbs its interpreters into itself, and the autobiographer no less than the critic becomes part of the total, ever varying event which is the work, and thus also of the response to and effect of that work which is the reading process. Each autobiography is a provisional version of events, and reflects not only on its raw materials but on the author who selected them.

There is therefore a certain irony in the fact that the earliest English novelists should have resorted to fictional autobiographies in order to authenticate the truthfulness of what they had to say. Defoe with his narrators, Richardson with his diligent letter-writers, pay authorial lip-service to the superior value of non-fictional narrative, with some consequent absurdities. In *Pamela*, for example, Richardson finds himself forced to account for his heroine's obtaining both paper and time with which to produce the novel in which she is appearing. The absurdity lies in the need to placate the literal-minded reader. Other novelists, however, were prepared not only to recognize but to encourage artifice. Fielding's awareness of the arbitrary nature of novel-writing is evident in the stylised organisation and interpolations of *Tom Jones*; while in *Tristram Shandy* Sterne both satirises Richardson's concern with plausibility and elaborates upon it, conversing with and haranguing his readers, and even involving them in the action, in one case dismissing a lady reader from the room, and thus from the book itself, while continuing to address his other readers until her return. Moreover, the novel originates in a satire upon autobiography as such.

But in the naturalistic conventions of the Victorian novel such sophisticated authorial freedom degenerates into moralising and facetiousness. The element of play turns into a feeling of uneasy responsibility for the moral tone of a readership. For a novel to be respectable it had to be "true to life." The Protestantism of the age, with its distrust of art as being potentially idolatrous, encouraged the study of the world as it was seen to be. Fidelity to recognizable experience was a mark of the serious Victorian novelist (the exaggerations and the symbolism employed by Dickens are atypical); and their role was to be that of recorders of events to which they could personally attest – Thackeray's use of Arthur Pendennis as narrator of *The Newcomes* and *Philip* being a characteristic instance. But the need for authenticity brooks no compromise: the same author's shuffling of his puppets back into the box at the end of *Vanity Fair* entirely lacks the debonair insolence of Fielding or Sterne. He is, in effect, apologetic by default.

It is through the developing use of relativity of viewpoint that the provisional nature of truth is conveyed in Victorian fiction. The experiments in diverse first-person narrative found in eighteenth-century novels as different as *Humphry Clinker* and *Clarissa* are developed not only in *Wuthering Heights* and, to a modified extent, in *Bleak House*, but in the work of such lesser writers as Wilkie Collins and Mrs Craik. The latter's *A Life for a Life*, while as moralistic as her popular *John Halifax, Gentleman*, through its alternating narratives by heroine and hero ensures the reader's awareness that while the truth of both characters is absolute for themselves, it is relative with regard to each other. A balance between fact and fiction is struck within the novel itself.

But the majority of Victorian novelists are content with a single authorial point of view, truth in fiction being treated as of the same kind as historical truth, and as that found in biographical writings. In the late nineteenth and early twentieth centuries the publication of memoirs proliferated, memoirs being records of things seen rather than of the nature of the seeing. Those of the Countess of Cardigan, for instance, conclude with the confident statement that she had done everything worth doing and known everyone worth knowing, for *My Recollections* (1909) is the autobiography of an achiever, a "deedy" person (to quote Ivy Compton-Burnett, whose own potential autobiography was so perfectly absorbed into her seemingly objective novels). Such works range from the ghost-written stories of film stars, sportsmen and radio celebrities (frequently rather touching in their artless insincerity) to the recollections of Cabinet ministers, politicians and generals, anxious to state their case and to "get the record straight." That particular rigid linear metaphor is instructive in its avoidance of such qualities as shading and ambiguity and of other people's points of view; but all such "factual" accounts are probably more misleading than are avowedly subjective ones. Literal-minded, their authors regard the truth as unconditional and within everybody's reach, treating their material as fixed and inanimate, matter for exploitation merely.

Indeed, a novel may be far more revelatory of its author than is a formal autobiography, especially in the case of reticent temperaments: the respective autobiographies and fictional writings of Siegfried Sassoon and Anthony Powell come to mind in this respect; and a fusion of the two modes of writing, as in Jocelyn Brooke's *The Military Orchid* (1948) and its successors, can preserve an author's privacy more effectively than can their separation. We know Trollope as much through *Barchester Towers* and *The Way We Live Now* as we do through his singularly prosaic autobiography.

Certainly the nineteenth century does not yield many autobiographies of sustained intensity and subjective exploration. *The Prelude* is unique as an examination of the growth of a poet's mind; but to conduct a similar examination in prose seems to have been beyond the literary and imaginative resources of the age. The more intimate autobiographical writings, such as those of Ruskin and Carlyle, tend to be fragmentary and discursive (both were written in old age); other writers are more interested in the explication and resolution of a particular issue in terms of developing experience, Newman and J.S. Mill being obvious cases in point. The writings of De Quincey apart, nineteenth-century autobiographies do not extend the boundaries of consciousness, perhaps because the peculiar validity of subjective vision was undervalued in a literary and moral climate still largely innocent of a sense of psychological relativity. Popular Protestantism discouraged exploratory self-examination in favour of the life of faith exhibited in good and heroic deeds.

But with the collapse of moral and religious certainties as the century drew to a close, the value of personal testamonies took on a new significance as witnessing to beliefs which had to be held in spite of, rather than because of, external evidence. The kind of faith in personal feeling voiced in *In Memorian* was to be the justification of a number of twentieth-century autobiographical writings which, while using the techniques and dramatic selectivity of the novel, do so in the name of a deeper truth than that of verifiable evidence. Their authors create an art form which to some extent resolves the misleading dichotomy between truth and fiction which has attended the course of the English novel to the present time; it is one which asserts and demonstrates the relativity of human experience in all its forms, but which none the less makes it possible to use the concept of the absolute in a way that continues to have meaning.

For if to adopt a specifically religious attitude by committing oneself to a church or creed is to accept a formulation or embodiment of truth as constituting a valid image of an absolute truth which is in itself unknowable, then the ability to recognize the continuing relativity of that provisional absolute marks the difference between bigotry and genuine faith. Although religious or spiritual autobiography is necessarily limited in its appeal (in so far as, to the unbeliever, the formulations accepted by the convert can only constitute another fiction), much depends on the honesty of the account of the quest as to whether the record be accessible and persuasive or not: at its best, as in an autobiography like C.S. Lewis's *Surprised by Joy* (1955), the reader is left as free in the text as though it were a novel; there is no inartistic bludgeoning at work, and as the story is that of a spiritual search and ends with that search's fulfilment, it is possible to participate in it without any sense of prior commitment.

Particularly interesting in this connection are the autobiographies of John Cowper Powys, Edwin Muir and Kathleen Raine. Different though their authors are in temperament, all three books reflect the tension between the propagation of a philosophy or a belief and the manner of its growth in the individual consciousness. Fact and the imaginative interpretation of fact combine to produce a personal reading of experience. But discussion of them needs to be prefaced by an account of certain other twentieth-century authors in whose more hybrid autobiographical writings the overlap of fiction and reportage results in a realisation of the

inseparability, where self-portraiture is concerned, of subjective interpretation and objective record. The achievements of these writers emphasise the necessarily artificial nature of the truth as the artificer conveys
it, and provide a perspective from which to assess the stature of the more
introspective autobiographies of the other three.

II

Artifice is not the same thing as mendacity. The latter tends to be casual
and unpremeditated. It can also be unintentional, though none the less
misleading for that. Rambling, unsupported reminiscences, however
entertaining, test the reader's credulity in a moral as well as rational sense
(the recollections of Ford Madox Ford are notoriously pleasurable in this
respect). But in autobiographical form the freely associative portrait of the
self-with-others relies on a perceptiveness that offsets its unreliability as
court-room evidence. Such a book is introverted only in that it stresses
"These I have known" rather than "This I have done". At its best it
amounts to a species of historical fiction, which, through the very nature
of its inventiveness (or unreliability) throws as much light upon its author
as upon its subject.

    Among the most accomplished examples of this kind of book are the
various autobiographical writings of George Moore. One says "various"
advisedly, for Moore chose to exhibit himself in a wide variety of roles –
as *enfant terrible* and exponent of all things French in *Confessions of a
Young Man* (1886); as amorist and connoisseur in *Memoirs of My Dead
Life* (1906); as the disenchanted, wry, amused participator in the Irish
Literary Revival in the masterly *Hail and Farewell* (1911–14); and as the
crotchety but genial bookworm of *Conversations in Ebury Street* (1924),
(the kind of fictional portrait essayed more sourly and self-critically by
Gissing in *The Private Papers of Henry Rycroft*). It is a recognizable
genre, a fictive *persona* licensing the expression of ideas for which the
author does not have to be directly accountable; rather, he turns himself
into a work of fiction – a dangerous game to play. A common factor in all
Moore's autobiographical works is a baffling mixture of wiry sensitivity
with a moral complacency that would be repellent were it not offset by the
self-mockery which makes Moore, for all his self-display, a writer who
remains in dialogue with his readers.

    This blend of fiction and autobiography, which might be considered
Moore's peculiar contribution to either mode of writing, was to yield
other interesting examples in succeeding decades. An ingenious one is to
be found in *Swan's Milk* by Louis Marlow, published in 1934. "Louis
Marlow" was the pen name of Louis Wilkinson, who published a number
of novels under it, including *Two Made Their Bed*, *The Devil in Crystal*
and *The Lion Took Fright* – he had an eye for an arresting title. *Swan's
Milk* purports to be the biography of one Dexter Foothood, who is
Wilkinson himself; and in it he includes non-fictional accounts of a

number of his friends, including the Powys brothers, Somerset Maugham and Oscar Browning. A sequel, *Forth Beast!* (1946) includes pseudonymous accounts of his four wives. In these books the distinction between fact and fiction is hard to draw, since "fact" is recorded as being "fiction" or a fictional character as belonging to "fact"; but the book provides an amusingly self-critical and realistic portrait, especially in those passages where the "author" (Marlow/Wilkinson) discourses with his "subject" (Foothood) as to the latter's limitations, motives and approach to life. The play of irony is subtle. Wilkinson shares with Moore a strong sense of the incongruous and an air of spontaneity that has in fact been artfully contrived; he deserves better than to be remembered solely as the first biographer of the Powys brothers.

Both John Cowper and Llewelyn Powys were adept at getting their personal lives into print in semi-fictional ways. Llewelyn in particular is a writer who is innately and perennially autobiographical; the family christened as "Luluising" his instinctive (and Proustian) capacity to refer all his experiences back to the touchstone world of childhood. This obsession with the past informs not only his essays and polemical writings but even his travel books. He employs direct autobiography in two modes. *Skin for Skin* (1925) is the record of little over a year, that in which he was smitten with tuberculosis; and it shapes a time of potential chaos into a literary artefact which could almost be taken for a novel. *The Verdict of Bridlegoose* (1927) on the other hand is a relatively uncomplicated piece of reportage with commentary. Llewelyn Powys is not an introspective writer; rather he is a great self-projector, imposing his inner vision on all he sees. But he sees with great immediacy, and in his best work the personal mythology and the objective observation play against each other in an illuminating way.

In *Love and Death* (1939) these two elements coalesce. Sub-titled "an imaginary autobiography," it combines a first-person account of Powys' grave illness at the time of its composition with the narrative of a boyhood love affair, the latter being rendered in language of fervid eloquence. The contrast between love and death is the more forcibly drawn for their being presented simultaneously, the author's real-life situation blending with his fictional creation. But the idyll is not in fact a youthful one: it derives from Powys' recently concluded love affair with the American poet Gamel Woolsey. By describing a contemporary relationship as though it belonged to the distant past, Powys subordinates it to a pre-existent personal myth. *Love and Death* really deserves the ascription "autobiographical novel" since not only as autobiography is it a novel, the resultant novel is itself autobiography: the arts of historical record and prose fiction exchange functions. By the very nature of its composition the book questions the role of verifiable fact in the evaluative process of remembering. It is possible to regard it either as a triumphant assertion of the creative sovereignty of the imagination, or as evidence of a deep-rooted emotional dishonesty.

The imaginative manipulation of autobiographical material is seen at its most assured and ostentatious in the autobiography of Osbert Sitwell, a book in which authorial control is absolute. *Left Hand, Right Hand* was issued in four volumes between 1945 and 1949. It is appropriate to think of it as a narrative edifice, in view of the author's architectural interests and use of architectural metaphor; but he also employs musical analogies and self-consciously conducts the verbal symphony he has contrived. Here the personal drama of his relationship with his father links together a series of graphic, if at times ponderously written, accounts of his ancestry, and of the various religious and social pressures in his family background and upbringing – in short, the moral and social ambience in which he grew up. The figure of Sir George Sitwell takes on the character of some great *monstre sacré* in a novel; the three Sitwell children are heroes and heroine in a drama of parental oppression and tragi-comic misunderstanding. The social world of Edwardian England and the post-war world of artistic and literary London provide backgrounds for this dramatic set-piece. The book is colourful, informative and informed, witty, and rich in vignettes and anecdotes; but one thing is missing. There is no sense of intimacy, of mystery or spiritual quest. As in Virginia Woolf's novel, *Jacob's Room*, the room is meticulously evoked; but where is Jacob? [1]

Osbert Sitwell, like George Moore and Llewelyn Powys, seems more concerned to exhibit than to understand: in all three writers the limited nature of their recollections is the occasion for the biographer to examine and interpret the material they leave unrecorded. But other writers, while not pre-empting the biographer's work, appear at a first reading to forestall it. To recognize the essentially selective nature of the remembering process, and to welcome it as the basis of each personality's unique response to commonly held human experience, is the mark of those autobiographers whose writings benefit most from the influence of the novel. If collectivism, both political and social, characterises the twentieth century, so also does the emergence of the individualistic autobiographer: the quest for a theme, a structure even, such as the critic may detect in a novel, becomes the mainspring of the writer's quest for meaning in his or her personal story.

III

"Only when one has lost all curiosity about the future has one reached the age to write an autobiography." Evelyn Waugh's comment at the commencement of *A Little Learning* (1964) emphasises the unconditional, contemplative perspective of the more serious autobiographical writers. They deal with their experience for its own sake, as rigorous in their detachment as if engaged upon a work of fiction. In the autobiographies of John Cowper Powys, Edwin Muir and Kathleen Raine the quest for meaning forms the connecting thread in narratives that cover a variety of landscapes and social situations; and it is the imaginative ordering of that material which constitutes the essence of what they have to say.

In the case of Powys one sees a remarkable instance of a born novelist treating his own personality as a fictional character, not by putting it into a novel but by subjecting it to the kind of analytic appraisal which the magisterial novelist bestows upon his creations. His book differs from most autobiographies in for the most part jettisoning any attempt to produce a coherent, verifiable linear chronicle: it is deliberately vague and imprecise, it pours forth like lava, typical in this of the author's essentially oratorical genius. Although written with syntactical formality, it conveys the quality of the spoken voice: it is very much a confessional work, its candour, however, serving to protect rather than to expose the author's privacy. Its method is related directly to an incident recorded early on in the book, when Powys recounts how, on his last day at Sherborne School, after years of persecution as an eccentric, he deliberately played the zany to confound his enemies. But such extravagance has a serious purpose.

> A ninny I fancy is a person who feels and looks like an undignified fool, while a zany is one who carries this peculiar cult into his *behaviour* and even makes an art of it. Cannot you see that there is a deep and subtle *irony* in all this ...? Cannot you see it is the profoundest of all religious gestures, and far the oldest?[2]

Powys' autobiography is unusual in blending an introspective revelation of quirks, phobias and perversions with an intent and analytical romanticism that has not a little in common with the aesthetic perceptions and speculations of Marcel Proust. Naturally enough it is the "neurotic" aspect of the book which has attracted most attention; but this is in fact subservient to the main theme, one common to Powys' numerous books of popular philosophy, which is the discovery of an attitude to life that will keep the various neuroses at bay. (And the attitude described in the final pages of the *Autobiography* was to prove effective: the author survived his book by almost thirty years, and lived into a serene and productive old age.)

In deciding to treat himself as a character in one of his own novels, Powys heightens his effects, just as he does in them, through drastically selective emphasis rather than through exaggeration; and, as in *Wolf Solent*, he creates a character whose inner world totally determines the form of the outer. He examines himself as though he were an invented character; and he does virtually create one in *Autobiography*, which in this respect might well be regarded as yet another of his novels. This fictive presentation is furthered by the book's wealth of descriptive prose, its sensitivity to sights and smells, to the suggestive quality of particular places, all rendered as though to present them for the first time, because newly invented, to the reader's eye. Powys does not assume his readers' participation in a shared world: he *tells* his story, writing here, as he does in his novels, with a leisurely particularity as though to children. And this specialised, invented effect is furthered by his decision to omit any account of the women who played such an influential part in his life – his mother, sisters, wife, and various lovers. The omission is, biographically, of great significance, in illuminating Powys' attitude to women and the woman's world, an attitude which emerges as part veneration, part defiance; but the omission also furthers the sense of self-enclosure which those readers not enchanted by the author's character and style find so repellent an aspect of the book. The consideration for others (if such it be, and attributable in some eyes to indifference rather than to concern) did in any case free him to write without restraint about his inner world. In a letter to his sister Marian he announces that

> It will not have very much about myself – except in so far as my experiences sensations ideas feelings over-tones, sins, vices, weaknesses, manias, recoveries, books, places, pictures, scenes, surroundings lend themselves to a sort of Faustian Pilgrimage of the Soul – or a sort of Goethean Pilgrim's Progress towards the City of God![3]

His autobiography's reticence as to times and outward events is offset by a marked specificity concerning moments of visionary experience (if this is what the ecstatic insights he records amount to) and the play of chance – it is the casual, non-sequential, illogical, non-aesthetic aspects of life which interest Powys, "that under-tide of life-reaction which by degrees reveals, to a mind that learns to watch for its revelations, a secret of awareness which cannot be overrated."[4] The difference from the autobiography of Osbert Sitwell could scarcely be greater. But Powys' account of himself is notably lacking in nostalgia or *Sehnsucht*: the ecstasy he seeks does not come from another mode of being but is latent in his response to everyday experience. Such emotions as nostalgia are to be used and enjoyed as a means to appreciating the present moment in which one has the pleasure of indulging in nostalgia. Powys' early poetry and prose is steeped in *fin de siècle* morbidities, but in his maturity he learned to put such imaginings to practical use. And the ecstasy he cultivates is an escape from an ever-present dread of life, part of a life-long battle against fear. The quest is as much a matter of flight as it is of seeking.

> The great thing is to have faith in our power of forgetting, faith in that magical reservoir of Lethe which we all cherish in our being at a deeper level even than our torment. If anyone asked me what is the most precious gift that Nature has given us, I – worshipper of Memory! – would reply; "the art of forgetting!"[5]

The resultant attitude to life, if "pagan" in its sense of the magical, is irreverent and irreligious, implacably opposed to the idea of an absolute, monarchical God. "Chance, not destiny, rules us, swirling the litter and the debris into endless insignificant patterns that form and re-form, only to dissolve even as we gaze at them."[6] It is not a belief to encourage a sense of self-importance.

Powys contrasts his attitude to life with that of the ambitious professionals, the activists:

> For them the urge of life is towards being successful and being heard of. For me the urge of life is towards enjoying the mystery of the elements and the magic of erotic sensuality.[7]

Again and again he undercuts the tendency of the autobiographer towards self-justification. "I am not a homosexualist – I would shamelessly confess it to you, reader, if I were!"[8] And he is unusually frank about his excretory functions: "It presents itself to me as a *sine qua non* of any honest recital in this kind that it should at least not totally rule out the intimate miseries and reliefs of this diurnal passing of matter through the body."[9] (Neither in fact nor in fiction have the majority of writers concurred with him in this opinion.) But at the same time as he offers to share so much of his experience, Powys can concede its limitations, "my tendency to live entirely in my own self-created world, a world composed of my response to books and my reactions against an energetic capitalist society."[10] He was not a clergyman's son for nothing: his entire autobiography, confessional though it is, is something of a sermon, a sermon of the kind that permeates his philosophical writings.

> The grand secret of enjoying yourself with a free heart is to get rid of ambition, rid of even the most trifling competitions with other poor devils. But we must have our pride; and we must have a very deep pride. We must have a pride in simply being ourselves outside and beyond any conceivable competition.[11]

But the hortatory note never gets out of hand. The paragraph continues and concludes with the words, "Luckily for me I have inherited from my father a towering pride; but not a pride in anything in particular."

John Cowper Powys' *Autobiography* is rather like his lectures: it constitutes a performance on a grand scale, given by a man who can use candour and self-analysis with superb virtuosity in order to project a self-portrait suffused in the light of its achieved experience. It is a talking book, and one whose quest ends as a redoubled appreciation of the day-to-day enjoyment of physical existence. And it expresses an elementalist philosophy which Powys shared (and it is one of the few things in a literary sense that he did share) with his brother Theodore, the eremitical author of *Mr Weston's Good Wine*. "Human sensations are Nature's self-expression. They are the earth's awareness of herself."[12] The self-torturing, self-proclamatory personality comes to rest in the life of rocks and plants and water. It is a progress charted in the development of Powys' novels likewise: in his case the work of autobiography and of fiction is the same.

IV

The unashamed subjectivity and self-display of Powys' autobiography is in sharp contrast to *The Story and the Fable* (1940) by Edwin Muir. It would be hard to find a more contrasting personality than this quietly-spoken, incisive yet gentle Scot. An astringent literary critic, Muir brings to the account of his boyhood, literary career, marriage and artistic and political involvements a clarity of analysis that can take on a subdued but none the less moving emotional colouring. His Orkney childhood was to be, as a country childhood so often is for imaginative writers, the touchstone for his later life; one thinks of Llewelyn Powys in this connection, and also of Arthur Machen's *Far Off Things* (1922) and *The Innocent Eye* (1933) by Herbert Read. In all three cases, as in many others, the magic fades in the succeeding volumes. But Muir did not provide a sequel, for his autobiography did not stop with his young manhood, but went on until middle life; he then added an extension for the enlarged edition, *An Autobiography* (1954). But Muir refuses to think in purely linear terms: it is the visionary nature of the author which determines the shape and nature of his book. Certainly *An Autobiography* is as quietly moving at its close, when Edwin and Willa Muir decide to leave Czecho-Slovakia following the Communist takeover, as it is when concerned with the young man's early days in Glasgow and London.

For all its unity of tone the book is not without its theme of innocence versus experience: who could forget the contrast between Muir's life on the farm on Wyre and his life in Glasgow with "the crumbling houses, the twisted faces, the obscene words casually heard in passing, the ancient, haunting stench of pollution and decay, the arrogant women, the mean men, the terrible children." But the realism is not only pictorial. "After a while, like every one who lives in an industrial town, I got used to these things; I walked through the slums as if they were an ordinary road leading from my home to my work." [13] Such quiet prose only makes the contrast more painful. And no less unsentimental are the childhood passages. The account of the pig-killing is as hideous as the pictures of the bone factory at Fairport; but even the lyrical passages are clear and accurate, as in the description of the child's sight of some new-born lambs.

> Some bloody, wet, rag-like stuff was lying on the grass, and a little distance away the two lambs were sprawling with their spindly legs doubled up. Everything looked soft and new – the sky, the sea, the grass, the two lambs, which seemed to have been cast up without warning on the turf; their eyes still had a bruised look, and their hoofs were freshly laquered. They paid no attention to me when I went up to pat them, but kept turning their heads with sudden gentle movements which belonged to some other place. [14]

Here the observation, while organised from an adult sensibility, notes what the child would see in terms of the child's presuppositions: that "cast up" is exactly right for one who has grown up on a small island. The language is plain and homely, with only one word of more than two sylla-bles, and that one the familiar "everything"; all the adjectives are con-nected with day-to-day domestic life – "rag-like," "spindly," "bruised," "laquered." But the final phrase, so natural in its place, and so unconditional, gives the whole passage a feeling of visionary power. The poems of Blake come irresistibly to mind.

Muir recognizes that it is impossible to re-create a child's innocent vision directly. What he gives one is the child's perspective rendered in terms of how a mature mind would interpret it, as when he speaks of "zones of childhood" in which the quality of seeing and remembering differ as the child grows up: "spring was only a few vivid happenings, not a state, and before I knew it the motionless blue summer was there, in which nothing happened."[15] The child thus becomes the author's fictive creation, distanced from him; but since those responses are related to the present memories of the adult Muir, the fictive nature of memory, while recognized and allowed for, is qualified yet again in terms of the validity of present experience. Thus childhood is not to be left behind and mourned, but integrated into adult life. Muir's autobiography has a singular wholeness.

The original title, *The Story and the Fable*, neatly balances the factual and fictional elements in autobiographical writing. Muir makes it plain what he means by it.

> It is clear that no autobiography can begin with a man's birth, that we extend far beyond any boundary line which we can set for ourselves in the past or the future, and that the life of every man is an endlessly repeated performance of the life of man. It is clear for the same reason that no autobiography can confine itself to conscious life, and that sleep, in which we pass a third of our existence, is a mode of experience, and our dreams a part of reality. In themselves our conscious lives may not be particularly interesting. But what we are not and can never be, our fable, seems to me inconceivably interesting. I should like to write that fable, but I cannot even live it; and all I could do if I related the outward course of my life would be to show how I have deviated from it; though even that is impossible, since I do not know the fable or anybody who knows it.[16]

Thus for Muir the life of fact is, if not delusive, then incomplete and without a key; it is out of such an awareness that religious quests arise, and it is not surprising to read at the end of *An Autobiography* that "I discovered that I had been a Christian without knowing it."

> As I look back on the part of the mystery which is my own life, my own fable, what I am most aware of is that we receive more than we can ever give; we receive it from the past, on which we draw with every breath, but also – and this is a point of faith – from the Source of the mystery itself, by the means which religious people call Grace.[17]

The work of fiction which is the autobiography, by moving from an immersion in Nature to the acceptance of Grace, receives its authorisation in the fact to which it seeks to approximate, the word in the Word.

V

In the autobiography of Kathleen Raine, on the other hand, we find that the concepts of Nature and Grace are, initially at any rate, fused. A convinced Neo-Platonist, she is unusual among contemporary writers in possessing both a metaphysic and a profound emotional commitment to it; her work is disconcerting in its uncompromising seriousness and in its lack of any self-protective irony. Hers is a singularly naked book, without a trace of exhibitionism; its sincerity is evident, and yet it too raises the question of what manner of truth can be expected of the autobiographer. As with John Cowper Powys, one is left wondering whether the very frankness does not aim to repel further biographical enquiry.

The book appeared in three instalments, called *Farewell Happy Fields* (1973), *The Land Unknown* (1975) and *The Lion's Mouth* (1977). An act of emotional exorcism, the work was written as a whole in 1962 "at a time when the writing of my story seemed to me the only way in which, by seeking to understand my life, I could go on living it."[18] The occasion was the ending of the author's complex and well-nigh disastrous relationship with the writer Gavin Maxwell. But what gives the autobiography its peculiar interest is not so much the human story, painful and psychologically interesting though that is, as the record of a spiritual quest which turns out to be more like a spiritual haunting. Here the life-illusion, the dominant dream, is given an independent reality.

Kathleen Raine's thesis is essentially the same as that of Edwin Muir. In the Introduction of 1973 she claims that she is "trying to give the essence of the life which it has been mine to live (and of what other life can I tell, since each of us has direct knowledge only through the self we are) ..."[19] That "mine to live" is significant: she is conscious of being fated, of being in the power of spiritual laws which it was her destiny to overlook and thus to disobey. The book is an act of reparation to the gods; for so she interprets what in other writers would be a mere case of personal misunderstanding. For her, autobiography concerns a "journey of consciousness"; and that consciousness reflects a deeper life from which it springs. Her precise sense of the numinous is seen in her account of a well in her aunt's garden in Northumberland, the landscape which formed her childhood paradise.

> The well must I think have been very old; the roughly-hewn well-head which covered the spring might have dated from the forgotten monastery; and simple as it was it spoke a language entirely strange to me at that time, not of nature, but of a different kind of meaning, which I recognized because this primitive shrine (for the well had, for me, a kind of numinosity) was raised upon a marvel of nature itself whose magic it served to enhance. I shared, as I drew my water, the wonder of those who had built the well-head, recognizing in it the expression of a mind for which, as for my own, a spring was something pure, mysterious, more than natural.[20]

In describing this childhood world Kathleen Raine also defines it: what in other writers would be merely personal reminiscence, she interprets in terms of myth.

It is this persistent other-worldliness which, while it gives this auto-biography its peculiar authority, accounts for the dislike some readers have for it. The author's dismissive description of her parents' home at Ilford sounds disdainful, even though she herself hastens later on "to repent" (in Charles Williams' phrase) "of the inevitable." For her "Ilford" is a spiritual state:

> the place of those who do not wish to (or who cannot be) fully conscious, because full consciousness would perhaps make life unendurable.... The phrase which describes the state of those who 'cannot call their souls their own' is not without truth, and often for social and economic reasons which are beyond the control of the sufferers.[21]

An adherence to her own point of view does not result in solipsism.

Her case was that of a sensitive girl brought up as an adolescent in an environment totally at variance with her childhood one; and she is prepared to generalise from it as a manifestation of the loss of Eden, part of the "fable" discerned also by Edwin Muir.

> Those who choose the vision of perfection choose to experience the pain of deprivation as the lesser evil; or perhaps there is no choice. ... And ultimately the many are sustained by those images of a lost perfection held before them by the rememberers. Such, as I un-derstand it, is the whole and sole purpose of the arts and the justification of those who refuse to accept as our norm those unrealities the world calls real.[22]

The human consequences of such a burden and such a belief were to be painful, complex and destructive; and not least among the book's virtues is the honesty with which the tragic outcome is faced. The very formality of the prose makes the candour more impressive. Especially frank and painful is the account of the relationship with Gavin Maxwell, which forms the climax of the book.[23] It describes how, through her mistaken belief that they shared an understanding of their imaginative world, she blinded herself to his failure to return her love. A mystical intuition distorted an emotional response; or, say, an imaginative reality was in conflict with a material one. The resultant guilt is left to confront a fundamental question, "Which is the stronger, the tangled weaving of destiny, the navel cord, cause and effect and inheritance, or the grace of that water rising always pure from a source deeper than the roots of those weeds?"[24] In this author's mind there can be no doubt as to which is the true answer.

Kathleen Raine writes in metaphors deriving from a northern land-scape, the landscape of her dream world; and in Neo-Platonic thought metaphor betokens reality, "a language in which bird and beast and tree

were themselves the words, full of otherwise inexpressible meaning."[25]
So in her autobiography, although "memory has now amended the
pattern of the outer to fit the inner reality,"[26] the tale recorded is anything
but fictional.

> Descriptions of one state of consciousness in terms of another must,
> to those who have not themselves known the experience, always
> give the impression of being figurative or poetic; so it always must
> be when, in whatever field, ignorance passes judgement upon
> knowledge. But those who know are unanimous in reporting that
> such changes of consciousness are not of degree, but of kind; not
> some strong emotion or excitement but a clarity in which all is
> minutely perceived as if by finer sense.[27]

It is this conviction which energises what might otherwise, in the first two
volumes at any rate, seem an aloof, even a self-indulgent record; indeed,
in its grave, musical cadences, its unashamed concern with nobility and
beauty, the book recalls *Marius the Epicurean*. But Kathleen Raine's
intellectual probity and her hold on physical reality (she read the Natural
Sciences Tripos at Cambridge), rescues her work from the languor that
informs Walter Pater's. Her artistry, however, is as deliberate as his;
moreover, the crisp archaism of her style, the careful selection of
episode and landscape to set forth her story, her discarding of the
superfluous detail or irrelevant event, are in keeping with, and embody,
her belief in an absolute spiritual world which reveals itself through
memory, prompting, and desire. For her, there is no contradiction
between truth and beauty. "The charm of science to me, at all events, was
aesthetic; and perhaps metaphysical."[28] The statement is in no way
apologetic.

VI

John Cowper Powys, the totally open-minded sceptic, sceptical even of
scepticism itself; Edwin Muir, the obedient disciple of an inward vision;
Kathleen Raine, the penitent and exalted exponent of the objectivity of
spiritual experience: all three articulate their personal history in terms
which give to it the accessibility and applicability of imaginative fiction.
What gives their work its particular value is their responsive, and responsible, attitude to their experience. They apply their individual tastes
and temperaments to the elucidation of a personal vision, so that it may
be available to those prepared to respond to it. In their hands autobiography records the growth of an attitude to life which, while constituting a working absolute for its holder, is none the less submitted to a
verification that concedes it to be relative. In Powys' case the relativity is
to other working absolutes, in that of Muir and Kathleen Raine to the
Absolute that is the source of their belief. But all three are equally
valuable as autobiographers in that they recognise the art of autobio-

graphy as involving a record, in personal terms, of that imaginative re-
shaping of experience which, in the novelist's hands, is called the art of
fiction. In their hands the two arts become aspects of each other.

GLEN CAVALIERO

NOTES

1. The careful composition of Sitwell's book is further evident in the two supplementary
   volumes, *Noble Essences* (1950) and *Tales My Father Taught Me* (1962) in which, in the
   first case, characters, and in the second, anecdotes regarded by the author as subordinate to the main design, are thriftily gathered to receive a fuller and independent
   treatment. *Left Hand, Right Hand*, is, for better or worse, one of the great monuments
   to the aesthetic approach to life.
2. John Cowper Powys, *Autobiography* (London, 1934), 3rd ed. 1967, p. 538.
3. *Autobiography*, pp. xix–xx.
4. *Autobiography*, p. 13.
5. *Autobiography*, p. 46.
6. *Autobiography*, p. 46.
7. *Autobiography*, p. 429.
8. *Autobiography*, p. 426.
9. *Autobiography*, p. 148.
10. *Autobiography*, p. 540.
11. *Autobiography*, p. 622.
12. *Autobiography*, p. 238.
13. Edwin Muir, *An Autobiography* (London, 1954), p. 15.
14. *Autobiography*, p. 31.
15. *Autobiography*, p. 32.
16. *Autobiography*, p. 48–9.
17. *Autobiography*, p. 281.
18. Kathleen Raine, *The Lion's Mouth* (London, 1977), p. 1.
19. Kathleen Raine, *Farewell Happy Fields*, (London, 1973), p. 6.
20. *Farewell Happy Fields*, p. 42.
21. *Farewell Happy Fields*, p. 170.
22. *Farewell Happy Fields*, p. 79.
23. It is significant that in one of his own autobiographical works, *Raven Seek Thy Brother*
    (1965) Maxwell should interpret literally, as the cursing of a rowan tree, an event which
    Kathleen Raine portrays as "a desperate heart's cry for truth" (*The Lion's Mouth*,
    p. 93).
24. *The Lion's Mouth*, p. 82.
25. *Farewell Happy Fields*, p. 25.
26. Ibid., p. 62.
27. Kathleen Raine, *The Land Unknown* (London, 1975), p. 118.
28. *Farewell Happy Fields*, p. 117.

I Do Believe Him Though I Know
He Lies: Lying As Genre and Metaphor
In Richard Wright's Black Boy

Since the publication of *Black Boy* in 1945, reactions to its authenticity have been curiously contradictory, often mutually exclusive. For many readers the book is particularly honest, sincere, open, convincing and accurate. But for others *Black Boy* leaves a feeling of inauthenticity, a sense that the story or its author is not to be trusted. These conflicting reactions are best illustrated by the following representative observations by Ralph White and W.E.B. DuBois. White, a psychologist, identified "ruthless honesty" as "the outstanding quality which made the book not only moving but also intellectually satisfying."[1] But DuBois noted that while "nothing that Richard Wright says is in itself unbelievable or impossible; it is the total picture that is not convincing."[2] Attempting to reconcile these opposing views, I wish to argue that both sides are correct, that the book is one of the most truthful accounts of the black experience in America, even though the protagonist's story often does not ring true, and that this inability to tell the truth is Wright's major metaphor of self. A repeated pattern of misrepresentation becomes the author's way of making us believe that his personality, his family, his race – his whole childhood and youth – conspired to prevent him from hearing the truth, speaking the truth, or even being believed unless he lied.

In terms of truth, we expect from an autobiography obedience to the conventions of the genre which hold that the story being presented is a significant part of a person's life, written in retrospect by the subject of the story, who purports to believe that he or she is telling a truthful version of the past. The reader expects, even enjoys, detecting misrepresentations, odd emphasis, telling omissions, and over and under determination, and will willingly overlook factual errors, but for most readers an autobiography is dishonest if the author does not seem to be trying to tell the overall truth. I agree with A.O.J. Cockshut's assertion that "the simple truth of accurate record of facts is clearly important; but as a rule this is overshadowed by other kinds. At the same time we are judging the autobiographer's central idea" which must have "its own momentous dignity" and must be "truly felt as working through the contingent and everyday."[3] For most contemporary readers worries about *Black Boy's* trustworthiness stemmed from questions of genre: although the book was clearly not called "The Autobiography of Richard Wright," its subtitle – "A Record of Childhood and Youth" – did suggest autobiography. The following descriptions of *Black Boy* reflect the confusion of readers: biography, autobiographical story, fictionalized biography, a masterpiece of romanced facts, a sort-of-autobiography, pseudo-autobiography, part fiction/part truth, autobiography with the quality of fiction, and case history.[4]

Some of these generic confusions were generated by Wright's statements about his creation; he meant the work to be collective autobiography, a personalized record of countless black Americans growing up with a personal history of hunger, deprivation, and constant racism. He also remarked that he decided to write his life story after giving an autobiographical talk to a racially mixed audience at Fisk University in Nashville in 1943. After the talk, he noted that he "had accidentally blundered into the secret black, hidden core of race relations in the United States. That core is this: nobody is ever expected to speak honestly about the problem.... And I learned that when the truth was plowed up in their faces, they shook and trembled and didn't know what to do."[5] A year later, Wright used the same metaphor when he wrote "the hardest truth to me to plow up was in my own life."[6] But speaking honestly about a racism endemic throughout America was more complicated, both for author and for reader, than Wright could have known, and, for many, a more delicate instrument than a plow was needed for harvesting the past. Using truthfulness as his watchword, Wright began *Black Boy* as an attempt to set the record straight, including his personal one, which already consisted of a number of "biographies of the author" or "notes on contributors" written by himself in the third person, sometimes with exaggerated accounts of his youth. In several interviews, as well as in "The Ethics of Living Jim Crow," an autobiographical sketch published originally in *American Stuff: WPA Writers' Anthology* in 1937, Wright had already given an incorrect birth date, and begun to establish a history overemphasizing the negative aspects of his early life.[7]

Most revelatory about the conflict between his intentions and the actual writing of his personal narrative is the following observation from a newspaper article called "The Birth of Black Boy":

> The real hard terror of writing like this came when I found that writing of one's life was vastly different from speaking of it. I was rendering a close and emotionally connected account of my experience and the ease I had had in speaking from notes at Fisk would not come again. I found that to tell the truth is the hardest thing on earth, harder than fighting in a war, harder than taking part in a revolution. If you try it, you will find that at times sweat will break upon you. You will find that even if you succeed in discounting the attitudes of others to you and your life, you must wrestle with yourself most of all, fight with yourself; for there will surge up in you a strong desire to alter facts, to dress up your feelings. You'll find that there are many things that you don't want to admit about yourself and others. As your record shapes itself an awed wonder haunts you. And yet there is no more exciting an

adventure than trying to be honest in this way. The clean, strong feeling that sweeps you when you've done it makes you know that.[8]

Although Wright seemed unsure of his book's generic identity, he never referred to *Black Boy* as an autobiography. His original title, "American Hunger," later used for his life story after leaving Memphis for Chicago, came after he had rejected *The Empty Box, Days of Famine, The Empty Houses, The Assassin, Bread and Water,* and *Black Confession,* all of which sound like titles for novels.[9] When his literary agent suggested the subtitle "The Biography of a Courageous Negro," Wright responded with "The Biography of An American Negro," then with eight other possibilities including "Coming of Age in the Black South," "A Record in Anguish," "A Study in Anguish," and "A Chronicle of Anxiety," which indicate his feeling that the book he had written was less personal, more documentary – a study, a record, a chronicle or even a biography – than autobiography.[10] Constance Webb reports that Wright was uneasy with the word *autobiography*, both because of "an inner distaste for revealing in first person instead of through a fictitious character the dread and fear and anguished self-questioning of his life" and because he realized he would write his story using "portions of his own childhood, stories told him by friends, things he had observed happening to others" and fictional techniques.[10]

Although some readers see Wright as unsuccessful in his struggle neither "to alter facts" nor to "dress up feelings," the book's tendency to intermix fiction and fact is clearly part of both Wright's personal literary history and the Afro-American literary tradition in which he was writing. The form of *Black Boy* partly imitates the traditional slave narrative, a literary type which allowed for a high degree of fictionality in the cause of abolition.[12] A number of major works of literature by black Americans, such as DuBois' *The Souls of Black Folks,* Toomer's *Cane,* and Johnson's *The Autobiography of an Ex-Coloured Man,* featured mixtures of genres, and Wright, simultaneously a poet, novelist, essayist, journalist, playwright, and actor, often used the same material in different genres. For example, "The Ethics of Living Jim Crow," first an essay, later appeared attached to the stories of *Uncle Tom's Children,* one of which, "Bright and Morning Star," is told in *Black Boy* as a tale which held the protagonist in thrall, even though he "did not know if the story was factually true or not."[13] When "black boy" says that the story is emotionally true, he reflects exactly the kind of truth he wants his readers to respond to in *Black Boy.* Several episodes recounted in "The Ethics of Living Jim Crow" are told in significantly different ways in *Black Boy,* and portions of *Eight Men* were once planned as part of that book. Some of the characters in *Black Boy* have been given fictional names, while Bigger Thomas, the central character in *Native Son,* was the real name of one of Wright's acquaintances.[14] That he used real names in fiction and fictional names in non-fiction is typical of Richard Wright who further confounded the usual distinctions between author and persona by playing the role of Bigger Thomas in the film version of *Native Son.*

Richard Wright makes clear that *Black Boy* is not meant as a traditional autobiography by presenting much of the story in the form of dialogue marked with quotation marks, which suggests the unusual degree of fiction within his factual story. Although critics often point to Wright's first novel, *Native Son* (1940), as the other half of *Black Boy*, another model for this autobiographical work was his just–completed *Twelve Million Black Voices: A Folk History of the American Negro in The United States* (1941). Writing *Black Boy* in the spirit of folk history seemed a reasonable thing to do, and Wright apparently saw no hypocrisy in omitting personal details which did not contribute to what he was simultaneously thinking of as his own story and the story of millions of others. Wright's claim to be composing the autobiography of a generic black child is reinforced by the narrator's particular reaction to racism: "The things that influenced my conduct as a Negro did not have to happen to me directly; I needed but to hear of them to feel their full effects in the deepest layers of my consciousness" (190).

Roy Pascal is correct in asserting that "where a lie is the result of a calculated intention to appear right or important, danger is done to autobiographical truth" and that "the most frequent cause of failure in autobiography is an untruthfulness which arises from the desire to appear admirable."[15] However, most of the omission in *Black Boy* is designed not to make the persona appear admirable, but to make Richard Wright into "black boy," to underplay his own family's middle-class ways and more positive values. He does not mention that his mother was a successful school teacher and that many of his friends were children of college faculty members; he omits most of his father's family background, and his own sexual experiences. Reactions from sensitive Southern whites are mainly left out, including those of the Wall family to whom, we learn from Michel Fabre's biography, "he sometimes submitted his problems and plans ... and soon considered their house a second home where he met with more understanding than from his own family."[16]

In addition to omissions, name changes, poetic interludes, and extensive dialogue, *Black Boy* is replete with questionable events that biographical research has revealed to be exaggerated, inaccurate, mistaken, or invented. Fabre's section dealing with the *Black Boy* years is characterized by constant disclaimers about the factuality of the story. Some omissions can be explained because the urbane ex-Communist who began *Black Boy* "wanted to see himself as a child of the proletariat" though "in reality he attached greater importance to the honorable position of his grandparents in their town than he did to his peasant background."[17] While these distortions are acceptable to many, especially in light of Wright's intention of using his life to show the effects of racism, there are numerous other manipulations less acceptable because more self-serving.

Most of these incidents are relatively minor, and so doubts seem unimportant; however, the misrepresentations in two of the book's most important episodes – the high school graduation speech and the story of

Uncle Hoskins and the Mississippi River – might be less acceptable. "Black boy's" refusal to deliver the principal's graduation speech rather than his own is apparently based on truth, but the version in *Black Boy* leaves out the important fact that Wright rewrote his speech, cutting out more volatile passages as a compromise.[18] The story of Uncle Hoskins does not ring true, for how could a boy whose life had been to that point so violent, be scared of his uncle's relatively harmless trick? One reason the tale feels false is that the story, complete with revelations about Uncle Hoskins such as "I never trusted him after that. Whenever I saw his face the memory of my terror upon the river would come back, vivid and strong, and it stood as a barrier between us," actually happened to Ralph Ellison who told it to Wright.[19]

For many critics, including Edward Margolies, these deliberate manipulations reduce *Black Boy's* authenticity as autobiography because they set up doubts about everything, the same doubts that resonate through the remarks of black writers from DuBois to Baldwin to David Bradley, all of whom have persisted in taking *Black Boy's* protagonist to be Richard Wright.[20] But "Richard Wright is not the same person as the hero of that book, not the same as 'I' or 'Richard' or the 'Black boy', not by several light years," argues James Olney, who refers to the book's chief character as "black boy," explaining that "by means of an encompassing and creative memory, Richard Wright imagines it all, and he is as much the creator of the figure that he calls 'Richard' as he is of the figure that, in *Native Son*, he calls 'Bigger.'"[21] Olney's idea that the central figure be treated as a single person referred to as "black boy," a literary character representing both the actual author as a child and the adult author – the famous writer imagining himself as representative of inarticulate black children – is finally convincing. That seems to be what Richard Wright meant to do, said he had done, and what he did.

Of course he was working in what we now see as dangerous areas, as recent literary history has shown. Black journalist Janet Cooke was labelled a liar, fired from the *Washington Post*, and relieved of her Pulitzer Prize for inventing a black boy in a series of articles on drug use; Clifford Irving was imprisoned for writing what he presented as Howard Hughes's autobiography; and Alastair Reid has recently been castigated for "cleaning up quotations," condensing, inventing personae and locations, and in general using new journalistic techniques in the *New Yorker*. But Wright's accomplishment in *Black Boy* is different, first because he announces his intentions – in authorial statements external to the text, and by title, quotation marks, use of symbolic and imagistic description, and well-organized plot – and second because he is manipulating his own story, not someone else's. Ellison's review–essay on *Black Boy*, "Richard Wright's Blues," begins with the refrain, "If anybody ask you/ who sing this song,/ Say it was ole [Black Boy]/ done been here and gone,"[22] a blues singer's signature formula that clarifies two important facts about the book. First, the protagonist is a literary character named "Black Boy" who bears the same similarity to Richard

Wright as the character Leadbelly, for example, does to the blues singer Huddie Ledbetter who sang about himself so often. Second, Ellison's refrain forewarned that the identity of the protagonist would be called into question by critics who would wonder who the elusive hero was and where he went. Unlike Ellison, who sees *Black Boy* as a talking blues, it is for me a be-bop jazz performance in which Wright uses his life as the melody on which he could improvise.

Part of the complication about lying in *Black Boy* – who is lying and to whom – derives from the interplay between audiences, the resonances between the actual audience, the authorial audience, and the narrative audience, to use Peter Rabinowitz's terms.[23] The actual audience is the group of real humans holding *Black Boy* in their hands as they read. The authorial audience is the group Wright imagined himself addressing. The narrative audience, which Gerald Prince calls the narratee (*narrataire*), is the group of people to whom the narrator is speaking.[24] Sorting out these audiences is particularly confusing but interesting in *Black Boy* because the book is autobiographical and therefore the relation between author and narrator is more complicated than in much fiction, and because both author and narrator are black. The important questions about the race, sex, and assumptions of the reader in the text are difficult to answer absolutely, but it seems clear that Richard Wright relates to the authorial audience as "black boy" does to the narrative audience. Because Wright's actual audience at Fisk University was racially mixed, and because he cited his speaking there as the specific impetus for writing the book, it is logical to assume that the authorial audience is composed of both black and white members. Because the book is dedicated to "ELLEN and JULIA," Wright's white wife and interracial daughter, it seems reasonable to assume that he thought of his authorial audience as being both male and female, black girls as well as black boys.

The question of the narrative audience is more complex, but I believe that the readers inscribed in and by the text, the audience to whom "black boy" is speaking, is also racially mixed. This audience is in one sense made up of all of the people described in the book, black and white, who failed to understand the narrator during his lifetime. At other times the narrator is addressing himself only to a white audience, as in the following presentation of schoolboy boasting, glossed for the white reader:

> "Man, you reckon these white folks is ever gonna change?" Timid, questioning hope.
>
> "Hell, no! They just born that way." Rejecting hope for fear that it could never come true.
>
> "Shucks, man. I'm going north when I get grown." Rebelling against futile hope and embracing flight.
>
> "A colored man's all right up north." Justifying flight. (90)

Although the authorial audience includes males and females, the narrative audience seems limited to males, as the narrator makes plain in such statements as "It was degrading to play with girls and in our talk we relegated them to a remote island of life" (90).

These distinctions between audiences are important because the actual reader's attempt to react to the book properly, that is in the right spirit, is somewhat like the narrator's attempts to react properly to the different values in the black and white worlds. Lying to white people is one thing, lying to blacks another. And, as Wright discovered after his speech in Nashville, telling the truth to a mixed audience is more dangerous than separating the truth into white and black versions. When *Black Boy's* authorial and narrative audiences converge, the reader is the least likely to question the authenticity of the story. As the two audiences move apart, the reader begins to feel uneasy, partly because of trying to decide which audience to join.

Many critical objections to *Black Boy's* methods of getting at the truth come from those who instinctly feel something strange about the work, not so much in its generic confusions, as in its tone and in what Albert Stone senses when he writes that "a proud and secret self presides over the text, covertly revealing itself through event, style, and metaphor."[25] When confronted with *Black Boy's* deviations from absolute biographical truth, less sophisticated readers, such as students, are seldom bothered. They sense that discrepancies uncovered by reading other texts have little bearing on the truth of the text at hand. Nevertheless, the same students often respond unfavourably to what they perceive as inauthenticity arising from within *Black Boy*. And part of their dislike of and distrust for "black boy" grows from the sense of the times that "narrative past ... has lost its authenticating power," as Lionel Trilling observes. "Far from being an authenticating agent, indeed, it has become the very type of inauthenticity."[26] Caring little about the crossing of generic boundaries, students are disturbed by the idea that "life is susceptible of comprehension and thus of management," as Trilling further remarks.[27] In short, they are uncomfortable with *Black Boy*, not because it is not true, but because for them it does not ring true. They experience what Barrett Mandel calls "dis-ease with the autobiography. It seems as if the author is lying (not, please, writing fiction), although readers cannot always easily put their finger on the lie."[28]

The lying they sense centres on these three concerns: "black boy" is never wrong, is falsely naive, and is melodramatic, three characteristics of what Mandel refers to as autobiography in which "the ratification is negative – the light of now shines on the illusion the ego puts forth and reveals it as false."[29] Mandel believes that most autobiographers are basically honest, but those who are not give themselves away through tone: "Since the ego is in conflict with the truth, the reader very often gets that message. The author has created an illusion of an illusion.... The tone is forever slipping away from the content, giving itself away."[30] While Mandel does not include *Black Boy* in the category of dishonest autobiographies, instead citing it as a typical reworking of the past, many critics have echoed my students' concerns. For example, Robert Stepto finds fault with two early incidents in which "black boy" insists on the literal meaning of words: when he pretends to believe his father's injunction to kill a noisy kitten, and when he refuses ninety-seven cents for his dog because he wants a dollar. "The fact remains that *Black Boy* requires its readers to admire Wright's persona's remarkable and unassailable innocence in certain major episodes, and to condone his exploitation of that innocence in others," writes Stepto. "This, I think, is a poorly tailored seam, if not precisely a flaw, in *Black Boy's* narrative strategy."[31] Rather than seeing these episodes, and others like them, as examples of bad faith or as rough edges in the narrative fabric, I see them as deliberate renderings of the terrible dilemma of black boys, and their need to dissemble about everything, especially about the nature of their naiveté. Wright's persona is confessing, not boasting. His family life and his difficulty with hypocrisy made lying at once a constant requirement for survival, and a nearly impossible performance, especially for a poor liar whose tone gives him away.

The inability to lie properly, exhibited in countless scenes, is "black boy's" major problem in adjusting to black/white relations in his youth. Asked by a potential white employer if he steals, "black boy" is incredulous: "Lady, if I was a thief, I'd never tell anybody" (160), he replies. *Black Boy* is filled with episodes in which its hero is unable to lie, forced to lie, caught between conflicting lies, not believed unless he lies. Poorly constructed lies are appropriate metaphors to portray a boy whose efforts to set the record straight are as frustrated as his grandfather's attempts to claim a Navy pension, which is thwarted by bureaucratic error for his whole life. Falsehoods are an apt metaphor for the speech of a boy who distrusts everyone, himself included.

Black Boy's opening, in which Wright describes how his four-year old self burnt his grandmother's house out of boredom and experimentation, is cited by virtually every commentator as an allegory for the fear, rebellion, anxiety, and need for freedom of the hero, as well as for the motifs of fire, hunger, and underground retreat. After the fire, which destroys more than half of the house, the child delivers this recollection:

> I was lashed so hard and long that I lost consciousness. I was beaten out of my senses and later I found myself in bed, screaming, determined to run away.... I was lost in a fog of fear. A doctor was called – I was afterward told – and he ordered that I be kept abed, that I be kept quiet, that my very life depended upon it.... Whenever I tried to sleep I would see huge wobbly white bags, like the full udders of cows, suspended from the ceiling above me. Later, as I grew worse, I could see the bags in the daytime with my eyes open and I was gripped by the fear that they were going to fall and drench me with some horrible liquid.... Time finally bore me away from the dangerous bags and I got well. But for a long time I was chastened whenever I remembered that my mother had come close to killing me. (13)

Albert Stone perceptively notes that the last line of this passage represents "a striking reversal." "Where the reader expects a confession that
the boy has tried (although inadvertently or unconsciously) to attack his
own family, one finds the opposite. Such heavy rationalization clearly
demands examination."[32] The adult autobiographer is not justifying
setting houses on fire; rather he is trying to show graphically and suddenly
how distrustful a child of four had already become. The episode does not
ring true because it is not necessarily literally true. In fact Wright used a
contradictory description in "The Ethics of Living Jim Crow," written
eight years earlier. Describing a cinder fight between white and black
children, he claims he was cut by a broken milk bottle, rushed to the
hospital by a kind neighbour, and later beaten by his mother until he "had
a fever of one hundred and two.... All that night I was delirious and could
not sleep. Each time I closed my eyes I saw monstrous white faces
suspended from the ceiling, leering at me."[33] The cinder fight is retold in a
later section of *Black Boy*, though in this version the hero's mother takes
him to the doctor, and beats him less severely.

Like Nate Shaw in Theodore Rosengarten's National Book Award
winning *All God's Dangers*, who distinguishes between stories "told for
truth" and those "told to entertain," or the old time musician, Lily May
Ledford, in Ellesa Clay High's *Past Titan Rock: Journeys Into An
Appalachian Valley*, who says "I never tell a story the same way twice, but
I tell the truth," Richard Wright has borrowed the rhetoric of the oral
historian in consciously fictionalizing the story of the burning house and
his subsequent punishment, while sending the reader signals that he has
done so. He wants the reader to feel that there is something not quite
right about the whole scene. That the three-year old brother can see the
folly of playing with fire when the four-year old "black boy" cannot, that
the reasons for setting the fire are as spurious as the explanation – "I had
just wanted to see how the curtains would look when they burned" (11) –
that the nightmarish description of white bags filled with foul liquid are
obviously meant to be symbolic, and finally that the boy is chastened, not
by his actions, but by the thought that his mother had come close to killing
him – all these signals are meant to paint a truthful picture of a boy who
later came to hold "a conviction that the meaning of living came only
when one was struggling to wring a meaning out of meaningless suffering"
(112). The opening scene suggests the whole atmosphere of the book, a
desperate fear of meaningless visitations of violence without context, a
life of deliberate misrepresentations of the truth and complete distrust of
all people, a world in which "each event spoke with a cryptic tongue"
(14). Throughout *Black Boy* Wright presents a lonely figure whose life
does not ring true because "that's the way things were between whites
and blacks in the South; many of the most important things were never
openly said; they were understated and left to seep through to one" (188),
so that all actions are tempered by a sub-text, though obvious to everyone, a strategy which the author claimed to have discovered when he
delivered his Fisk University oration.

Whenever the narrator questions his mother about racial relationships, she is defensive and evasive. "I knew there was something my mother was holding back," he notes. "She was not concealing facts, but feelings, attitudes, convictions which she did not want me to know" (58), a misrepresentation which disturbs "black boy" who later says "my personality was lopsided; my knowledge of feeling was far greater than my knowledge of fact" (136). While he holds back or conceals facts, he is usually straightforward about emotional feelings, even though he can say "the safety of my life in the South depended upon how well I concealed from all whites what I felt" (255). Worrying less about factual truth, Wright was determined to stress the emotional truth of Southern life to counteract the stereotypical myths shown in the song which prefaced *Uncle Tom's Children*: "Is it true what they say about Dixie? Does the sun really shine all the time?"

One of the particular ironies of *Black Boy* is that the narrator's constant lying is emblematic of the truth that all black boys were required not only to lie, but to lie about their lying. In the boxing match between "black boy" and a co-worker, this pattern is played out almost mathematically. The two black boys are coerced into a fight they both know is false, based on lies that are obvious to all. Much of the shamefulness of the whole situation is that they are forced to pretend that they are neither aware that the situation is false, nor that they know the whites know they know. These paradoxes are clearly analyzed in Roger Rosenblatt's essay "Black Autobiography: Life as the Death Weapon":

> They had been goaded into a false and illogical act that somehow became logical and true. At the end of their fight, Wright and Harrison *did* hold a grudge against each other, just as their white supervisors had initially contended. The madness of the situation did not reside in the hysteria of the onlookers, nor even in the confusion of defeat and victory or of power and impotency on the parts of the boxers. It resided in the fact that a lie became the truth and that two people who had thought they had known what the truth was wound up living the lie.[34]

Although personal and institutional racism was everywhere evident, Southern whites generally maintained that they treated blacks more humanely than did Northern whites, that they understood blacks and knew how to deal with them, and that they were friendly with blacks (as evidenced by their calling them by their first names), all of which blacks were supposed to pretend they believed. Whites deliberately set up situations where blacks were forced to steal, and not only did they like to be stolen from, they forced blacks to lie by repeatedly asking them if they were thieves. "Whites placed a premium upon black deceit; they encouraged irresponsibility; and their rewards were bestowed upon us blacks in the degree that we could make them feel safe and superior" (219), notes the narrator. When "black boy" forgets to call a white co-worker named Pease "Mister," he is caught in a trap from which the usual escape is "a nervous cryptic smile" (208). The boy's attempt to lie his way out of the situation fails, despite his ingenuity in turning the false accusation into an ambiguous apology:

> If I had said: No, sir, Mr. Pease, I never called you *Pease*, I would by inference have been calling Reynolds a liar; and if I had said: Yes, sir, Mr. Pease, I called you *Pease*, I would have been pleading guilty to the worst insult that a Negro can offer to a southern white man. I stood trying to think of a neutral course that would resolve this quickly risen nightmare....

> "I don't remember calling you *Pease*, Mr. Pease," I said cautiously, "And if I did, I sure didn't mean ..."

> "You black sonofabitch! You called me *Pease*, then!" he spat, rising and slapping me till I bent sideways over a bench. (209)

Episodes like this make clear that inability to tell the truth does not make black boys into liars. Instead the frequent descriptions of the protagonist as a prevaricator reveal to white readers the way blacks used lies to express truths, used, for example, the word "nigger" to mean one thing to white listeners, another to black. The elaborate system of signifying, of using words exactly the opposite of white usage (bad for good/ cool for hot), of wearing the mask to cover emotions, of the lies behind black children's game of dozens – all of these are behind the motif of lying in *Black Boy*. Wright's metaphoric use of lying is made more complex by his awareness that a history of misrepresentation of true feelings made it difficult for black people to be certain when they were merely dissembling for protection, when they were lying to each other, or to themselves. "There are some elusive, profound, recondite things that men find hard to say to other men," muses "black boy," "but with the Negro it is the little things of life that become hard to say, for these tiny items shape his destiny" (254). What sets him apart from his contemporaries is his difficulty with the lying they find so easy: "In my dealing with whites I was conscious of the entirety of my relations with them, and they were conscious only of what was happening at a given moment. I had to keep remembering what others took for granted; I had to think out what others felt" (215).

The actual audience must narrow the gap between the narrative and authorial audience; the reader of *Black Boy* must strive to be like the narrator of *Black Boy*, must keep what is happening at a particular moment and the entire history of black/white relations – the content and the context – together in his or her mind. Wright's context includes the need to speak simultaneously as an adult and as a child, to remove everything from his story that, even if it happened to be true, would allow white readers to maintain their distorted stereotype of Southern blacks. He was searching for a way to confess his personal history of lying, forced on him by his childhood, while still demonstrating that he could be trusted by both black and white. His solution is what Maya Angelou calls "African-bush secretiveness":

> "If you ask a Negro where he's been, he'll tell you where he's going." To understand this important information, it is necessary to know who uses this tactic and on whom it works. If an unaware person is told a part of the truth (it is imperative that the answer embody truth), he is satisfied that his query has been answered. If an aware person (one who himself uses the strategem) is given an answer which is truthful but bears only slightly if at all on the question, he knows that the information he seeks is of a private nature and will not be handed to him willingly.[35]

What makes *Black Boy* compelling is its ability to remain autobiography despite its obvious subordination of historicity. Although a reader may not be aware of the complexities of "black boy's" "African-bush" slanting of truth, or know about the book's fictionalizing, there is, nevertheless, something unmistakably autobiographical about *Black Boy* that convinces even the unaware. What makes this true is the way the author signifies his lying through rhetoric, appeals in writing to both black and white, as he was unable to do in his speech at Nashville. One of the patterns of the book's lies involves just such a distinction between speaking and writing.

Wright's claim to be speaking for the millions of inarticulate children of the South is in an ironic way reinforced by the constant difficulty the narrator has with the spoken as opposed to the printed word. Although it is a love of literature that saves "black boy," he is constantly threatened by speaking. Often out of synchronization, he speaks when he should be quiet, or is unable to utter a word when questioned; his words slip unaware from his mouth, flow out against his will. But just as often he is totally paralyzed, unable to produce a phrase. In answer to his early questioning – "What on earth was the matter with me ... every word and gesture I made seemed to provoke hostility?" (158) – the narrator answers, toward the end of the book, "I knew what was wrong with me, but I could not correct it. The words and actions of white people were baffling signs to me" (215).

The problem with the spoken word begins with the narrator's killing the kitten because of the pretence of not reading his father's command as figurative, and continues with the melodramatic description of himself begging drinks as a six-year-old child, memorizing obscenities taught to him in a bar. Later he learns "all the four-letter words describing physiological and sex functions" (32), and yet claims to be astonished, while being bathed by his grandmother, at her reaction to his command: "'When you get through, kiss back there,' I said, the words rolling softly but unpremeditatedly" (49). Wishing to recall those words, though only vaguely understanding why he is once again being punished so severely, "black boy" says "none of the obscene words I had learned at school in

Memphis had dealt with perversions of any sort, although I might have learned the words while loitering drunkenly in saloons" (53). This explanation is weak and unconvincing, given his earlier description of himself and other children stationing themselves for hours at the bottom of a series of outdoor toilets, observing the anatomies of their neighbours.

Forced to declare his belief in God by his family of Seventh Day Adventists, "black boy" mis-speaks again and again. "'I don't want to hurt God's feelings either,' I said, the words slipping irreverently from my lips before I was aware of their full meaning" (126). Trying to keep his grandmother from questioning him about religion, he hits upon the strategy of likening himself to Jacob, arguing that he would believe in God if he ever saw an angel. Although this plan was imagined with the purpose of "salving ... Granny's frustrated feelings toward him" (128), the result is that his words are misconstrued. His grandmother thinks he *has* seen an angel, and "black boy" once again has "unwittingly committed an obscene act" (131). His explanation is another example of his difficulty in speaking as others did: "I must have spoken more loudly and harshly than was called for" (131).

Called before a teacher to explain a schoolyard fight with two bullies, the protagonist says, "You're lying!," which causes the teacher to reply, "Don't use that language in here" (137), even though he is right. Once again daydreaming, the narrator interrupts his family's "arguing some obscure point of religious doctrine" (147) with a remark which he says "must have sounded reekingly blasphemous" (137). This time his grandmother is in bed for six weeks, her back wrenched in attempting to slap her grandson for his statements. Again "black boy" is an innocent victim, beaten for not allowing his grandmother to slap him – his physical, like his verbal skills, out of rhythm with his family. He is slapped for asking his grandmother, on a later occasion, what his dying grandfather's last words were, and for replying to the question "What time have you?" with "If it's a little slow or fast, it's not far wrong" (173). "Black boy's" poor sense of timing makes him feel unreal, as if he "had been slapped out of the human race" (210), makes him resemble Ellison's invisible man who believes that his condition "gives one a slightly different sense of time, you're never quite on the beat. Sometimes you're ahead and sometimes behind. Instead of the swift and imperceptible flowing of time, you are aware of its nodes, those points where time stands still or from which it leaps ahead."[36] Ellison's words, which are also suggestive of the sense of time essential to jazz, describe the narrator who is out of phase with everyone until he can control the timing of his life through the syncopated rhythms of *Black Boy*.

In light of the repeated pattern – swift physical reprisal delivered to the totally astonished narrator for speaking out of turn – it is surprising to read the following justification for his resorting to threatening his Aunt with a knife: "I had often been painfully beaten, but almost always I had felt that the beatings were somehow right and sensible, that I was in the wrong" (118). This confession sounds false because "black boy" never seems to admit that he is blameworthy for anything. "Nowhere in the book are Wright's actions and thoughts reprehensible," objects Edward Margolies, echoing a number of others.[37] Robert Felgar makes a similar point when he remarks that "the reader does tire of his persistent self-pity and self-aggrandizement."[38] An early reviewer argues that "the simple law of averages would prevent any one boy from getting into as many situations as we have related in this story, and one senses with regret, that it is hard to know where biography leaves off and fiction begins."[39] What these critics see as foolish self-pity is most apparent in the heavily melodramatic description of the familiar playground game of crack-the-whip, which the narrator describes in life or death terms: "They played a wildcat game called popping-the-whip, a seemingly innocent diversion whose excitement came only in spurts, but spurts that could hurl one to the edge of death itself.... The whip grew taut as human flesh and bone could bear and I felt that my arm was being torn from its socket" (122).

Here the author is depicting a children's game using the kind of rhetoric usually reserved for a slave narrative – a cruel overseer whipping a runaway slave "to the edge of death." Wright's words are not self-pitying; instead he is presenting a naive youth who was never good at lying or exaggerating. The misrepresentation is so obvious that only a particularly inept liar would attempt it, a child who did not want to be good at lying. Only an outsider such as "black boy" to the established systems of lying by both races, a representative of the many black adolescents then coming of age – what Wright hoped would be a new generation of the children of Uncle Tom, no longer willing to accept the old lie that the best way to fight racism was to lie through both omission and commission – could fail to distinguish between melodrama and genuine oppression, and to be surprised at the power of his words.

Black Boy should not be read as historical truth which strives to report those incontrovertible facts that can be somehow corroborated, but as narrative truth, which psychiatrist Donald Spence defines as "the criterion we use to decide when a certain experience has been captured to our satisfaction; it depends on continuity and closure and the extent to which the fit of the pieces takes on an aesthetic finality."[40] The story that Richard Wright creates in *Black Boy*, whatever its value as an exact historical record, is important both in telling us how the author remembers life in the pre-Depression South and in showing us what kind of person the author was to have written his story as he did. Although he is often deliberately false to historical truth, he seldom deviates from narrative truth. "Consistent misrepresentation of oneself is not easy," writes Roy Pascal, and in *Black Boy* Wright has made both the horrifying dramatic and the ordinary events of his life fit into a pattern, shaped by a consistent, metaphoric use of lying.[41] "Interpretations are persuasive," argues Donald Spence, "not because of their evidential value but because of their rhetorical appeal; conviction emerges because the fit is good, not because we have necessarily made contact with the past."[42]

In *Black Boy* Wright creates a version of himself whose metaphor for survival and for sustenance is falsehood. But the multiple lies of the narrator, like the fibs of children trying to avoid what they see as irrational punishment, are palpably obvious. They are not meant to deceive; they are deliberately embarrassing in their transparency. For the protagonist, whose home life was so warped that only when he lied could he be believed, Alfred Kazin's dictum – "One writes to make a home for oneself, on paper" – is particularly true.[43] The author's manipulations of genre and his metaphoric lies produced a book about which DuBois's assessment was, in my judgment, exactly backward: although much of what Wright wrote is not literally true, the total picture is ultimately convincing, taken in context. For all his lying, "black boy's" essential drive is for truth, and his constant revelation of how often he was forced to lie should be judged according to the standard set forth by Marcel Eck in *Lies and Truth*: "We will be judged not on whether we possess or do not possess the truth but on whether or not we sought and loved it."[44]

TIMOTHY DOW ADAMS

NOTES

1. Ralph K. White, *"Black Boy*: A Value Analysis," *Journal of Abnormal and Social Psychology*, 42 (1947), 442–3.
2. W.E.B. DuBois, "Richard Wright Looks Back," *New York Herald Tribune weekly Book Review*, 4 March, 1945, p. 2; rpt. in *Richard Wright: The Critical Reception*, ed. by John M. Reilly (New York: Burt Franklin, 1978), p. 133.
3. A.O.J. Cockshut, *The Art of Autobiography in 19th & 20th Century England* (New Haven: Yale Univ. Press, 1984), p. 216.
4. For these terms see, in Reilly, the following: Gottlieb, Creighton, DuBois, Garlington, Bentley, Richter, and Hamilton, pp. 122–76.
5. Quoted in Michel Fabre, *The Unfinished Quest of Richard Wright*, trans. by Isabel Barzun (New York: William Morrow, 1973), p. 578.
6. Fabre, *Unfinished Quest*, p. 578.
7. Fabre, *Unfinished Quest*, p. 250.
8. Quoted in Fabre, "Afterward," to *American Hunger* (New York: Harper & Row, 1977), p. 138.
9. Alternate titles cited in Constance Webb, *Richard Wright: A Biography* (New York: G.P. Putnam's Sons, 1968), pp. 206–7 and in Charles T. Davis and Michel Fabre, *Richard Wright: A Primary Bibliography* (Boston: G.K. Hall, 1982), p. 56.
10. Fabre, *Unfinished Quest*, pp. 254 and 578.
11. Webb, p. 198 and pp. 207–8.
12. For a discussion of *Black Boy* and slave narratives see Robert B. Stepto, *From Behind the Veil: A Study of Afro-American Narrative* (Urbana: U. of Illinois Press, 1979); Sidonie Smith, *Where I'm Bound: Patterns of Slavery and Freedom in Black Autobiography* (Westport, Conn.: Greenwood Press, 1974); and Stephen Butterfield, *Black Autobiography in America* (Amherst: U. of Massachusetts Press, 1974).
13. Richard Wright, *Black Boy: A Record of Childhood and Youth* (1945; rpt. New York: Harper & Row Perennial Classic, 1966), p. 83. Parenthetical references within the text are to this edition.
14. See Webb, p. 402 and Richard Wright, "How 'Bigger' was born," foreword to *Native Son* (1940; rpt. New York: Harper Perennial Classic, 1969).

15. Roy Pascal, *Design and Truth in Autobiography* (Cambridge: Harvard U.P., 1960), pp. 63 and 82.
16. Fabre, *Unfinished Quest*, p. 47.
17. Fabre, *Unfinished Quest*, p. 6.
18. Fabre, *Unfinished Quest*, p. 54.
19. Webb, p. 419.
20. Edward Margolies, *The Art of Richard Wright* (Carbondale: Southern Illinois U.P., 1969), p. 16.
21. James Olney, "The Ontology of Autobiography," in *Autobiography: Essays Theoretical and Critical*, ed. by James Olney (Princeton: Princeton Univ. Press, 1980), pp. 244–5.
22. Ralph Ellison, "Richard Wright's Blues," *Shadow and Act* (New York: New American Library, 1966), p. 89.
23. Peter J. Rabinowitz, "Assertion and Assumption: Fictional Patterns and the External World," *PMLA*, 96 (1981), 408–19.
24. Gerald Prince, "Introduction à l'étude du narrataire," *Poétique*, 14 (1973), 178–96.
25. Albert E. Stone, *Autobiographical Occasions and Original Acts* (Philadelphia: Univ. of Pennsylvania Press, 1982), p. 124.
26. Lionel Trilling, *Sincerity and Authenticity* (Cambridge: Harvard Univ. Press, 1972), p. 139.
27. Trilling, p. 135.
28. Barrett J. Mandell, "Full of Life Now," in Olney, *Autobiography: Essays Theoretical and Critical*, p. 65.
29. Mandel, p. 65.
30. Mandel, p. 66.
31. Stepto, p. 143.
32. Stone, p. 126.
33. Richard Wright, "The Ethics of Living Jim Crow," in *Uncle Tom's Children* (1938; rpt. New York: Harper Perennial Library, 1965), pp. 4–5.
34. Roger Rosenblatt, "Black Autobiography: Life as the Death Weapon," in Olney, *Autobiography: Essays Theoretical and Critical*, p. 173.
35. Maya Angelou, *I Know Why The Caged Bird Sings* (1970; rpt. New York: Bantam, 1971), p. 164.
36. Ralph Ellison, *Invisible Man* (1952; rpt. New York: Vintage, 1972), p. 8.
37. Margolies, p. 19.
38. Robert Felgar, *Richard Wright* (Boston: Twayne Publishers, 1980), p. 46.
39. Patsy Graves, *Opportunity*, 23 (July 1945), rpt. Reilly, p. 173.
40. Donald Spence, *Narrative Truth and Historical Truth: Meaning and Interpretation in Psychoanalysis* (New York: W.W. Norton, 1982), p. 31.
41. Pascal, p. 189.
42. Spence, p. 32.
43. Alfred Kazin, "The Self As History: Reflections on Autobiography," in *Telling Lives: The Biographer's Art*, ed. Marc Pachter (Washington, D.C.: New Republic Books, 1979), p. 89.
44. Marcel Eck, *Lies and Truth*, trans. by Bernard Murchland (New York: Macmillan, 1970), p. 160.

INDEX